Cinema, Emergence, and the Films of Satyajit Ray

The publisher gratefully acknowledges the generous support of the Eric Papenfuse and Catherine Lawrence Endowment Fund in Film and Media Studies of the University of California Press Foundation.

The publisher also gratefully acknowledges the generous contribution to this book provided by the University of Minnesota.

Cinema, Emergence, and the Films of Satyajit Ray

KEYA GANGULY

University of California Press

BERKELEY   LOS ANGELES   LONDON

University of California Press, one of the most distinguished
university presses in the United States, enriches lives around the
world by advancing scholarship in the humanities, social sciences,
and natural sciences. Its activities are supported by the UC Press
Foundation and by philanthropic contributions from individuals
and institutions. For more information, visit www.ucpress.edu.

University of California Press
Berkeley and Los Angeles, California

University of California Press, Ltd.
London, England

Library of Congress Cataloging-in-Publication Data

Ganguly, Keya.
    Cinema, emergence, and the films of Satyajit Ray / Keya Ganguly.
        p.   cm.
    Includes bibliographical references and index.
    ISBN 978-0-520-26216-4 (cloth : alk. paper)
    ISBN 978-0-520-26217-1 (pbk. : alk. paper)
    1. Ray, Satyajit, 1921–1992—Criticism and
interpretation.   I. Title.

PN1998.3.R4G32   2010
791.4312'33092—dc22   2009052479

19   18   17   16   15   14   13   12   11   10
10   9   8   7   6   5   4   3   2   1

This book is printed on Cascades Enviro 100, a 100% post consumer
waste, recycled, de-inked fiber. FSC recycled certified and processed
chlorine free. It is acid free, Ecologo certified, and manufactured by
BioGas energy.

Printed in Canada

For Baba

Contents

Illustrations

Acknowledgments

A labor of love, this book was completed under trying circumstances. To my father, who is no longer with us, and to my sister, who, despite her ongoing illness, read my chapters in between visits to the Mayo Clinic. To my mother, whose keen botanist's eye no less than her early schooling at Shantiniketan under the artist Nandalal Bose, influenced my reading of Bengali culture. To my grandmother, Kamala Devi, whose stories of living in seclusion in the very midst of the Europeanized urbanity of my grandfather's experience as a civil service officer in India, I continue to absorb.

A number of people gave me the opportunity, in encouraging environments, to present my ideas about Ray. I should like to thank them here, though I cannot do justice to all of the ways their questions, comments, and suggestions have influenced the outcome: Elleke Boehmer, Kenneth Calhoon, Corey Creekmur, Nicholas Dirks, Gayatri Chakravorty Spivak, Dilip Gaonkar, Martina Ghosh-Schellhorn, Priyamvada Gopal, Suvir Kaul, Ranjana Khanna, Gautam Kundu, Neil Lazarus, Philip Lutgendorf, Colin MacCabe, Negar Mottahedeh, Laura Mulvey, Graziella Parati, Rajagopalan Radhakrishnan, Sharmila Sen, Parna Sengupta, Czaba Toth, and Rashmi Varma. I should also like to acknowledge the friendship and support of Rick and Cathy Asher, Janaki Bakhle, Chris Chiappari, Tim Heitman, Robert Hullot-Kentor, Sukeshi Kamra, Michal Kobialka, Neil Larsen, Elise Linehan, Jeane McGinn, Madhuchhanda Mitra, and Zohreh Sullivan. Silvia López, Neil Lazarus, and Benita Parry read and commented on various drafts of the chapters, and I am deeply grateful for their ideas and insights.

The two outside readers for this project, Richard Terdiman and Partha Mitter, deserve my gratitude on two counts: first, for their scholarship, which I have long admired, and, more proximately, for providing extremely helpful, enthusiastic, and thorough reports in a short space of time. My editor at the University of California Press, Mary Francis, has stood behind this project for many years. Her advice, patience, and promptness in dealing with all its aspects made working with her a genuine pleasure.

The Satyajit Ray Film and Study Center (FASC) at the University of California, Santa Cruz, provided me with access to stills from the collections of Sandip Ray, Tarapada Banerjee, Amanul Huq and Cutty Lethbridge. I was fortunate to obtain the assistance of the curator of the archive, Dayani Kowshik, and media assistant, Jason Palines, who worked on the images reproduced here, as well as last-minute help with illustrations from Josef Lindner, preservation officer at the Academy Film Archive of the Academy of Motion Picture Arts and Sciences. Dilip Basu, founding director of the Ray archive, provided incalculable support by commenting on the chapters and helping me select production stills to go along with the arguments. He also introduced me to Sandip and Lalita Ray, whose kindness and hospitality in giving me access to Ray's study (now a shrine to his immense creativity), I will always treasure.

Research support was provided by the College of Liberal Arts at the University of Minnesota in the form of a Grant-in-Aid fellowship in 2004, a single semester leave in 2006, and an "Imagine" fund subvention grant in 2009 for image reproduction and licensing fees. I want to thank the IT fellow in my department, Brynja Gudjonsson, for her prompt and consistent technical assistance. I had the opportunity to teach a class on Ray in 2005, and two of the participants in that class, Samuel Johnson and Patrick Flanagan, especially convinced me through their seminar papers that it is not necessary to know Bengali or Indian culture to produce sophisticated analyses of Ray's films. Gabriel Shapiro, another student who does know quite a bit about South Asia and its regional cinemas, has been an energetic, indefatigable, and enormous source of help at every stage of this project.

To Timothy Brennan, my comrade-in-arms (in every sense of this phrase), whose love, patience, humor, and intellectual integrity is a constant model. This book is dedicated to the memory of my father, who took us as children to see *Goopy Gyne Bagha Byne* (The Adventures of Goopy and Bagha). He would probably have greeted its appearance with a chuckle, quoting from the classic Ray song: *dekho re nayan mele, jagater bahaar* (open your eyes and look at the wonders of the world).

Note on Romanization

A comment is necessary on my transliteration of Bengali and, occasionally, Sanskrit words. I have followed Ray's usage where relevant (such as *Doyamoyee* or *Doya* although *Dayamayee* or *Daya* would have been the more standard Sanskritized transcription of the name). Since this is a book on cinema and critical theory rather than linguistics, I have taken the liberty of distinguishing between the palatal and dental *s* (pronounced in the same way in Bengali) through the respective use of *sh* and *s;* this too goes against accepted convention. On a few occasions I have resorted to diacritical marks (for example, *momo citté,* instead of *mama chitte* [in my heart]) when not doing so might cause more awkwardness.

Introduction

The Light of the New Moon

What was "modern," what was indeed "avant-garde," is now
relatively old. What its works and language reveal, even at their
most powerful, is an identifiable historical period, from which,
however, we have not fully emerged.
  —RAYMOND WILLIAMS, *The Politics of Modernism*

Avant-gardism is a luxury we cannot yet afford in our country.
  —SATYAJIT RAY, *Our Films, Their Films*

POINTS OF DEPARTURE

A short scene in *Charulata* (1964) depicts Bhupati, the heroine Charulata's
husband, discussing the vocation of the writer with his cousin Amal. The
latter has given the fanciful title of *Amabasyar Aalo* (The Light of the
New Moon) to one of his impassioned bits of writing. Amal and Charu
(Charulata's abbreviated name) share a love of literary essays, and the intimacy it sparks between them leads to the romantic complication that is at
the core of this classic film in Satyajit Ray's wide-ranging oeuvre. In this
scene, as well as throughout the film, the practical and rational Bhupati, a
newspaper publisher, is revealed to be more interested in political events
in the world than in the issue of creative license; he consequently regards
Amal's effort as florid and, moreover, nonsensical. As he quite reasonably points out, blocked by the earth's shadow the new moon never casts
any light, so there is no earthly reason, so to speak, to expostulate about
it. More than a description of geoselenic relations, the light of the new
moon designates the oddity, the impracticality, and, indeed, the illogical-
ity of the idea, and Ray uses it to set up a contrast between possibilities,
however improbable, and hard-nosed reality. But the phrase also serves as
an extended metaphor for the contrary forms of imaginativeness that go
under the sign of the improper, the incorrect, and the illogical—that which
rhetoricians call "catachresis." The impossible idea of the light of the new
moon helps to situate my goal in this book, which is to examine the utility
of a conception of modernism and the avant-garde, conventionally seen as

1

ill-suited to a discussion of Ray's cinema (or Indian culture at large), for understanding the nature of his visual experiments.

In other words, to propose an exploration of Ray's films by the terms of the avant-garde might, I recognize, seem as unlikely as the notion of the new moon's light. This is not willfully to deny that the ideal and outlook of the avant-garde have in a general sense been inherited from debates in Europe; by the same token, they have seldom been applied to the expressive strategies found in Ray's works. However, what is largely a problem of naming—"modernism and the avant-garde"—has been misunderstood as a problem of substance and thereby held out as a caution against misappropriation. It is, of course, easy to see why vanguardist developments in the second half of the twentieth century in countries such as India would be thought of as either following from an earlier avant-garde in Europe or as a distinct phenomenon without any connections to the aesthetics of modernism and therefore bereft of its political impulses.

My efforts will be to show that neither view is conceptually or historiographically adequate (if, by historiography, we mean to indicate an approach to the writing of history as opposed to chronology itself). Aside from the fact that the historical avant-gardes of the early twentieth century were themselves inspired by intellectuals from across the globe, the more important point is that the bitter rejection of capitalist modernity was widespread throughout the entire span of the last hundred years and led to varying inflections, as well as crisscrossing influences, in the disparate milieus in which the spirit of the avant-garde flourished. The full aspects of its world-historical critique can only be accounted for by taking the twentieth century as a total conjuncture and geopolitical whole, not simply a developmental scheme in the unfolding of Europe and its "others."

As Raymond Williams illustrates in the first epigraph, the story of modernism and the avant-garde is by now old; it also comes with specific historical and geographical associations in place and particular agents who are brought to mind whenever the terms *modernism* and *the avant-garde* are invoked. It conjures up places like Paris, Berlin, and New York, for example; literary figures such as Charles Baudelaire, Bertolt Brecht, and T. S. Eliot; artists such as Marcel Duchamp, Constantin Brancusi, and Andy Warhol; or movements such as *Der Blaue Reiter*, surrealism, constructivism, and pop art. In addition to being a familiar story, this version has a definitely European (and, later, American) flavor. But there are at least two other ways of plotting the tale of modernism. One takes up the trajectory of a *cinematic* modernism, which, even though it is largely neglected in the most influential accounts of radical artistic and cultural experiments of the period, is surely of continuing interest if we consider that cinema is the most paradigmatic of modern expressive forms, whose very constitution depends on the mediation of art by technology and conditions of mass production and reception. At the same time, films also exemplify, on occasion, a recoil from traditional conceptions of art, all of which is pertinent to the arguments I seek to advance.[1]

The second narrative, deriving in part from the specific encounter of cinema and *aesthetic* modernism, brings us closer to the ways that, as a mode of understanding and practice, the impulses spurring cinematic modernism travel outside what we conventionally take to be "the West."[2] More to the point, it puts us in contact with Ray, whose films, I contend, exemplify what Williams called the "one general property" of the avant-garde, which was, he said, to "pion[eer] new methods and purposes in writing, art and thought."[3] I will go further and say that Ray's films do this in a manner that may well be seen as thoroughly reformulating prevailing distinctions and descriptions of the avant-garde in its cinematic articulations. Thus, quite in opposition to thinking that the avant-garde is best understood as the disenchantment or youthful revolt of modern European subjects, it must, as Williams also suggests, be set against a backdrop of global social ferment and upheaval prompted by (a) the various anticolonial movements of the early part of the twentieth century; (b) the energies of the commitment to internationalism within independent art and cultural institutions in France, Italy, the Soviet Union, India, Latin America, and the Caribbean; and (c) the resistance to the discourse of modernization among European and Third World intellectuals alike. The effects of modernity, although felt differently inside and outside Europe, were nonetheless perceived as a common plight and a shared predicament to be contested by artists and intellectuals worldwide.

In a conversation with the British film critic Derek Malcolm, published in *Sight and Sound*, Ray offered the following description of the method and purpose of his cinema: "I certainly like to follow a simple, classical structure. My films are stories first and foremost, because India has a great tradition in that respect. Of course a certain amount of commitment is unavoidable. But I never want to be a propagandist. I don't think anybody is in a position to give answers to social problems—definitive answers at any rate. Besides no propaganda really works."[4] In the tension that stretches across words such as *unavoidable, commitment, definitive answers*, and *propaganda*, several conflicting ideas make their presence felt. By themselves these ideas are not remarkable, inasmuch as they signal what has now become commonplace in our understanding of the limited extent to which artistic practices can serve as instruments of social change within the context of capitalist modernity. But if the ready response to the question of commitment in many circles is that art with a transformative social goal belongs to an earlier age, not ours, this reaction is itself the historical and political product of a modernism against which the avant-garde movements struggled in the first three decades of the twentieth century. It was the avant-garde's specific response to modernism's failure to bring aesthetic practices back into a confrontation with society that has, as we know, come to inform attitudes toward the political efficacy, or lack thereof, of artistic forms. These attitudes, I might add, have since bled over into the disposition of postmodernism that Fredric Jameson has termed the "cultural logic" of late capitalism; and they remain on the horizon in this incarnation, still demanding scrutiny.[5]

Williams reminds us that although it now seems paradoxical or un-timely to refer to ideas that go back almost a hundred years by a term that translates as "advance guard," what is crucial in any reflexive stock-taking of the avant-garde is not its temporal or definitional origins, whether in film or the other arts, but the fact that we have not yet emerged from this historical period. This leads us to recognize that the avant-garde is poorly understood if we restrict the term to issues of provenance, intention, or effect. Instead, what Williams emphasizes are the "internal pressures and contradictions" that first emerged in the avant-garde moment though they have actually "intensified" in the present.[6] With this he designates a con-ceptualization of the avant-garde that forgoes embedding it in this or that moment or tendency. The ideas that form its basis were not sui generis but the result of material constraints and conditions of possibility (it would be generatively idealist to assume otherwise). Also, the overall political orientation of the avant-garde is by no means settled as progressive, as the program of the Italian Futurists, the literary production of Wyndham Lewis, or the theoretical writings of Friedrich Nietzsche would suggest.[7] Accordingly, any contemporary assessment of the avant-garde proceeds less by requiring guarantees about the term's political or geographical past than by thinking through its afterlife in the present, an afterlife that is subject to the same pressures and contradictions that had earlier deter-mined the circumstances of its promulgation.

This relates directly to Ray's uncertainty about the status of his work. In making the statement that "a certain amount of commitment is unavoidable," he avows the notion of commitment (albeit in a qualified manner), but what is more, he casts it as inescapable, even inevitable— along lines that imply the kinds of "internal pressures and contradictions"

Williams had proposed as also impelling the historical avant-garde. The impossibility of aesthetic forms to divorce themselves from social realities can be seen as the reason Ray distances himself from "propaganda" in the remarks above—that is, from art that has set itself off from society in the conviction that it possesses the remedy for social ills or, as he puts it, has "definitive" answers. This aspect of Ray's comments is worth highlighting for its recognition that the vexed relationship between artworks and the sociohistorical dynamics subtending them makes any claim for their precise political status impossible. The same principled reasoning guides his statement that serves as my second epigraph. In saying that *"Avant-gardism* is a luxury which we cannot yet afford in our country," he rejects the label and the Kantian end-in-itself of autotelic form—*l'art pour l'art*—valorized in certain strains of avant-garde film. Underscoring his location as an Indian director, Ray signals the political distance that now separates the label from anything it may have once conveyed even as he recalibrates the meaning of artistic engagement.

By the 1980s (when this conversation was published), an aura of Euro-American effeteness and decadence had already settled over the idea of the avant-garde, lending it a corresponding sense of exhaustion that he had no wish to endorse. Accordingly, if decadence is a luxury the West could afford, the situation in "our country," Ray avers, rendered it an untenable aesthetic choice for him. It is in the context of these two modes of thought—propaganda and aestheticism—that we must read his hesitation about the meaning of commitment, on the one hand, and autonomy, on the other. Doing so also enables us to read his films against the grain of his own utterance about *avant-gardism*, a position that has less to do with repudiating the term or its underlying imperatives as such than with opposing the sensibilities that have come to be associated with it.

To the extent that the avant-garde's (failed) historical mission was to lead art back into society through a break with tradition and the inculcation of new ways of seeing—including new ways of seeing the old—Ray's project is, in fact, remarkably consistent with it. For his cinematic intentions are declared along the same lines in the proposition immediately proceeding from his demur about avant-gardism: "What we can do—and do profitably—is to explore new themes, new aspects of society, new facets of human relationships. But if you want to do that, and be serious and artistic about it, you cannot afford to sugar your pill for the masses who are used to tasty morsels of make-believe."[8] In emphasizing the new *not* for the sake of aesthetic experimentation alone but as a means of intensifying the newness of the social—that is to say, as an aesthetic registration of

Indian modernity—Ray confronts his contradictory predicament. Unable to settle for providing the "tasty morsels" that might satisfy the appetites of mainstream audiences, he was also unwilling to cater to the political demand that India's emergence be represented in ways that fit conventional thinking.

In his excellent biography Andrew Robinson narrates the objections to Ray famously raised by the Bombay film actress Nargis Dutt (who played the heroine in the 1957 Hindi blockbuster *Mother India*, directed by Raj Kapoor, and who later became a member of India's Upper House of Parliament, the *Rajya Sabha*). The anecdote is worth repeating here as indicative of the personal obstacles Ray faced but also as symptomatic of the banality that persists to this day when modernist forms of refusal go against accepted notions of art and entertainment. I quote from Robinson's excerpt of the interview in which the actress-parliamentarian repeated her charge (made during a parliamentary debate) that Ray was responsible for "distorting India's image abroad":

INTERVIEWER: *What does Ray portray in the Apu trilogy and why do you object to it?*

NARGIS: He portrays a region of West Bengal that is so poor that it does not represent India's poverty in its true form. Tell me something. Which part of India are you from?

INTERVIEWER: *UP [Uttar Pradesh].*

NARGIS: Now, tell me, would you leave your eighty-year-old grandmother to die in a cremation ground, unattended?

INTERVIEWER: *No.*

NARGIS: Well, people in West Bengal do. And that is what he portrays in these films. It is not a correct image of India.

INTERVIEWER: *Do people in West Bengal do such a thing?*

NARGIS: I don't know. But when I go abroad, foreigners ask me embarrassing questions like "Do you have schools in India?" "Do you have cars in India?" I feel so ashamed, my eyes are lowered before them. If a foreigner asks me, "What kind of houses do you live in?" I feel like answering, "We live on treetops." Why do you think films like *Pather Panchali* become so popular abroad?

INTERVIEWER: *You tell me.*

NARGIS: Because people there want to see India in an abject condition. That is the image they have of our country and a film that confirms that image seems to them authentic.

INTERVIEWER: *But why should a renowned director like Ray do such a thing?*

NARGIS: To win awards. His films are not commercially successful. They only win awards.

INTERVIEWER: *What do you expect Ray to do?*

NARGIS: What I want is that if Mr. Ray projects Indian poverty abroad, he should also show "Modern India."

INTERVIEWER: *But if the theme and plot of Pather Panchali are complete[ly] within the realm of a poor village, how can he deliberately fit "Modern India" within it?*

NARGIS: But Mr. Ray can make separate films on "Modern India."

INTERVIEWER: *What is "Modern India"?*

NARGIS: Dams . . .[9]

If the *ressentiment* expressed by Nargis is not to be taken seriously (seeing as her principal qualification for speaking on behalf of "Modern India" was that she played "Mother India" in a melodramatic Hindi film), it at least reveals the distance between Ray's "art house" practice and the ideology of transparent representation underlying her views.[10] As Roland Barthes reminded us back in the 1950s, this is an ideology that, in passing itself off as natural, makes dominant interests seem universal. In this way setting off the notion of "India's poverty in its true form" from what "people in West Bengal do," Nargis adopts a lofty, moralizing tone about the need for positive representations geared toward "foreign" consumption, while also casting aspersions on Ray's motives for making films.

Triteness notwithstanding, Nargis's statements also hint at a sense that prevails in some strands of scholarly writing. In them one often finds that there are properly authorized versions of India, the Third World, and so on; that only a few are allowed to offer them; and that these versions must conform to accepted notions of emergence, influence, and effect. So while the actress's reference to dams as an appropriate subject for depicting "Modern India" on the screen may invite derision, it bespeaks an anxiety not restricted to the credulous about the meaning of modernity and the modes of narration appropriate to it.

The art critic Geeta Kapur has been among the influential voices to wade into the waters of Indian modernism and modernity. According to her, "The fact that the modern never properly belongs to us as Indians, or we to it, does lead to anxieties of misappropriation."[11] The presupposition that the modern does not "properly" belong to Indians leads Kapur to Ray himself. She arrives at a reading of two of his films in the course of surveying the ideas and work of different artists—from Raja Ravi Varma, the nineteenth-century painter, and the directors of the early Marathi film *Sant Tukaram* (1936),[12] to Ritwik Ghatak, the activist filmmaker and Ray's compatriot from Bengal (along with a host of other, more contemporary, visual artists). Her broad argument is that a liberal, anti-imperialist state such as India's stymies the emergence of a radical cultural politics or a "cultural front" because it has managed to assimilate opposition and render it inert. She offers the following perspective with Ray in mind:

> If we extend the argument about the consequences of what has been called, after Antonio Gramsci, the "passive revolution" to analogous developments in the realm of contemporary arts, we find that Indian modernism has developed without an avantgarde. A modernism without disjunctures is at best a reformist modernism. The very liberalism of the state absolved the left of confrontational initiatives on the cultural front. Similarly, the very capacity of newly independent India to resist up to a point the cultural pressures of the cold war era makes it less imperative for artists to devise the kind of combative aesthetic that will pose a challenge to the Euro-American avantgarde.[13]

Kapur raises a number of issues that deserve to be considered in more detail because they affect her assessment—and ours—of Ray's politics and his placement within the discourse of modernism. First, we must consider the proposition that the passive revolution in Indian cultural politics was, in fact, so passive as to thwart confrontational politics avant-garde style, leaving only the possibility of a "reformist modernism." Whatever the merits of this assertion, the secondhand allusion to Gramsci (Kapur does not refer to Gramsci's elaboration, merely to its derivative uses) has certain liabilities. This is not because the idea of passive revolution is inapplicable here but because Gramsci's views on avant-garde movements—both progressive and reactionary—were offered in the same context as his conceptualization of passive revolution under the Risorgimento.[14] That is to say, the conditions of passive revolution were, for Gramsci, neither necessary nor sufficient to explain the political orientation of avant-garde movements (such as the Italian Futurists, whose radicalism he applauded initially but later rejected for its "aristocratic spirit"). So, futurism could not only arise but also be transformed under the very shadow of the bourgeois imperatives of Italian reunification; the conditions of passive revolution had little impact on the movement's political tendencies.[15] Indeed, Italian Futurism, given its ultimately reactionary character, could hardly be called *"reform-*

ist," leaving us to conclude that the incomplete social transformation induced by a passive revolution cannot, by itself, serve as the index of the value-determination of avant-garde politics. And if this was the case in Gramsci's Italy, there is every reason to see similar patterns in the Indian situation as well.

Kapur's operative assumption seems to be that an Indian avant-garde worthy of its name should have devised a "combative aesthetic" and that it fell short as a collective, "left" initiative—the only form capable of issuing a challenge to a "Euro-American" avant-garde. As the Italian example shows, however, the lack of a movement politics, albeit regrettable, cannot bear the burden of the distinction between revolutionary and reformist inclinations in the designation of avant-garde practices themselves. To think this is to reproduce the instrumental logic of Nargis's demand for films about dams by adopting preconceived notions about the "use value" of combative aesthetics. A great deal depends in any analysis on what one considers transgressive within the modern.[16] Moreover, there are specific art-historical battles over the nature of Indian modernism, particularly in relation to the Bengal Renaissance, the name given to the aesthetic culture that developed alongside the social reform movements of the nineteenth and early twentieth centuries (and a generative source of influence on Ray's life and practice). Some have referred to this culture as a truly renascent and Bengali imperative, others as something else entirely.[17] These disputes take disciplinary shape or reflect regional political conflicts over civilizational value and can appear somewhat beside the point in the present context.

For us the question is, How do we understand the practices and problems engaged by these debates without muddying the waters? The welcome assertiveness with which Kapur maps the highly uneven terrain of contemporary cultural practices in India entails an attempt to read both motivation and effect into her portrait of Ray. She consequently depicts him as belonging to the generation of post-Independence artists inclined to "perpetrate a set of self-deceptions" in the very process of "fill[ing] the ideal role of an Indian artist within the progressive paradigm of the 'first decade.' "[18] With this we are taken back to the initial gesture in her argument: to set the discussion of Indian modernism by the terms of passive revolution. But despite appearing to be a materialist gesture whereby the correct note is struck about the relationship between state and society, the relative autonomy of the aesthetic sphere and its contradictory, *in*organic dimensions are given short shrift by Kapur's positing unmediated correspondences between the liberalism of the Indian state and Ray's "liberal and reformist ethics" (220). In this respect Kapur ends up displaying some of the commonsensical literalism of Nargis's position.

Take, for instance, the following sentences, in which Kapur measures Ray's "national status" relative to his cinematic account of rural Indian life in the Apu trilogy: "There has been unmitigated trust extended to Ray's conscience story via Apu. But there is also the methodological ruse one can elicit from it: the truth-effect in the inadvertent form of an ethnographic allegory that will give us the clue to ramified cultural meanings—through reverse allegorical readings that work the text against the grain with political intent. While likening the Apu trilogy to an ethnographic allegory it becomes possible then to ask what significant displacement, what civilizational subversions it introduces in our notion of the contemporary" (225). Negotiating the twists and turns in this passage while wending our way through the terms *ruse, truth-effect, inadvertent form, ramified cultural meanings,* and *reverse allegorical readings*—which, we are told, "work the text against the grain"—we arrive at a declaration posed as a question: "it becomes possible then to ask." But there is no real question here, as the ending of the sentence indicates. Instead, what is given with one hand is taken with the other. Thus, the "revolutionary socialism" of Ghatak, whose film *Jukti, Takko ar Gappo* (Debate, Argument, and Story, 1974) she sees as "rejecting the overdetermination of the aesthetic," can be set against Ray's reformist realism (203–4).[19] As for Ray, he is seen, vis-à-vis his films of the 1950s (the Apu trilogy) and *Devi* (1960), as being paradoxical: "the very progressivism in the Apu trilogy . . . [is seen] to become diffused, to settle into a splendid hypostasis of hope" (228). By rendering hope into a metaphor of perennial deferral, Kapur locates Ray's films within "the ideology and norm of realism" (210). Using modifiers such as *subliminal* and *destinal* (213–14), she urges readers to enter a place that has already been predetermined in order to accept the indictment that Ray participated in "a romantic, even orientalist discourse" staged on an opposition between "the *indigenous* and the *universal*—euphemisms in Ray's case for the regional and the international" (207, Kapur's italics).

By now it is probably clear that I wish to offer a different answer to the question first asked by Williams in the essay that Kapur adapts as her own title: "When was modernism?" In taking this question from Williams, however, what was positioned as unsettled in his examination of the period and its pitfalls appears to have reached stasis in Kapur's study as she works her way through the predicament of contemporary cultural expression in India. The problematic of modernism is, in her hands, routed through a crypto-nativism that is all the more vaunted for its apparent engagement with Williams's theoretical positions, even though the ends have been determined in advance. So, although Kapur has cogently isolated issues that remain vexed, her representation of Ray serves as a cautionary tale.

By way of a final contrast between my approach and existing criticism, let me allude one last time to Kapur's discussion of Ray's film style and place it against the remarks of Ashish Rajadhyaksha, another Indian critic who has written more influentially on cinema.[20] First, here is Kapur:

> Ray is of course quite easily situated in film lineage. I am referring to the composite, broadly realist movement in cinema signalled by Renoir (to whom Ray apprenticed himself when he came to India in 1949 to make his film *The River*) and theorized by Andre Bazin, the philosopher-critic of existential persuasion. He is closer to the Italian Vittorio De Sica whose lasting intervention in cinema history via *Bicycle Thieves* (1947) influenced Indian filmmakers (Bimal Roy's *Do Bigha Zameen*, 1953, being the first evidence). With "classical" Hollywood directors like John Ford as the baseline, Ray picks his way through several options, aligned to realism on the one hand and to the new wave on the other. Finally, however, he retracts from the logical extension of both tendencies, particularly the latter which while incorporating realism gives itself over to modernist surrealism (as in Luis Bunuel [sic], Alain Resnais). Like the Japanese masters Kenzi [sic] Mizoguchi, Yasujiro Ozu and [Akira] Kurosawa, he finds a cultural location from where he can clarify, or even rigorously demystify, the means of representation. He offers the belief that art lends transparency to history and arrives at a near-classical repose. (221)

Now here is Rajadhyaksha on the same "broadly realist" impulse of Indian cinema and Ray's relationship to it:

> Realism, then, was for the most part a subterfuge: a means of weighting certain kinds of symbols of the contemporary with certain kinds of desires or apprehensions, all the while restaging earlier genres—the social reformist movie and its religious counterpart, the devotional movie—as full-blown melodrama. Ray himself—contrary to the common perception of his Renoir/De Sica persona—was not at the time averse to these genres or to the idea of updating them.[21]

If we give any credit to Rajadhyaksha's observation later on in the same essay that "Ray's retrospective vision was one of the high points of Indian cultural modernism, to the extent that India has had such a thing,"[22] we are better prepared to contend with the degree to which even critics who admire one another sometimes get entangled in mutually incompatible positions: Kapur regards Ray as naively pursuing a transparent realism while Rajadhyaksha speaks of the "subterfuge" involved in restaging realism as a modernist strategy of *détournement.* Such inconsistencies have less to do with the substantive difficulties of the realism-modernism debate than with an inadequate conception both of how ideas and movements travel as modes of critique and metacritique and of what is at stake in them.

My effort will be to engage a theorization of the avant-garde as it comes into contact with Ray's cinematic experiments from a perspective that refuses the assumptions and emphases revealed in either of the positions adduced above. I find psychological explanations of the contemporary ultimately uncompelling, whether in the psychosocial imputation of "desires or apprehensions," as Rajadhyaksha sees it, or the psychobiographical attribution of faith in "the ethical regime of authenticity" that, according to Kapur, stops Ray short of "effecting an upheaval in the structural formations designated as the Indian civilization and making a radical intervention in the historical process on hand."[23] Somewhat to the sidelines of the debate over whether Ray's films are realist, modernist, or both, my argument will follow a discontinuous strand of thinking about image and history.

In pursuing this strand of thought, I take my philosophical leads from the experiments in *thinking the visual* worked out in early Soviet film theory, especially by Sergei Eisenstein, and also from the ways that a preoccupation with transforming perception and reality is taken up in the "material aesthetics" of the Frankfurt School. We may recall that the theorists of the Frankfurt School who wrote on film (such as Walter Benjamin, Ernst Bloch, and Theodor Adorno, as well as their associates such as Siegfried Kracauer or Hanns Eisler) took many of their cues from the overall Soviet effort to find correlates of the goals of Marxist dialectics in the practice of the image, recognizing for their part that what remained unaddressed in Marx's analysis of capitalism was a theory of the superstructure.[24] It is in this particular theoretical context that an emphasis on the avant-garde reenters the discussion of technology and cultural form (pursued, as well, by Williams and Barthes). Such an emphasis also promotes an understanding of a new type of reception to cinema centered not on the meaning of parts to a whole but on how the spectator's attention is caught by the work's constituents and principles of construction. If, to paraphrase the opening of Adorno's *Negative Dialectics,* modernism only lives on because the moment to realize it has been missed,[25] I argue that in reprising missed opportunities, Ray's films give us a different template for understanding the crisis of contemporary existence in the avant-garde's terms of a crisis of aesthetic experience. I should say, too, that it is because of my interest in exploring the historicity of cinema as a social form that I am neither persuaded by nor compelled to follow recent debates in film studies over so-called changes in its object of analysis.[26]

POINTS OF CONVERGENCE

To establish the standpoint of analysis that articulates the various chapters of this book, let me return to a key qualification in Rajadhyaksha's description of Ray as a modernist. Saying that this description was true only to the extent that India has "had such a thing" as modernism, Rajadhyaksha temporizes both about the nature of Ray's directorial innovations and about the relationships between theory and practice. For he goes on to represent Indian modernism as orphaned, the result of a derivative encounter with European ideas that was not only belated but also incomplete: "This modernism had no debate between Brecht and Lukacs to inform it, it built no neo-realist citadel of truth, had no Adorno-like warnings about a totalitarian culture industry."[27] Let us set aside for the moment the fact that these debates are as much the inheritance of Indian as German or Hungarian intellectuals. Even more significantly, the argument posits an absence in India of conditions for articulating a specifically modernist response to modernity. But this is to misunderstand the directional flow between ideas and realities. Surely, it is neither the exchanges between Brecht and Lukács nor Adorno's critique of the culture industry that renders the trajectory of modernism so powerful but the actual, material pressures to which they were each responding?

It is crucial to see that the discourse of modernism as a historical, political, and experiential critique of modernity rests not on the sophistication of ideas (however attractive) but on the degree to which this discourse is prompted given circumstances to take up the challenge to thought under capitalism. If we are guided, in this as in other instances, by Marx's fundamental insight that being determines consciousness and not the other way around, we are enjoined to avoid the trap of the German ideologists Marx took to task in the nineteenth century. We have thus to recognize that it is the twentieth-century reality of mass culture, technological modernization, and the emergence of bourgeois social interests in India that makes modernism an appropriate model for understanding Ray's place within the panoply of aesthetic responses to modernity. The trajectory of modernism, then, must be seen as spurred on by contradictory and concrete experiences of the modern (in India as much as anywhere else) rather than the potency of intellectual ideas—Brecht, Adorno, or Lukács notwithstanding.

Any other way of parsing the issue represents an idealist view of our relationship to the past that risks repeating the errors of a history of ideas that mistook the adventures and misadventures of *Geist* (which we may gloss as consciousness) to be the basis of human history itself.

The challenge of specifying the contours of Ray's modernism therefore remains open. So even if Kapur is right to say "the modern never properly belongs to us as Indians," this observation turns on the weight of the adverb *properly*. What would it mean to belong properly, seamlessly, unproblematically to the modern? If there were a proper predication either of the experience or its narrativization, Williams's question "when was modernism?" would be rendered moot (as would Kapur's avowed allegiance to the standpoint of his investigation). A better, more historically nuanced account of the travails of modernism as it moves outside the space of European modernity, and as it comes to embody the particular sociohistorical dynamics and contradictions of peripheral and semiperipheral societies, is to be found in the Brazilian literary critic Roberto Schwarz's brilliant use of Adorno's aesthetic theory to comment on the encounter between aesthetic forms and the alienated totality that goes by the name of modernity everywhere. Schwarz provides his explanation in an essay written in 1980 entitled "Misplaced Ideas: Literature and Society in Late-Nineteenth Century Brazil." He emphasizes the simultaneous historical novelty and dissonance created by the belated arrival of European ideas in Brazil, which he refers to as their "ill-assortedness" that is at the same time "recognizably Brazilian in [its] peculiar distortion."[28] We should note that the stress here is less on the difference or incommensurability of Brazilian experience from the European case than on the lack of coordination between the ideology of capitalism and its adaptive possibilities.

According to Schwarz the specificity of Brazilian modernity was *not* that it did not obey the rules of the universalizing logic of capitalism (contra the superficial theories of "alternative modernities" that abound) but precisely that, in doing so, it took over and rearranged existing modes of political and social life.[29] In providing an account of the late arrival of the literary form of the novel in Brazil, Schwarz is by no means proposing a theory of belatedness; or, more precisely, he proposes a theory of belatedness that is not about cultural backwardness but about combined and uneven developments within capitalist social formations worldwide. The delayed arrival of Brazil into the world system of capital, he argues, results in a productive contradiction he calls a "misplaced idea." For the ideologies of the modern do not map themselves out comfortably in new locations.

They take hold in a jumbled and disorderly manner, exposing sociohistorical contradictions peculiar to the location and, in doing so, succeed in posing original problems in art and culture that surpass the conceptions that produced them in the first place. Schwarz argues that there is a narrative logic to the displacement of capitalism's structural logic onto social forms, and, as a key example, he cites the contrast between French and Russian literature vis-à-vis the emergence of the realist novel. Faced with their Russian counterparts, he says, "even the greatest novels of the French realism seem naïve. And why? In spite of their claims to universality, the psychology of rational egoism and the ethics of Enlightenment appeared in the Russian Empire as a 'foreign' ideology, and therefore, a localized and relative one. Sustained by its historical backwardness, Russia forced the bourgeois novel to face a more complex reality."[30]

In elaborating on how a belated encounter with an alien ideology resulted in a genuine renovation of form, Schwarz allows us to refocus on Ray's cinema by the light of a theory whose function is not to prescribe the definitional criteria of what counts as avant-garde. Instead, Schwarz enables us to get a firmer grasp on how, in *improperly* affirming European ideas, the conception of a (belated) avant-garde can be retrofitted to illustrate the experience of capitalist modernity in "foreign" locations—in all of the ill-fitting ways that the exportation of an expressive ideology transforms ideals of aesthetics and politics. In much the same manner that I earlier described Amal's literary experiment on the light of the new moon, the ensuing chapters flesh out the contours of how, as a "misplaced idea," Ray's films permit us to take up an ill-assorted gamble on reconceiving the possibility of political art.

In *Theory of the Avant-Garde* Peter Bürger asserted that the concept of the avant-garde only becomes meaningful as an attack on modernism's pretensions toward artistic autonomy, itself a function of the consolidation of capitalism in industrialized Europe. As he saw it, the avant-garde arises out of the division of labor that, under capitalist organization, separates art and society, public and private, as well as work and leisure. This bold emphasis on the division of labor under capitalism as the precondition of the avant-garde is frequently overlooked, both in restricting the parameters of the avant-garde to Europe and in asserting that post–World War II movements of literature and the arts worldwide express a hitherto unprecedented "hybridity" or "double consciousness" that is purely cultural. But while Bürger's theory does not suffer from the myopia of presentist views of global cultural traffic, it can be challenged on two counts: one, for its failure to address the non-West's impact on the avant-garde's initial emergence, and two, for its lack of analysis of the world market and the international division of labor that has accompanied capitalism's penetration of the globe from the time of its inception. With specific respect to the former, it is now generally acknowledged that there are demonstrable influences of non-Western cultures, specifically African, Caribbean, and Asian drawing and sculpture, on the practices associated with the historical avant-garde in Europe. In fact, the forceful borrowings from *haiku* poetry in surrealist forms, African rhythms in avant-garde musical compositions, or Chinese pictorial genres in Soviet cinematic ideas about montage are, we know, constitutive of the European discourse of primitivism, as well as other modernist statements.

The larger implications of redrawing our conception of the avant-garde are, however, still missed if we only claim the subsidiary status of "also ran" in making these connections between source and adaptation. Rather than simply introducing a "transnational" inflection to the circulation of ideas (which carries with it a hint of resentment about the status of non-Western cultural achievements), I seek to establish a historical case that emphasizes social contradictions and antagonisms. Also, a self-conscious history of the present, stripped simultaneously of Eurocentric preconceptions of cultural value and relativistic understandings of cultural difference, must contend with the shared experiences of modernity around the globe, and it is in this embodiment that Ray's cinema presents a powerful illumination of modern vicissitudes very much in and through their localized placement.

Unlike the views of influential European and American theorists of the avant-garde (such as Bürger, Hans Magnus Enzensberger, Renato Poggioli, Rosalind Krauss, Clement Greenberg, or T. J. Clark), my argument is that the lament over the impossibility of socially committed art under capitalism is in fact contradicted by the expansive and anti-imperial social imagination found in Ray's films (as well as other expressions of protest literature from various parts of the globe). This is why, in many respects, I see no particular advantage in pitting Ray as a "reformist modernist" (à la Kapur) against Ghatak or some other, more recent, director produced in the hothouse, activist environment of the Indian Film Institute in Pune (where Ghatak taught for a few years and developed a following that has emerged as the dominant voice of independent Indian cinema). My overall contention is that, contrary to the philosophical exhaustion and pessimism of their earlier European counterparts, films such as the ones examined in this book continue to struggle toward a revitalization of the "lifeworld," even under capitalist existence and very much as a redoubt against it.

How to think of progress without reducing it to economic advancement? How to aspire to enlightenment without abstracting it in the direction of an "obtuse" rationality? How to rescue an ideal of community from the debris of mass culture? These are the many faces of aesthetic commitment in the ways that Ray elaborates it.

What I have said so far is in keeping with Fredric Jameson's proposals in *Signatures of the Visible*. In that collection Jameson averred that the only way to conceptualize the visual is to grasp its historical emergence. Moreover, he argued that particularly in the contemporary world film represents the exemplary locus for understanding the mediation of historiographic concerns by aesthetic or formal ones. This is also to say that categories such as modernism, realism, or postmodernism make only a modicum of sense when used as periodizing labels. On the contrary, these categories must be historicized as subsumptions of the relationships among space, time, and the mode of production, no less. Jameson's attempt to sever cultural analysis from an exclusive preoccupation with style and to reorient us toward the radical proposition that history is transmitted through form gives us a different perspective on the center-periphery model of cultural transmission. It suggests that cultural practices from the periphery are not so much constituted by their distance from the dominant cultural order as marked by the same social and historical contradictions that make the distinction legible in the first place: between center and periphery, First and Third World, culture and its margins.

Along these lines it may be proposed that Ray's modernism exemplifies precisely such a reformulation of conventional distinctions between form/content and center/periphery, so that it becomes possible to read his films less as representative examples of Third World cinema than as definitive meditations on the ways that film transmits historical perception, including the perception of being modern. Jameson's analysis also permits us to replace the directional imperative behind our understanding of Ray's modernism—as a filmic style "borrowed" from great European directors such as Fellini, De Sica, or Bergman—with a perspective that can take closer account of his directorial "signature," without attributing a subordinate status to his efforts. As I will try to establish in chapter 5, a film like *Mahanagar* (The Big City, 1963) attests both to his borrowings from Fritz Lang and his surpassing of Lang's vision. And although Ray's formal innovations in editing tempo or camera movement have been observed often enough, much less has been said about his stress on cinema's refraction of the ways that organic social relations are everywhere deranged under capitalist modernity.

Within such a broadly materialist perspective Ray's treatment of the well-worn subject of the debate over tradition and modernity extends only to the nominal level of narrative content. Likewise, his portrayals of nineteenth- and twentieth-century social mores are, I would argue, only the means for more philosophical propositions about the retroactivity of historical understanding. Instead of discussing whether Ray's filmic narratives accurately capture historical or thematic realities, I think we are better served by looking at his efforts to intensify the language of cinema and push it to its limits as a refutation of the allure of bourgeois art (whose foundational impulse is to make life bearable through the magic of narrative). In this way his cinema makes it possible to explore what the image can do to critique reason, a somewhat abstract idea that rests on a distinction familiar to readers accustomed to Hegelian terms: between cinema as a positive form *in itself* and that which exists critically, self-consciously, and *for itself*.[31] Ray's films exemplify the latter, in that they are not so much "about" what is India, modern Bengali womanhood, colonial Indian history, and so on (even if conventional film and literary scholars, historians, and others have almost exclusively used such affirmative considerations to refer to them). That is to say, his works do not so much *reflect* historical, aesthetic, or cultural problems as present critical, dialectical conceptualizations of the continuities between art and experience.

To say that Ray's cinema is conceptual rather than representational is to distinguish between differing notions of *mimesis* poised between the classical, conventional sense of the mimetic (going back to Aristotle) as that which reflects or imitates reality and a dialectical understanding of mimesis (in the tradition of Lukács and Adorno, despite their differences) as an immanent perception of the mutual entanglement of subject and object. My effort in the chapters that follow will be to chart the complicated course involved in analyzing Ray's films along the latter lines without, one hopes, diminishing the pleasures of the texts themselves or explaining away their difficulties. Ray's work must also be read against the backdrop of an international post–World War II *cinéaste* environment that gave rise to independent film movements in places such as France, Latin America, Japan, and Africa. Many if not most of these movements were impelled, at least in part, by a need to question the role of art in modern societies, and the questions they posed were similar in both form and substance to approaches taken by the early European avant-gardes.

As a result, the analytic leads I pursue return to these early approaches, questions, and settings; by that token they are hardly new but are also very much outside trends in film scholarship—which, if one looks at work in postcolonial film criticism in particular, is largely presentist and exceptionalist in its bent, often in the name of disavowing Eurocentrism. To the degree that my discussion returns to an earlier conjuncture in Europe in order to situate Ray's cinematic experiments, the time of this undertaking is perhaps out of joint. His own reliance on European sources also seems at odds, at least temperamentally, with current scholarly regimes that keep beckoning us to "provincialize Europe."[32] Nonetheless, such a redrawing of the lineages not only of Ray's cinematic project but also of the social vision of independent aesthetic movements in the Third World is, I would submit, both necessary and overdue, and part of an emergent critical imperative to rethink the problem of "world literature" as an integral component of the lineages of the present.[33]

Theoretically speaking, the reason to go back to an older model of ciné-aesthetics informed by the likes of Eisenstein, Benjamin, Kracauer, or Béla Balázs (who were not all "European" in quite the ways that some postcolonial scholarship would like to reduce them, since one was a Soviet, the others Jews from Germany and Hungary, respectively) is its contemporary relevance. In reading this body of work, I am always struck by the fact that its materialist insights have not, despite continually recycled assertions about their outdatedness, been superseded by other approaches to film criticism. Indeed, the opposite is true, especially when it comes to understanding expressive forms that attempt to foreground the problem of social and historical contradiction. If this sounds like an odd way to begin a book on a Bengali director and his cinematic practice, it is because I want to signal a set of overlapping theoretical and political contentions advanced in these pages. The first, as I have already begun to outline, has to do with arguing in favor of dialectical thought and its relevance for understanding non-Western and postcolonial cultures. The second is a corollary of the first, and it guides the thematic arguments of my chapters. It is based on thinking that although the critical choices one makes can always be attributed to taste and formation alone, the stakes and consequences sometimes extend beyond the issue of personal preference. In the present instance I am convinced that it is no longer possible, if it ever was, to discuss Ray's films outside of the context of an internationalist New Wave cinema movement and, therefore, *not* as representative of "Indian cinema" in any strong sense (even though he remains in my estimation the most accomplished Indian filmmaker to date). I also think it is time to redirect the conversation about Third World cinema away from the emphasis on multiculturalism and cultural difference, on the one hand, and, even more, from the fixation on subjectivity and identity, on the other. The effects of these emphases have, at least in practice, been antithetical to serious critique.

More than anything, such emphases have impelled us to cordon off Indian cinema (or the African novel, for that matter) in its own, now newly exalted cultural province, rendering, say, debates with German Expressionism impertinent to its concerns. But breaking contact in this artificial way has had negative consequences. Not only did Ray share some of the sensibility and social goals of his expressionist forebears, however distant they may have been from his location and subject matter, but it is also the case that his work, along with theirs, directs attention away from thinking of the avant-garde as merely interested in novelty or rupture. At base the idea of an avant-garde (both insist) has less to do with capturing the new for its own sake than in retraining our perception of the old, almost as an antidote to the forms of reprogramming that capitalism imposes on its subjects. Specified in this manner, the avant-garde represents neither a set of known artists nor a historically delimited artistic experiment alone but an overall *outlook* that, in the words of Benjamin, sought to trace "the revolutionary energies that appear in the outmoded: the first factory buildings, the earliest photos, the objects that have begun to be extinct."[34] This commitment to the old and to the past—albeit seen in a different, noninstrumental and critical light—is expressed most clearly in one of the best-known texts associated with the European avant-garde movement, Louis Aragon's early surrealist novel *Paris Peasant*, in which Aragon sees himself as speaking on behalf of "places that were incomprehensible yesterday and that tomorrow will never know."[35]

As we will see, many of Ray's films express the same conviction about the need to recognize the past anew, not in a nostalgic reprisal but, paradoxically, as a repository for the future; in addition, they provide a reflexive commentary on cinema as a homeopathic intervention: on how the filmic apparatus can *cut into* the ideology of accepted conventions of sight itself. With the emergence of cinema the debate about what constitutes such a redirection of perception shifts to a specific consideration of the film medium's capacity to further the aims originally expressed by the avant-garde via painting, sculpture, installations, and other media. Cinema comes to represent the subjective and objective potentiality sought insofar as it reflexively mediates means and ends. So, if the fundamental ambition of the avant-garde was to provoke a new type of reception to the work of art—from an overreliance on meaning or correspondence to a focus on the artwork's constituent elements and principles of construction—the film medium finally permitted this reorientation given that its technological bases and its representational capacities are only intelligible in terms of each other. Solely in the context of a technologically mediated, image-ridden society does the homeopathic potentiality of film to expose the ideologies of vision by "penetrat[ing] the world before our eyes" become evident. This is Kracauer's phrase, and I use it to flag my reliance on his arguments about cinema.[36]

It should be said that although Kracauer has once again emerged as an important source for critics such as Mary Ann Doane, Miriam Hansen, and the late Dagmar Barnouw, his voluminous writings are completely ignored in postcolonial discussions of film and culture. But I would submit, for reasons that follow, that he is critical in locating Ray's works within an anticlassical, antimimetic understanding of the medium. Specifically, what is of fundamental importance here is that Kracauer's theory is not just abstractly related to Ray's films. In other words, my invocation of his work stems not just from an ex post facto desire to lend weight to the book by dressing it in the trappings of critical theory. On the contrary, I refer to Kracauer because *his* theory was elaborated with Ray literally in mind (giving the lie to the notion that critics associated with the Frankfurt School were all unmitigated Eurocentrists). It is by now mostly forgotten that Kracauer began and ended his major work, *Theory of Film*, by alluding to Ray in his basic contentions regarding the materialist ontology of cinema. Almost at the beginning of the book (in the preface) he states: "From Lumière's first film strips to Fellini's *Cabiria*, from *Birth of a Nation* to *Aparajito* [Ray's second film], . . . practically all important cinematic statements have been made in black and white and within the traditional format."[37] The book ends with another reference to Ray as the director who made it possible to argue for a conception of cinematic universality without doing violence to the specificities of location, time, and story. Indeed, Kracauer gives Ray almost the last word in establishing what the cinema can do to capture the world for everyone, comparing Erich Auerbach's conception of the modern novel as the form in which "the elementary things which men in general have in common" with his estimation of Ray's works as having penetrated "ephemeral physical reality and burn[ed] through it" (311). Consequently, it is neither a matter of fetishizing European theory on my part nor of exoticizing the "other" on Kracauer's that is at issue in interpreting Ray's films by the light of his theoretical formulations. The point is rather that Kracauer's large-scale conceptions of the cinematic medium were offered with Ray's cinema as one of his foundational examples, though this historiographic fact may come as a surprise to some.

With this I can say a little more about the framework of analysis Kracauer enables. For him the specificity of the filmic medium resides in its immanent, indexical relationship to reality. Furthermore, the world of film "is a flow of random events involving both humans and inanimate objects" (1). It is important to recognize that in proposing these concrete links between the world of film and the world of reality, Kracauer was not subscribing to a semiotic framework of signs and signifiers but working from a fundamentally different tradition of Weimar thought that took aesthetic experience to be symptomatic of the historical crisis of experience. From Kracauer's apocalyptic standpoint, then, cinema both embodies the experience of modernity and renders its catastrophe in an expressive form, though his goal was neither to psychologize this nor to transform it aesthetically. Instead, he sought to historicize the cinema as "an approach to the world, a mode of human existence" (li).

To the extent that for the historical avant-garde, turning away from the ideology of artistic autonomy—the ideology of "art for art's sake"—had less to do with affirming experimental techniques than with highlighting how art ciphers sociohistorical contradictions, cinema emerged as its handmaiden. This is because it is the first medium, ushered in by technological developments (since it derived from photomechanical techniques), that reflexively represents the very modernity that birthed it. Thus, if the fate of art is seen as symptomatic of broader changes in the structure of experience and the avant-garde stands as the doomed response to this crisis, cinema can be said to reveal this mutually constituted destiny well into the present, even, and perhaps especially, in its non-Western locations.

POINTS OF ARRIVAL

I have spent this time on the relevance of conceptual formulations relating to the avant-garde and their implications for examining Ray's work because I think such a historical and theoretical lens is crucial both for an adequate understanding of his films and for a contextualization of the development of cinematic institutions in India. It is important to remember that the early twentieth-century debates in Europe and their transformation into arguments about the specific nature and role of cinema were not that distant in time from the emergence of Indian cinema itself. Within six months of discovering the capacities of cinematic projection and exhibiting their filmstrips in Paris, the Lumière brothers had sent their representatives across the globe—with their first reels (*The Arrival of a Train in*

Ciotat Station and *Leaving the Factory*) being shown in Bombay in 1896. So whatever the utility of pondering whether or not the novel emerges belatedly in India (and the epistemological or political consequences of this), when it comes to Indian cinema, we have to note that its development was largely contemporaneous with its European counterparts. Calcutta (now renamed Kolkata, though I prefer to follow the older spelling for its historical resonances), the site of Ray's political and aesthetic investments throughout his life, had its first movie theater in 1898, and its precursor, the British-run Bourne and Shepherd photographic studio there, dates back to 1868.

These international influences soon acquired local color, and, with his production of *Raja Harishchandra* (1913), Dadasaheb Phalke introduced the first Indian feature film, explicitly advocating the nationalist philosophy of *swadeshi* (indigenous production and self-sufficiency). Phalke was struck by the pedagogic possibilities of the medium after seeing Alice Guy's French film *The Life of Christ* (1910), while at the same time his motives remained consistent with the Brahminical rhetoric of his orthodox Maharashtrian milieu. Crucially, the vanguard properties of the medium were subordinated to the emergent imperative of profit-making (quickly realized thereafter by the large-scale popularity of the genre of "mythological" films that formed the bulk of Indian cinema in the early part of the twentieth century). In something of a paradox, the imperative to inculcate a Hinduized worldview—as part and parcel of the discourse of anticolonial, anti-Western nationalism—was derived at the intersection of Indian and European sources, given that Phalke's inspiration for rendering the myth of King Harishchandra was sparked by a version of Guy's film made for the Pathé company, a French outfit that had cornered the global market for selling film stock. Phalke was apparently prompted by the thought that if Jesus could be the subject of films in the secular West, then the adventures of the Hindu gods could furnish an inexhaustible supply of source material for Indian films.

The impetus for Bengali cinema came from the remake in 1917 of Phalke's *Raja Harishchandra*, while a different, more activist, tendency expressed itself in film with Dhiren Ganguly's *Bilet Pherat* (1921), in which the problem of Westernization was thematized through a satire of the manners and pretensions of an Anglicized Bengali bourgeoisie. Formed within the universalizing and cosmopolitan outlook of Rabindranath Tagore's university in Shantiniketan, Ganguly can be thought of as the forerunner to Ray, not only in terms of his outlook but also in his self-conscious intention to politicize the institution of cinema. Perhaps inevitably, his own fate recalls that of many other avant-garde efforts from the same period, seeing as his representation of communal violence in *Razia Begum* (the story of a female Mughal ruler who falls in love with a Hindu subject) resulted in its being censored.

What I have said so far intimates not only the material and historical contingencies that defined the international crisscrossing of medium, story, and circumstances of Ray's emergence; it also betokens the economic and political realities of a milieu that today would hardly be recognized (given the disfavor with which any discussion of internationalism is now received). Nonetheless, the specificity of Ray's practice only gains its legibility from this early history, as well as from the cultural and political environment of the postwar period—in which ideas germinated and traveled across new wave movements in France, Germany, Eastern Europe, Africa, Latin America, and India. There were, of course, peculiarities attached to geopolitical realities of the North and South, as well as core and periphery, but an overall commitment to a collective, progressive vision of a world was, as I suggested earlier, present throughout. As an example of this commitment the Calcutta Film Society (which Ray founded along with others such as fellow artist Chidananda Das Gupta in 1947, the year of India's independence) served as an important site for shifting the conversation about modern art and culture from its mooring in European thought and experience and reanchoring it in non-Western texts and realities. To undertake this project in a way that was a substantive effort at raising consciousness rather than an empty gesture of nativist appropriation, Ray and Das Gupta understood that they first had to educate the Calcutta literati in the various European and Soviet traditions of cinema; only then could an alternative tradition express its full force, though it had by no means to be merely parasitic. Fully accepting that a conventional education in European (or at least British) traditions was par for the course for literate and urban Indian readers, Ray wanted more, both for and from his native audiences. To this end, India's first film society introduced audiences to the films of American directors such as Frank Capra, John Ford, and John Huston, as well as those of Eisenstein, Vladimir Pudovkin, and De Sica. It is, of course, true that for Ray, as much as for anyone else, cultural literacy was a matter of specialization and the stuff of the cultivation of an intelligentsia as opposed to the education of the masses. He also understood that even if colonialism had dictated that middle-class Indians be inculcated into the manners of the British (able to recite, at will, snatches of Shakespeare or Wordsworth or speak knowingly of the exploits of Billy Bunter and the mysteries of Enid Blyton), a more nuanced appreciation of classical and modernist experiments in European art and literature was required of a visually literate audience. Therefore, that aesthetic experience is a *conceptual* problem is something that Ray understood very well. Taking my cue from him, I attempt to get beyond the banal afterimage that the high culture–low culture debates seem to have imprinted on us and to put conceptuality back on the table.

In many of his writings Ray alludes to the predicament of being a Third World director who had to confront the chasm between experimental, antitraditional modes of storytelling, which form the guiding principle of independent aesthetic practices, and the penchant for mass cultural, profit-driven narratives of mainstream cinema in India—where there was very little appreciation for self-consciously radical or progressive art. Keeping faith with Ray's own inclinations, we might be in a better position to contend with the experimental quality of his practice if we recognize in it a futural dimension for which there is as yet no counterpart in reality. On this reading cinema has the potential to be politically progressive not when it tries to *adequate* the textual and the historical but when it fully accepts that the surplus of signification resides less in the vicissitudes of representation (which would bind them to their own time) than in the contradictions of historical existence that possess what Marx called "general validity." Regardless of their generality, such contradictions take specific forms, as he explains in the *Grundrisse;* their universality is, by this token, a product of particular "historic relations."

Commentators have pointed out that Ray's cinema must be seen as a by-product of the Nehruvian project of nation-building, with its cosmopolitan impulses. But this genteel cosmopolitanism also came into contact with (and felt the impact of) the grassroots consciousness-raising style adopted by the Leninist programs of cultural empowerment of the Indian People's Theatre Association (IPTA) and the Progressive Writers Movement. In post-Independence Calcutta, especially, the IPTA and the Progressive Writers held the kind of sway—because of several Left Front governments—that remains relatively unmatched elsewhere. These local cultural factors aside, Ray's cinema evinces the influence of a more broadly global artistic and cultural zeitgeist extending beyond the boundaries of his location. This larger frame of reference demands that we see Ray in terms of more than a merely contextual experiment with the visual image; instead, his work becomes paradigmatic when he is placed within a wider artistic and political conversation that attempted to rethink the conditions of possibility of art under capitalism. Ray's politics, albeit not as explicitly subversive as that of his contemporary fellow-director Ghatak (for example), can thus be discerned not by looking for already constituted cinematic topics that advertise themselves as overt protest but by understanding that his was what Eisenstein had called "an ideational cinema"—a conceptualization of the world rather than a representational reaction to it.[38] This is not to say that Ray's conceptual take was either realized or realizable, nor do its limitations render his vision romantic or reformist. Indeed, many of his films betoken the failure of modernity to bring with it enlightenment and salvation or even to effect a satisfactory negotiation between old models of thinking or being and new horizons of possibility.

Closer to the particular film-theoretical leads I follow in this book, the shift from affirmative to nondocumentable, negative realities is what Kracauer avers is uniquely possible in the filmic medium's capacity to explode the real, promoting in its stead the disenchanted vision of a Sancho Panza who exposes "the Donquichoteries of ideologies and intentional constructions."[39] This suggests an approach to the medium that has less to do with subjective representation than with objective revelation. Or again, as Kracauer puts it, the power of the filmic medium lies in laying things bare and in its "gravi[tation] toward the expanses of outer reality—an open-ended, limitless world."[40] On this view film functions less as portrait or representation than talisman of the surrounding world, along with other technological innovations such as the telegraph, telephone, railroad, automobile, and photograph.[41] The medium's affinity with the physical world is premised on the effects on the viewer and in terms of the subject, who is simultaneously barred from authentic experience and shocked into witnessing at every turn the transformation of life into spectacle.[42] While there is much more to be said about material aesthetics and the extent to which Ray's films bear witness to such a commitment, it suffices here to designate a constellation of arguments about the relationship of critical theory to a postcolonial *grammar* of the cinema as articulated in Ray's works.

By the time of his death in 1992, Ray had won every major international film award (including an Oscar for lifetime achievements), and there are several studies of his life and work.[43] But even when he is invoked as one of the great modernist auteurs, this is immediately followed by a potted critique of auteur theory. By this means, Ray's achievements can be assimilated within a critique of auteurism—seen as an intentionalist paradigm that, in practical terms, overinflates the role of the director in the assembly-line process that more accurately characterizes filmmaking.[44] And then there are critics who do not concern themselves either with industry considerations about who does what during the production process or with mounting a critique of auteurism qua humanism. For them Ray is seen wholly in terms of the degree to which he was or was not a classical realist filmmaker. In this approach, he is regarded as having borrowed techniques from his European and American counterparts in order to represent the dilemmas of rural and urban life in modern India. On the other hand, he is seen as someone whose films are so authentically Indian they are simply incommensurable with forms of meaning and being—and therefore of interpretation—in the so-called West.[45]

The complexity of Ray's work cannot be grasped on the terms above and without attending to the formal aspects of his films. This essential premise of my overall argument has less to do with getting caught up in the intricacies of shot structure, montage, or cinematography than with realizing that the recursive turns of his films—in and out of form, function, and narrative—render some variety of formalist explication necessary. Moreover, Ray's filmmaking expresses his metacritical commitment to the idea that story worlds do not by themselves embody a cinematic predicament; the latter has to be elicited by means of reflexive strategies and techniques. But the question of form also constitutes ciné-aesthetics per se and is fundamental to reckoning with cinematic objects, which reveal again and again that our appreciation of filmic events centers not only on what is portrayed but how and why. In fact, Ray himself proposed a strong version of the need to *think with the cinema* (as opposed to thinking *about* it) when he approvingly cited Chaplin on the importance of the apparatus: "When a camera is placed on the floor and moves about the player's nostrils, it is the camera that is giving the performance and not the actor."[46]

Still, at the end of the day Ray's work is more faceted in its dimensions than any single study or emphasis can hope to assimilate. Critical responses to his films vary as much today as they did when they first drew attention (among reviewers more than scholars), though it is not that our comprehension of the worlds they evoke is now either predetermined or, by contrast, beyond us in some ineffable way. My strategy is thus to approach his films less with comprehensive discussion in mind than with a situated examination of the distinctive form of postcolonial modernism they exemplify.

To this end I look at six of his films selected for their illustrative and argumentative value. In four of the chapters I focus on films that shed light on the dialectics of Indian, particularly Bengali, modernity at the turn of the nineteenth century (a point in history that Ray returns to in several of his films), when the signs of India's entry into the modern were spectacularly punctuated by the mutual reinforcements of colonialism, capitalism, and the struggle for national sovereignty. In Ray's hands this historical moment is conjured up retroactively as a telescoping of the problem of existence itself, now inevitably framed within and by the actuality of an emergent capitalist modernity, as well as within and by the technological mediation of cinema. We are thus given a very specific moment of historical transition and emergence and a very deliberate investment in recursively capturing the predicament of being caught between an old and new order. In all but two of the films I discuss, these historical and subjective crises are rendered as the predicament, most pointedly, of women, who emblematize what it is to be positioned on the brink of an emergent sensibility of newness, change, even freedom, but burdened, as well, by a sense of historical loss. In the two remaining chapters (on *Jalsaghar* [The Music Room, 1958] and *Apur Sansar* [The World of Apu, 1959]) my interest is in the reversal of Ray's directorial perspective: from the feminine to masculine dilemmas of experience. The particular gender inflections aside, with each film under discussion my goal is to interweave narratological concerns with Ray's experimental attempts to work out the dialectic between movement and image, duration and meaning.

In my first chapter I present a reading of what is perhaps Ray's most familiar film, *Ghare Baire* (Home and the World, 1984). Its popularity within critical circles and in class syllabi on the literature of modernity can probably be explained as a by-product of the interest in issues of nationalism and consciousness that has flourished, however ambivalently, over the past two decades. Ray's take on the problem of consciousness continues a theme he had first explored in his 1964 film *Charulata* (The Lonely Wife). *Ghare Baire* self-consciously evokes its earlier counterpart, *Charulata*, and in doing so bears witness to the dialectical shift that the twenty years separating the making of these two films produced in his cinematic perspective. Moving from a treatment of subjective contingencies of gendered perception in *Charulata* to a reflection on the objective conditions of history (whose burden is imposed on women in very particular ways) *Ghare Baire* serves as an elaboration of the problem of catastrophe. Overall, I am concerned with distinguishing between reading *Ghare Baire* as a tragic portrait of feminine subjectivity and an allegory about the redemptive potential embedded in catastrophic figurations. The tension underlying competing visions of the place of women in the struggle over Indian independence is both etiolated and, I argue, overcome in Ray's remake of a novel by Rabindranath Tagore.

Chapter 2 returns to Ray's first experiment with the problem of reflexivity, especially as it designates the arena of perception and the cinematic and historical mechanisms by which vision, often presumed to be neutral, is modernized, given a historical inflection, an epistemological weight, as well as local color. *Charulata* is a film that labors exquisitely over these issues, reflecting on what is captured by the camera and how what is photographed is made intelligible to the viewer by musical means. The eye of the camera and the eye of the female protagonist are the dual points of emphasis in my examination of the contrary aspects of modern Indian consciousness worked out in this, Ray's most accomplished film (and one that he professed to be his best). Meditating on the cultural and gender-specific entailments of the phenomenological dimensions of human experience such as aurality, temporality, and visuality, I draw attention to the reorganization of these dimensions and to the reflexive commentary the film enables on technologies of vision. My argument is that this film gives us an entirely new formulation of the relationships between form and content, in the process displacing the question of cinematic representation onto philosophical considerations of time and space, subject and object, narrative and memory.

Chapter 3 examines the fate of religiosity as it comes into conflict with the increasingly Europeanized and secularized worldview that was part and parcel of British rule in India. But Ray's intervention in *Devi* (The Goddess, 1960) is not staged as a critique of gender ideology alone, even if this has been the mainstay of most interpretations. No less is it a straightforward indictment of Hinduism itself, although this was the reason the film provoked the ire of the Indian censor board upon its release in 1960. Instead, Ray literalizes the trope of woman-as-goddess in order to underscore its catastrophic extravagance as a metaphor for both womanhood and religious devotion. *Devi* is a formal exploration of the annihilating magic of the cinema and its ability to conjure up the twin fetishes of religion and the commodity. Ray's preoccupation here with what can only be called "baroque" ornamentation offers a statement about the impossible predicament in which belief finds itself in the modern era. This impossibility pertains as much to belief in the power of the feminine as to the power of the divine, caught as each is between the extremes of doctrinal obsession and secular zeal, myth and enlightenment.

Following this line of argument, chapter 4 takes up a single though paradigmatic proposition: if cinema, as the quintessential medium of the twentieth century, encodes the sociohistorical contradictions of our time, what is the role of music (or other cinematic "attractions") in deepening or exposing them? To ask this is to recall that films encode meaning in ways that are very different from other modern systems of communication, particularly literature. This chapter expands on the argument that the goal of Ray's cinema is not to render the pathos of a disappearing past, or reconcile us to the present, but to intimate the as-yet unrealized future. The idea that cinema is a hieroglyph of alienated social relations, and that ciné-music functions as the code that on occasion permits the surface of this reality to be penetrated, is central to *Jalsaghar*. Retelling a fairly familiar story about the shifting meanings of decadence in the transition from a feudal to a modern social order in Bengal, Ray deploys motifs derived from the traditions of North Indian classical music and dance as a counterpoint to reinforce, as well as undercut, the largely conventional representation of Indian history in the film's plot.

Chapter 5, on the 1963 film *Mahanagar* (The Big City) takes us into a very different diegetic orbit although the conceptual and epistemological problems posed in this film are fully consistent with the ideas of emergence and crisis that occupy me in the other chapters. Here I focus on the narrative connections Ray draws between the inevitability of *gharoa* (or household) life in lower-middle-class circumstances exemplified by the drudgery of the protagonists' existence and the disconnected temporality or pace demanded by metropolitan, capitalist modes of being. But these narrative preoccupations are also explicitly formalized—in relation to the image itself. In this way, instead of emphasizing elements of narrative construction (which settles on a fairly predictable set of familial conflicts), the text underscores formal constructs: camera movement, editing, and self-conscious allusions to film history. As a result *Mahanagar*, which has been seen by some critics (like Pauline Kael) as a less-than-rich film is, I argue, deliberately so because Ray uses the medium to convey a critique of the demand for filmic "depth" and "richness"—ideals that, at the thematic level, are constitutively unavailable to subjects whose lives are precariously balanced between *bhadralok* (middle-class) niceties and sheer poverty. The bareness of the form of life narrated is thus elucidated through the thinness of the film's own formal appearance. My intention is to extend the argument about "imperfect cinema" proposed by Julio García Espinosa in order to consider Ray's formulation of a cinematic aesthetic proper to the imperfections of life itself in Third World contexts.

By focusing on a very different kind of film, the last one in the "Apu trilogy," as the object of my final chapter, I want to resist the impression of a teleological unfolding both of Ray's style and subject matter—since all three of the Apu films are set in post-Independence India (as contrasted with the colonial locale of four of the six films discussed in this book). Based on a popular Bengali novel by Bibhutibhushan Bandopadhyay, this film is much more than an individual or local story about self versus society, particularly in the ways Ray draws on his neorealist predecessors to offer a structural and universal critique of aesthetic ideology. In expressing this critique, Ray found himself remarkably close to the position made famous and familiar to us by the Frankfurt School: namely, that artworks cannot provide the consolation that life itself disallows. At the same time, doubling back in a comment on his own location, Ray also highlights the material and aesthetic constraints forced on a Third World director with limited resources at his command—as a reproof against the kitsch of conventional Indian cinema and as resistance to the dominant Hollywood or Bollywood ethos of filmmaking.

I conclude by focusing on the idea of "late style" *(Spätstil)* formulated in Adorno's unfinished book on Beethoven. Although neither Adorno nor any of the other figures in critical theory have been engaged by mainstream postcolonial criticism in any depth (there are some exceptions), the Adornian proposition of lateness was taken up by Edward Said in his last (posthumously published) book, *On Late Style*. Unlike Said I see lateness as more than a matter of "style"; it is, rather, a decisive concept for rethinking the configurational form of Ray's cinematic experiments, returning us once more, in a new way, to the idea of belatedness and its implications for cinema. As modern art lives out its life amid the contradictions of experience, including in its postcolonial variations, "late style" emerges as an aesthetic commentary on alienated existence.

1 Catastrophe and Utopia

Ghare Baire, *or the Household Goddess*

> Future mysteries will arise from the ruins of today's.
> —LOUIS ARAGON, *Paris Peasant*

REDEMPTIVE HISTORY/REFLEXIVE CINEMA

On July 25, 1915, the *New York Times* reviewed a biography of Rabindranath Tagore that quotes the poet advancing the following contrast between European and Indian women:

> In Europe homes are disappearing and hotels are increasing in number. When we notice that men are happy with their horses, dogs, guns, and pipes and clubs for gambling, we feel quite safe to conclude that women's lives are being broken up. . . . Our women make our homes smile with sweetness, tenderness, and love. . . . We are quite happy with our household goddesses, and they themselves have never told us of their "miserable condition." Why, then, should the meddlers from beyond the seas feel so bad about the imagined sorrows of our women? People make mistakes in imagining too much as to what would make others happy or unhappy. If perchance the fishes were to become philanthropists their tender hearts would find satisfaction only in drowning the entire human race in the depths of water.

The reviewer notes that Tagore seems to have possessed "sparkle and depth," although nothing is said about his droll assessment that "in Europe homes are disappearing." Close to a century later, it remains unclear whether these words would meet with anything other than dismissal. For some contemporary readers a sense of humor might not be enough to overlook Tagore's paternalism toward the "household goddesses" who apparently made Indian homes "smile with sweetness." Others might find it implausible to suggest that non-Western women enjoyed any advantages over their European counterparts, then or now. Still, the fact that times have changed, or that a feminist recasting of "the woman question" has made the notion of the happy housewife somewhat risible, does not negate the enduring resonance of Tagore's provocation: what makes women happy?

If Sigmund Freud's preference was to shift this question onto the unconscious territory of "what a woman wants," then we would have to say that the sexualized subjectivity at the heart of his approach retains only minimal contact with the philosophical problem that occupied Tagore: to wit, the thinking that civilizational discontent does not foreclose on the possibility of utopia, no matter how limited the terms of conceptualizing the search for a happier place. For Freud the answer to happiness was rooted in the unconscious and its directional imperatives—where happiness is a contingency of subjective being whose ends are only achieved negatively, with "civilization" or the "super-ego" performing the break between desire and social satisfaction. It is this notion of civilization with which Tagore takes issue; indeed, this is the import of his provocation. On his satirical take, if the European subject-as-fish wants to "drown" Indians in a sea of universalizing pretensions, it is in part because schemas about happiness and its objects are mutually unintelligible across cultures, Freud's assertions notwithstanding. But despite their dissimilar views about what makes people happy, Tagore and Freud agreed about the power of storytelling to contribute to it. In both their accounts stories are seen to exert a real force on consciousness, including on the experience of happiness. From this convergence of otherwise divergent worldviews we may glean that insofar as stories everywhere provide insight into incommensurable contingencies of desire and meaning, their incommensurability nonetheless touches on something that can be said to represent a universal form of experience. Moreover, we can only begin to take account of this generality if we get past binarisms such as East/West or primitive self/modern society, which have become, to borrow a phrase from a now-unfashionable Marxist lexicon, bad abstractions.

To shift the discussion of happiness from the terrain of the unconscious onto the site of sociality, then, we may propose that stories are not just the expression of sublimated desires in life (à la Freud) but experiential confrontations with death—taken as the denial of futurity. As such, they are inversely related to the possibility of happiness, and these confrontations recur in consoling, compensating, or conceptualizing guises within narrative at large. Death, as the terminus of life, is the ultimate contingency that storytelling seeks to keep at bay and in doing so relates to a collective vision of utopia disconnected from the individualized Freudian opposition of the life instinct/death drive [*Lebenstriebe/Todestriebe*].[1] Put in different terms, aesthetic experience universally pertains to imagining the experience of death in life as a necessary aspect of imagining a better, happier life itself. From this chiasmic perspective the opening "once upon a time" or concluding "lived happily ever after" of stories is not merely the fabulation of a mythic past or fantastical future but also a spatiotemporal animation of ideals of happiness, emergence, and freedom and their reverse coin: misery, unfreedom, or death. Together, these circumscribe the present and place limits on the possibility of conceiving happiness. Consequently, the utopian imagination—in every location in which it finds expression—has to contend with both privileged and negative registers of experience and emotion not only in order to distinguish between them but also to show their interdependence in configuring what is yet to come.

That the future is imagined through the past and present is, obviously, a familiar proposition, though perhaps it is fair to say that we are more accustomed to literary representations of this turn in hopeful terms that render the future as an ideal or perfected time. But a negative and dialectical (though not dystopic) possibility of conceiving the utopian as *catastrophic* is also available, even if it is a road less traveled in conventional assimilations of this genre.[2] In addition, then, to positive conceptions of utopia, we also find examples of shifts in temporality in story and history that stem from incident or "turn" *(strophe)*, disruption or counterturn *(antistrophe)*, and a denouement or final turn that includes disaster *(catastrophe)*. Persisting from classical Greek times, this latter configuration has, in various traditions and cross-cultural manifestations, come to represent the core of a critical conception of utopic possibilities—a utopia against the grain, so to speak. In *Ghare Baire* (The Home and the World), written in 1915 and translated into English in 1919 by his nephew, with assistance from himself, Tagore attempted to give form to the darker side of utopia, centering his exploration of happiness, life, and death, as well as envy, resentment, and betrayal, on the formulaic vehicle of a domestic triangle but with critical reversals in place about its meaning.

The standard reading of Tagore's novel has largely, if not to say exclusively, rested on seeing it as a meditation on nationalism and womanhood, with critics jostling to endorse or rebuke his deployment of the figure of woman as allegory of the nation. In this vein critics have either praised *Ghare Baire* as a reflexive palimpsest of nationhood and womanhood or regarded it as symptomatic of the patriarchal fixation on women as bearers of tradition.[3] In either case, what has largely been missed is the text's contrary imagining of historical emergence via a reflexive if conventional plot. Part of the reason for this elision has to do with difficulties in the mode of translation, whereby Tagore's elaborately layered views are flattened out into a simple correspondence between woman and nation. A more fundamental problem stems from the author's resort to the device of the *atmakatha* (autobiography or personal story), the literary expression of nineteenth-century bourgeois individualism par excellence, which lends itself too easily to quick analogies between voice, idea, and objectivity. And, although a broader contemplation of the novel is the subject of a different discussion, I would contend that in its constellated, allegorical form Tagore conveys a more radical set of meanings about the contradictions of nationalist consciousness than later interpretations, usually offered on the hackneyed terms of the personal and/as the political, women and/as the nation, and so on, have suggested.

Although it may not seem to be borne out yet, the focus of this chapter is on Satyajit Ray's 1984 cinematic translation of *Ghare Baire* rather than on the novel. But I have begun by alluding to the literary precedent because I want to flag the notion that the full complexity of Ray's revision can only be comprehended once it is set off against Tagore's earlier foray into the problem of catastrophe and utopia. The discussion that follows is structured largely as a series of contrapuntal readings of the novel and the film, although my goal is not to argue about appropriation or adaptation as such. Rather, I want to pursue a line of thought about dialectical reversal, and from this perspective, the fact that Tagore's novel serves as the filmic text's literary-historical precedent is a way to understand the film's own actuality. I submit that the specificities of cinematic form and meaning make it possible to examine what the film can do that the novel cannot, so the reason to read the two versions against each other has to do with wanting to resituate the novel by the retrospective light shed on it in Ray's film—as opposed to the other way around.

To say this, however, is to insist that the film's reality is discontinuous from the moment of Tagore's writing—which is an obvious enough statement, though it seems to require belaboring given the conventional assumption that Ray simply adapted Tagore's novel for the screen and, in effect, dealt with the same material. It is also to propose that the reality of the film does not pertain to its narration of the past (that is, the film is not a document of or about history) but to a conjunctural way of thinking about the past. In other words, the film is a contemporary statement, suggesting that, as an utterance in the world, it shares more with us as readers than it does with Tagore's context. In this sense it reflects a shift in the historical frame of reference that separates what came before India's independence in 1947 from its emergence thereafter. Recognizing this shift is, for reasons that I elaborate below, only made possible in the act of interpretive retrospection.

We can begin to think about the matter by first accepting that as an utterance the film belongs to our own historical moment. This, too, is less a chronological point than an epistemological given, even if almost three decades have elapsed since its release in 1984. But since historical temporality is a semantically driven field (that is to say, it depends for its meaning on organizing concepts that shape time), one can see that the film belongs to our time by juxtaposing it to the novel, which by the same token, reveals itself as the product of a different spatiotemporal regime. One might even go so far as to suggest that the novel now needs the filmic mediation to be understood, not in the sense of being comprehended as such but in the more restricted sense of offering a historical standpoint. All of this turns on our use of the term *conjuncture*, for if the conjunctural is taken as an episodic emphasis on history (characterized by what the *Annales* historians call "medium-term" developments such as the French Revolution or romanticism or post-Independence India), Ray's text, as well as any current discussion of it, must be seen as contained with a discursive framework that is distinct from the one Tagore both occupied and fictionalized. The former conjuncture—Ray's and ours—has been determined by the historical fallout of decolonization and the crisis of postcolonial life in ways that Tagore did not live to witness.[4] Thus only in this specific sense is it possible to take the full measure of the film's retroactive sensibility, a mode of seeing that it correspondingly urges on viewers. From this vantage point the complications of Tagore's utopianism are only legible *après coup*, although they help to refocus on the vicissitudes of post-Independence Indian history elaborated by Ray in an altogether different parsing of the meaning of utopia.

Part of Ray's experimentalism lies in the ways that his revision expresses a utopianism that is not only different from Tagore's but that can *only* be described as catastrophic, since this is the sole vantage point left from which to articulate anything resembling a critical conception of emergence, both cinematic and historical. Tagore, in his novelistic rendering of the dilemmas of nationalism, could not foresee how the future— our present—would unfold. Nevertheless, his vision of possibilities and impossibilities exemplifies a certain kind of gamble on historical futures, however unrealized. This is because the present is not only given by what came before; it also enables any prospect of what is to come. Thus the past and future have something in common: the bond of the present, in turn revealing that conceptions of history depend on a temporal orientation to the future and, crucially, vice versa. Such a consciousness of the recursive structure, as well as the conceptual organization of historical time, is what the intellectual historian Reinhart Koselleck amalgamated into the phrase "futures past" *(vergangene Zukunft)*, reflecting that any given present is at the same time a "former future." According to Koselleck all conceptions of modernity, revolution, emergence, and so forth depend on a temporal orientation, whether that is brought up to the surface or not. To the degree that a "future past" is self-consciously articulated within or by a particular account of history, it exposes the tacit normativity of temporal understanding and expresses what he argues is a truly novel, modern attitude toward time *(Neuzeit)* that only took shape in the past two hundred years.[5]

As much as we have learned to value the idea of an order of things in which, as Michel Foucault has popularized, all history is a history of the present, Koselleck's more radical contention is that from the standpoint of the past two centuries, all history is a history of the future. That is to say, historical intelligibility is only given by a *predictive* sense about a course taken or, for that matter, not taken. I find his argument quite compelling (even if it has not acquired the authority of Foucault's notions) because it rearticulates synchrony and diachrony without collapsing the two—a move that, despite the rhetoric about attention to historicity within forms of poststructuralist criticism, has rendered the task of interpretation presentist in essence. Koselleck, on the other hand, makes it possible to suggest that if modernity is thought of as underwritten by a temporal sensibility in which conceptions of the future dissimulate their reliance on a present and a past, we can then consider representations, including cinematic ones, in terms of the extent to which this relationship is made legible in the present. Such an epistemological framework lends a specifically diachronic perspective to interpretive activity, one that in the context of film theory and criticism opens up an entirely new way of looking at a "slice of life" in the cuts of celluloid. In contrast with much of what is standard reading practice in ciné-semiotics—with its all-too-convenient "bracketing" of the temporality of interpretation, as well as the cinematic text's existence within history—this way of interrogating the frame or the shot recontextualizes what is the otherwise decontextualized moment of analysis by reinserting *the text into history* (instead of the well-rehearsed notion of putting history into the text informing much of what goes in the name of conventional literary, cultural, or film history).[6]

If the past, present, and future have always to be considered in terms of each other, and, moreover, if they constitute a perspective on the passage of time itself, the key is to distinguish the anticipatory formulations in a given account or a given text from those that are retrospective or those that remain bound to their own time. Such a form of reflexive consciousness about temporality is, precisely, the token by which it can be proposed that Tagore's novel and Ray's film are *projections* into the future (as opposed to representations of the past) inasmuch as they articulate unfolding landscapes of cognition and recognition. Each text attains its relative reflexivity to the degree that self-understanding about historical emergence is marked in various ways by them. Particularly in Ray's case, this involves doubling back to account for historical desiderata, as well as their negation in the post-Independence era. Accordingly, one of the considerations for this discussion is to distinguish between Tagore's and Ray's respective visions of the future in order to determine how the conceptual category of a "catastrophic utopia" is revised in the shift from Tagore's worldview to Ray's critical negation of it.

To the extent that the novel is at issue here, the most obvious point to make is that the past casts its shadow on the present in the film's reprise of its plot. But the differences between the two have less to do with merely this nominal issue of a change in medium than with understanding that the very nature of historical consciousness has been transformed in the interregnum. This requires a different take on such notions as tradition and modernity (which have served as buzzwords in much of the criticism that sees these texts as analogs or simply adaptations). Also, along the lines I have begun to sketch, it requires specifying what it means to depict a redemptive understanding of pessimism through the vehicle of cinema—a medium and an institution that has a long and specific history itself, especially when it comes to reflections about temporality and consciousness.[7]

By way of beginning to untie the knot that has conventionally bound the film to the novel, one must note that the demarcation of the late nineteenth and early twentieth century from the post-Independence era—that is to say, the shift from Tagore's milieu to Ray's—designates, as I have already suggested, not merely a chronological change but a fairly radical overhaul of material and social conditions. Tagore's romantic view of the place of women in tradition or modernity is perforce a world apart from Ray's disenchanted outlook on the present, and it follows that our conjuncture—the one that we as readers and viewers share with Ray—bears witness only to commodified social relations disanchored from a traditional understanding of community, kinship, or society. The filmic text's return to Tagore's themes and to the familiar tale of Bengal's partition by the British demands to be seen less as an adaptation of older narratives than as a wholesale rewriting of them; it is the product not of fidelity to the original but of cinema's explosive capacity to express sociohistorical contradictions of the present. In this particular respect one may say that the film represents the problems of *its* time by reactivating the past, as well as anticipating the future (just as Tagore's novel remains emblematic of a different temporal configuration and the contradictions peculiar to it).

As I hope this line of thinking makes clear, one of my purposes in this chapter is to shift the ground on which issues such as the representation of female subjectivity, the status of women in nationalist discourse, or the question of gendered history have been debated with respect to this film—as if they merely required adjudication in terms of already established notions of correspondence with the real. This variety of criticism, centering on whether "Third World" narratives adequately represent "Third World" social realities, seems inadequate not only because Ray's cinema expresses a futural orientation to the world as a whole but also because the very notion of "representing" history in film is shot through with the contradiction that the medium of discussion has fundamentally transformed past events into present spectacles, mutating the object under scrutiny in the process. This is not merely a formalist quibble so much as an unavoidable fact that must be contended with if one is not to be guilty of naive representationalism. Not only does it have to be granted that film is its own medium, with its own rules and conventions, but also that it produces very different kinds of evidence about history that may indeed be more worthy of our consideration than whether a certain historical event has been faithfully retold. Given this preference, I take the diegetic aspects of *Ghare Baire*, its representation of a fairly traditional story of personal betrayal amid the well-documented political and social upheavals of the day, to be of interest only insofar as they open out onto deeper, conceptual problems having to do with the presentness of the past, the meaning of historical (im)possibility, and the price of selfhood in modernity overall.

Conceptually speaking, Ray's portrayal of reality in *Ghare Baire* provides us with some terms of a dialectical experiment. On one level the film is pitched as a testament to the possibilities of the catastrophic to tell us something about the future through the cancellation of a present determined by capitalist social relations. By this token neither an understanding of historical imagination nor the question of female agency or utopian emergence can be addressed as if these existed outside the "baleful systematicity" of the capitalist world system—a phrase Fredric Jameson uses in the context of examining what he calls the "geopolitical aesthetic," which he sees as defining postwar cinema around the globe. Although Jameson's arguments have influenced my thinking greatly, I differ from him in the weight I place on how to discern the "grammar," the specific logic of an aesthetic mode at odds with the system that necessarily underwrites it.[8] Indeed, that is where a dialectical emphasis must be placed: on variations from the rule, on contingent attempts to go beyond merely reflecting the system, to expressing "structures of feeling" (to use Raymond Williams's coinage) that resist or otherwise disturb it. This is by no means to declare that Ray's cinema subverts the system of capitalist social relations; rather, it is to discern the self-conscious and often compelling ways that any form of political art—bearing witness to its own degraded existence—must find to express a negative, critical relation to conditions at large.

On another level much of Ray's emphasis is on elaborating how the visual image and sound function as portents of the decay of experience in modernity. But he attempts neither to evade nor escape recognition of this decayed predicament; instead, he reinforces it at every level of filmic intervention—a practice of aesthetic *détournement* that is in equal part protest and the demarcation of possibilities. Before turning to these aspects, it may be worth pondering, briefly, the framework of intelligibility and the circuit of reception into which any contemporary encounter with Ray (or, for that matter, Tagore) is likely to occur. We would have to grant that the intertext constituted by the film and novelistic versions of *Ghare Baire* is among the better-known examples of "serious" cultural expression from India that circulates in the West. For example, Tagore's novel is routinely assigned in introductory "world civilization" courses (scores of Columbia University freshmen have been known to walk around Manhattan's Upper West Side with the Penguin Classics edition); this text serves on many other campuses as well to initiate the young and the restless into "cultural sensitivity" in anticipation of their becoming acceptably cosmopolitan by graduation. Likewise, film curricula throughout the North American academy often include Ray's text in the (usually condensed) "Third World cinema" section, in part because it is one of his later, easily available, works but also because impatient young minds are more easily coaxed into an encounter with otherness if it can be served up in color.

The relative familiarity of the film and novel makes a plot summary strictly unnecessary, though it may still be useful for readers to recall that both versions are set in Bengal circa 1905, the time of its partition by the British. The struggle between *ghar* (home) and *bahir* (the outside world) is staged as an ill-fated interpersonal drama featuring Nikhil, a wealthy landowner, or *zamindar*, who wishes his wife to emancipate herself by learning English and by emerging from the segregated quarters of an aristocratic household; Bimala, his wife, who reluctantly enters the process of becoming modern by leaving the confines of her comfortable but unenlightened domestic life, only to have her entire existence shattered by the betrayal of her innocence; and Sandip, Nikhil's boyhood friend, whose arrival as the demagogic leader of the *swadeshi* (home rule or nationalist movement) also provides the occasion for Bimala's betrayal at home, for Nikhil's disillusionment with his friend's manipulations that lead indirectly to his death, and, above all, for the disarray of the economic and political struggle against the British. Home and world are set apart less as antinomies than as complements whereby interior dissolution parallels exterior disintegration.

FETISH AND FUTURE

I propose that *Ghare Baire* provides a chronicle of the disruptions of modernity and, simultaneously, an intimation of a transformed future. As such, it exemplifies a catastrophic utopianism, a proposition best approximated as resembling a Möbius strip—suggesting the interdependence and inextricability of the catastrophic and the utopian. In considering this dual mode, the element of the catastrophic has first claim, so let me specify its dimensions by turning to the treatment of the central figure of Bimala. If Ray's portrayal hinges less on depicting her as a flesh-and-blood personality whose interiority can be plumbed for its revelation of psychological conflicts, it is only because this enables him to draw out the implications of the withering of subjectivity in a commodified world. While the point about Bimala being a flat rather than rounded character has often been made, that she emblematizes a critique of reified forms has never been noted. This is not, however, just another way to say that she is "objectified" but to contend with such objectification—such thingliness—on the specific terms of reification *(Verdinglichung).* If we know that reification is the fundamental subjective and objective reality of our collective existence in modernity, it is at the same time difficult to reckon with in the medium of daily life. The paradox at the heart of reality is that its truth-content (*Wahrheitsgehalt,* as Adorno put it) must now be rendered in a defamiliarized mode: as a problem of representation rather than in itself. At the crux of other modernist explorations as well, Ray's resolution to this problem of representability results in his treatment of Bimala as a construct for the abstraction of reification, as well as the marker of a more local historical narrative about the struggle over *swadeshi* (and the movement's failure to take up the issue of women's agency in the emergent Indian nation).

In Ray's telling, Bimala is both disposable and indispensable—disposable in the sense that she represents the relation of exchange at the heart of the commodity and indispensable in the sense that this relation now defines the very possibility of being. Consequently, her placement in the narrative is his attempt to work out the conceptual dilemma of how to encode an objective crisis through subjective means. Reiterating the opposition between outward appearance and experiential depth (or *Schein* versus *Wirklichkeit* as these terms were debated in nineteenth-century German Idealism, the source of many of the debates about representation we have inherited), Bimala intimates the utopian entailments of catastrophe, discerned in and through the very depthlessness of a flat character who bespeaks the essential contradiction of our own age, namely, the problem of exchange.

I will have occasion to elaborate further on the cinematic aspects of Ray's emphasis on Bimala-as-objectivity, but for now let me note that by effecting this turn in how we think about the content of forms, Ray redirects the binarism of appearance and reality to the Marxian orbit of commodity fetishism. The literal appearance of Bimala as a celluloid exposure overlaps with her display as a metaphoric expression of the misrecognition that underlies a social form of fetishism; according to Marx, this disguises a relationship between humans as a relationship among things. Contemporary sensitivities notwithstanding, to refer to commodity fetishism in this context is not to impose a "vulgar" reading from without since my argument is that the film itself invites us to read Bimala as such an allegory of modern fetishism. As I have already mentioned, that she is presented as an objectified figure to whose subjectivity we have little access has been acknowledged, and on this reading she has been seen as one in a series of "types" in Ray's explorations of the *nabeena* (new woman) in films ranging from *Devi* (1960) and *Charulata* (1964) to *Mahanagar* (1963). Indeed, the point is that Bimala *also* functions as an emblem of the nation, femininity, and the conflict between tradition and modernity. But to say this is to read only off the surface of the text and miss the larger import of Ray's highly stylized choices in framing her figure onscreen. Here, particularly, the liability of thinking of the novel and film as analogs and, moreover, as realist documents of the nationalist struggle is evident, resulting in the penchant of critics to regard Bimala as the overvalorized symbol of woman-as-nation. Reading her exclusively as an emblem of womanhood, purity, or emancipation, critics have indicted what they take to be Tagore's and, equally, Ray's patriarchal vision. Both men are seen as offering essentialized representations of women in their role as domestic or national icons.[9] But an epistemological distinction must be made between a representational mode that *belies* a problem and one that *critiques* it; that is, between betraying and exposing ideologies at work. I would submit that, in fact, Ray is critical of idealized notions of womanhood and his elaboration of femininity proceeds as an exposition of the problem of fetishism rather than as an essentialist or fetishistic representation on its own.[10]

Continuing along these lines, perhaps the first thing to say is that the argument about film fetishism has been around for decades, the bulk of it resting on asserted similarities between theories of female sexuality (in which the female body, seen as the source of castration anxiety, is subjected to fragmentation) and the discourse of narrative cinema. Within this perspective the fetishistic nature of the medium has been regarded as constitutive of the cinematic apparatus itself, premised as it is on the "cuts" of editing and a dialectic of presence-absence—or what psychoanalytic critics have sometimes referred to as the *fort/da* of the flickering image. Quite apart from this stress on the parallels between mechanisms of desire and imperatives of film editing or projection, however, there is a more primary aspect to fetishism that concerns the formation of *all* forms of consciousness under the sign of the commodity. On this more materialist reading, if one accepts Marx's basic insights into the commodity form, the particularity of cinema (regardless of notions of "suture" or "scopophilia") must, by definition, be subsumed under the universality of commodity fetishism as such. That is to say, since fetishism is constitutive of modern sociality in toto, it is less an aspect of representation per se than the totality subtending capitalist exchange.[11] It is on these terms that I would defend Ray's deployment of the logic of the fetish as a diagnosis rather than a symptom of the world of appearances, be it femininity, cinema, or the nation. What is more, even as he exposes the impossibility of the "true" portrayal of these false unities, he explores what a different configuration of aesthetic and social possibilities might look like in an alternative world, thereby embedding a utopian or futural element in his experiment.

Therefore, in opposition to theories of film fetishism that rely on the metaphoric or metonymic similarities between the fetish (be it sexual or anthropological) and the cinematic image, I see Ray as proposing that it is in the nature of mystified society to block the possibility both of genuine social relations and genuine subjective experience. Not only does his critique of fetishism underscore this mystification, but it also, and by this very token, takes cognizance of its own structural limit at representing the mutual reinforcement of what is possible to enunciate and what is beyond visibility—precisely because it has been reified. This antinomy is collocated at different levels: first in the vexed world of the film's diegesis, which is revealed as teetering on the brink of anticolonial yet reactionary religious violence, and next in the film's formalistic insistence on highlighting rather than eliding the impossibility of representing an unbroken self in the time of commodity fetishism.

If the fetish depends for its meaning on the condensation of imaginative possibilities, Ray's depiction of Bimala is a tour de force construction exactly to the extent that he does not represent her as merely a "stand-in" for certain static notions—such as the future, the new woman, the commodity, or the tragic. Rather, she becomes a dynamic conjugation of emergent ways of being, coalescing as a form of subjective possibility not yet conceivable in the world except as catastrophic, disastrous, or monstrous. Seen in this aspect, Bimala embodies a revelation: a projection into the future even though she is nominally cast as a figure from the past. Referred to at the end of the film (by her sister-in-law) as a *rakshasi* (demoness), her uncanniness bespeaks the future and the fear engendered by the unknown. As such a *rakshasi*—with its allied sense of the wild, the disagreeable, and the brazen—Bimala is thrust out of the "natural" space of wifehood and womanhood into the unnatural topos of the phantasmagoric. Her incapacity either to be the *grihalakshmi* (domestic goddess) or to step into the role of the *memsahib* (European woman) and, at a different level, to overcome the opposition of *pracheena/nabeena* (traditional woman/new woman) becomes the measure of her "dummy" character, gesturing toward the possible rather than the existent—what might *be* as opposed to what *is*.

Not belonging to either home or world, we might consider Bimala's resemblance to Walter Benjamin's construct of the "threshold goddess," guardian of the potentially transformative frontier that wavers between visible and invisible, real and unreal, and representing the vanishing point of the horizon between tradition and modernity. Within the space of the film this quality of *dis*-appearance is often rendered literally—with Bimala's onscreen image fragmented or doubled, whether in a photograph, a reflection in the mirror, or, as in the final scene of the film, in the liquidated, literally dissolving, figure of the woman-becoming-widow. In these ways Ray repeatedly remarks Bimala's unreality not just in the nominal sense that she is a character and not a personality but also to the extent that her history has no correlate in "facts" since she is an untimely conception intended to signal the future.

Let me further this argument by referring to a scene that fully realizes Ray's method of presenting Bimala as the sign of an all-encompassing

FIGURE 1.   Bimala at her toilette. Used by permission from Satyajit Ray Film and Study Center.

fetishism and ineluctable estrangement. In it she is pitted against her wid-owed sister-in-law, Bouthan (or "elder sister," as she is addressed in the di-egesis), their dual presentation emblematizing the catastrophe that attends the past as much as the present. Occurring early on in the film, this epi-sode reveals Bimala in medium shot, the dark lighting throwing her figure into relief as she is caught reflected in the Victorian mirror, arranging her toilette (Figure 1). The sequence of shots inaugurating this scene has a deliberately incandescent quality, as it opens on a cut to a candle burning on Bimala's dressing table and shows her (as she often is throughout the film) trying on her new manners, new clothes, new self, all brought on by Nikhil's exhorting her to become a modern woman and wife.

This highly charged moment in which viewers get their very first look at Bimala's emergence as a woman of the world is almost immediately dis-turbed by another presence as Ray, almost imperceptibly, shifts the frame to include Bouthan in the reflection in the mirror. Along with Bimala, she—who, given her secluded and discarded existence, can fulfill the role neither of modern woman nor of companionate spouse—becomes part of the picture. The shift in attention from Bimala to Bouthan is abrupt yet somehow seamless, the camera repositioned to admit the latter into view, in the process alienating both narrative and spectatorial focus. Subtly, as the shot tightens, the figure of Bimala is entirely replaced by her sister-in-law, who moves from being reflected in the mirror to being presented in a reverse shot in full view. The substitution of one figure (Bimala) by another (Bouthan) suggests the ways that those who are left by the way-side on the road to modernity also deserve our attention. It is as if the duration of a few seconds in which Bimala and Bouthan are both exhibited as reflections captures their dual presence and, notably, their dual absence. Each is a spectral figure albeit along different lines. Bimala represents a figure who is *not yet* possible, Bouthan a figure who is *no longer* so. With his etiolated focus on issues of temporality, this scene perfectly highlights Ray's preoccupation with the retroactivity of the past—its influence on the present, to be sure, but also its recalcitrance as a "former future," to invoke a distinction from Koselleck I alluded to earlier in this chapter.

So, if Bimala embodies the uncanniness of the future, Bouthan represents the intractability of remaindered time. This is brought out most poignantly in the dialogue (or, to be precise, in Bouthan's dramatic monologue addressed more to the viewer than to Bimala). As the camera lingers on her, Bouthan recounts her sad tale in her own voice. Trapped within the confines of a hypertraditionalism characterizing Bengali social mores in the nineteenth century, her destiny is presented as one that is no longer recognizable as a force on the present, though it returns as the repressed sign of a disavowed difference. Ray makes this point with care, endowing Bouthan with the power of speech and bringing her in from the margins of the plot to appear front-and-center. Diegetically, on the other hand, Bimala is indifferent to this plight, absorbed as she is in admiring her new self in the mirror. As distinct from the novel, where she is only rendered as apostrophe, the subject of an indirect address, Bouthan here recollects her fate in the first person; nevertheless, unlike Bimala, whose bildungsroman claims most of our attention, she signifies only the remains of the day.

The scene in question is imbued, like many others in the film, with an attendant sense of stillness and stagnation that deepens the sense of what the audience already knows to be a setting for imminent disruptions in the world abroad. Catastrophe is the mode du jour, not only in the home and the world but also in the narrative's delineation of time as the final contingency of disaster toward which it indicates a propensity to turn. Standing by the four-poster bed in Bimala and Nikhil's bedroom (another intimation, along with all of Bimala's toiletries and fashionable clothes, of a sexuality to which she has no access), Bouthan recalls the night of her husband's death. Her words express not just the tragedy of the past but also that of her irrelevance in the present. Ray uses the deliberately reflexive strategy of having her face the camera as she recounts her dying, dissolute husband's blank look and his last, devastating, query: "Tumi ke?" (Who are you?). The intensity of the scene is reinforced as the camera slowly closes in on the figure of Bouthan framed by the bed frame against which she leans. As she utters the words *tumi ke*, Ray shoots her looking out of the screen, though not directly at the audience, as if to chide the spectator no less than her dead husband for not recognizing her.

With his extraordinary understanding that the most profound cinematic moments are ones that pass us by, Ray has the minor character of Bouthan deliver the film's most important criticism against the contemporary world for its fatal neglect of the old. But although this is the film's cardinal lesson, it is rendered without any disruption of cinematic illusion or any overtly estranging gesture of breaking the fourth wall. A universe of misrecognition is intimated in the repetition of the question "Who are you?" and conveys the past's accusation to a present that has revealed itself to be inadequate to the claims of history on the real. And with this turn Bouthan, rather than Bimala, becomes the eccentric subject of history within the filmic space of *Ghare Baire*. In realizing Bouthan's widowed self as a developed character (albeit by no means the main focus of the narrative), Ray offers us a glimpse of the loss that she symbolizes in a modernity that has no use for her, underscoring the distance between such a melancholic figure and Bimala, who serves as Ray's take on the rather different historical problem of emergence.

It is reasonable to argue that Ray's strategy of dealing with the character of Bouthan acquires its salience precisely in its difference from Tagore's rendition. For film critics accustomed to paying attention to the import of details, it is inescapably significant that she appears on the screen almost from the beginning and remains a shadowy presence throughout, always signifying a deprecated traditionalism. In representing her as a subordinate member of the extended household who is deprived of her status as the "Bara Rani" (senior lady) on account of being widowed, Bouthan serves as a recalcitrant token of the past. A child bride first, and now a widow who must stand by and watch Bimala enjoy the pleasures of the present, she *is* the unhappy strain of the ditty that Bimala learns to sing from her English tutor, Miss Gilby, of the tale from "long, long ago." As an aside, we should note that the film's early scenes are entirely original in conception, since there is no counterpart in Tagore's novel to Ray's deliberate layering of time within diegetic space. The original story is set forth as a series of juxtapositions from the diaries of the primary characters, and

Bimala, Nikhilesh, and Sandip each speaks in his or her own voice. But the Bara Rani, as I have already mentioned, is only adduced, her existence implied by the other characters. In the film, by contrast, Bimala's remembrances (given in voice-over narration) provide the exclusive coordinates for the audience's introduction to the text's recursive temporal structure. Everything that unfolds is presented only in flashback and from Bimala's point of view even if, and especially because, she is not depicted in terms of a depth-psychological model of an interiorized subjectivity. But by assigning considerable screen time to Bouthan, Ray draws her out from behind the folds of Bimala's memory, as well as the curtains of time, thus refracting both temporal and subjective continuity.

If the notion of an unbroken self functions as a false totality that mystifies both subjecthood and nationhood, this falsity is most acutely brought out in the scene in which Bimala and Nikhil have their first, and most pointed, conversation about the changes wrought in their lifeworld by the disruptions of the world market. Not wishing to shelter his wife from either the pleasures of embourgeoisement or their costs, nor indeed to deny himself the enjoyment of being the agent of her worldly emancipation, Nikhil represents the means by which Ray ventriloquizes his own stance on the way that commodification thoroughly penetrates the existent, within the terms of the diegesis, as well as in reality. We can discern this in the scene immediately following Bouthan's lament about her fate, in which Bimala continues to ponder her new sense of self, consolidated by her emergent bourgeois tastes and, simultaneously, by her emergent interest in *swadeshi*. Here Bimala learns about the nationalist movement's attempt to challenge the stranglehold of the world market on India's domestic consumption from her husband, Nikhil, but this struggle is only made salient for her a little later on—by the subsequent, dramatic appearance of Sandip into her hitherto placid existence as a cloistered woman in the *andarmahal* (private quarters).

The transition to this scene occurs with Bouthan referring to Bimala as Nikhil's *mem putul* (foreign doll), viewing her transformation not only as mimicry but also as ill-advised. That she turns out to be correct when Nikhil is killed is not the end of the story but the beginning of a meditation by Ray on fissures within the discourse of nationalist consciousness on the question of self-rule and how to accomplish it. He also continues his critique of fetishism, attempting to work through the contradictions thrown into relief by the standoff between subjective desires and the object world. Bouthan has no place in this worldly scenario, and she leaves it with the telling phrase, "I have no tolerance for these foreign aromas" (Figure 2).

FIGURE 2. Bouthan (the Elder Rani) and the aromas of the foreign. Used by permission from Satyajit Ray Film and Study Center.

The aroma she abjures is the redolent air of the commodity world, an emergent horizon literalized by the sights and smells of foreign objects placed all over the baroque household in the diegesis. In this setting, even as Nikhil gives Bimala a lesson on Lord Curzon's divisive policy of partitioning Bengal and the goal of *swadeshi* to boycott foreign goods, Ray's camera work emphasizes the nature of objects and invokes the tales that *they* might tell, not because they are real but because of their fetishistic hold over existence.

As Bimala readies herself, she is again reflected in medium long shot in the mirror, doubly configured as depthless: as a projected image throughout and now as a reflection of the projection itself, her ephemerality reinforced by the camera, which is, of course, the instrument of Ray's propositional and even didactic intentions. If the idea of *le caméra-stylo* (camera pen) advanced by Alexandre Astruc in the mid-twentieth century was immensely influential on the consolidation of a theory of the film auteur, its operation here is as good an example as any of the argument that directors, very much in the manner of writers, express their directorial signature through thematic elements, as well as the movement of actors and objects within the space and time of the shot.[12] Surrounded by her newly tailored jackets, Victorian mirror, tortoiseshell comb and hairpins, French perfumes, and English dressing table—objects whose foreign provenance is commented on by Nikhil—Bimala is herself transformed into another object, not only of Nikhil's desire to be the instigator of her worldly emergence but also in terms of her self-display. In showing her as this objectified figure, Ray draws out the analogy between Bimala and the other objects around her and between her body as another decorative object and her self in relation to other commodities. She is a "thing among things"—to echo a phrase that Miriam Hansen attributes to Kracauer to describe how film reveals the functioning of commodities in modern life.[13] In this way Bimala serves as a cipher of the social, and her presence on the screen exists in tension less with other people than with other objects, exhibiting the luminosity of the still life rather than the roundedness of real historical personalities.

By reading along these lines I have attempted to bolster my general argument that Bimala defies resolution in terms of her adequacy or inadequacy as a political subject, that of "new woman." In opposition to realist constructions of self and identity, Ray's depiction refuses the framework of interiority and subjectivity (which from Lukács to Kracauer is seen to represent the bourgeois ideal of art); moreover, it calls our attention to the filmic medium itself. Going beyond this, I want to suggest that if the talk about fetishism is to hold, it must at all times take into account the nature of the cinematic image as its embodiment, an embodied materiality that perforce refuses subjectivist reductions. Like the fetish, cinema is a form premised not on depth but exchangeability. In fact, of course, both the technology of film and its spectatorship are defined by depthlessness—at a literal level by the projection of a flat image on a screen but also temporally, by the gap between image and spectator. So if the medium itself depends on the dynamic of the fetish—which hides as well as reveals in that it requires absent presences and present absences to produce meaning—this constitutive fact has to be referred back to what happens onscreen, as well as to the recursive turns between narrative concerns and the possibilities of form.[14]

CATASTROPHE AND EMERGENCE

My discussion of fetishism leads to a second, overarching, contention I want to advance in this chapter. This has to do with looking more closely at the means by which a transformed future is intimated by Ray's cinematic choices. A first viewing might suggest that it is fanciful to derive the notion of a utopianism, however catastrophic, from a story about the failures of *swadeshi*, especially given that the personal destiny of Bimala is revealed to be no less doomed. It is certainly the case that at the denotative level, the story world Ray recreates from his source material is tragic, even melodramatic, and centers on themes of betrayal, disappointment, and, ultimately, death. The narrative's tragic impulses, however, serve less to foreclose on emergent possibilities than to enable them, and it is in articulating such a vision that Ray marks both his distance from his literary predecessor and his own directorial signature on the discourse of cinematic modernism. As I have already indicated, the charge of representing the past becomes, in Ray's hands, a way to signal its claims on the present; consequently, tragic disruption provides if not a different actuality then at least a turn toward it.

Folded into this way of conceptualizing emergence is the generatively modernist supposition, very much akin to Marcel Proust's meditations on things past, that art signifies for us as a form of perception that, as Jameson has also averred, our "normal" ways of reckoning with the meaning of this or that reality are unable to comprehend the first time around. In this mode film has the potential to reckon with the real or the possible retroactively, as it enters through the corner of the eye.[15] In the space of the narrative Bimala's tragedy is already exhibited for us in the opening frames of the film in the long shots of a fire that is recognizable only at the end as a scene of conflagration. Moreover, the opening soundtrack is a musical composition in Raga Darbari, the grandest of Hindustani classical musical *ragas*, or "moods," that Ray uses here to set the stage for what is to follow. Both in the ways that as viewers we expect the beginning of any narrative to indicate the unfolding of time rather than its arrest, and in the fact that Darbari is a *raga* associated with the fourth phase of the day, which is to say its denouement, the spectator's senses are tricked into *not* noticing that the action does not unfold at all, just as the day does not begin. For the film actually begins at the end, proceeding only in flashback. These details in the setting of the film's spatiotemporal coordinates are, remarkably, only cognizable after the fact, once we have learned to recognize the retroactive force of events as remembrances of things past.

This retroactive sensibility is exemplified above all by Ray's presentation of Bimala, who, as we have seen, symbolizes the congealment of past, present, and future in her very appearance as fetish. To think more specifically about her as this kind of "retro-futural" configuration (an idea that returns us to his conception of a "threshold goddess"), we may be helped by Benjamin's somewhat underappreciated deployment of the fable of Scheherazade in his essay "The Storyteller."[16] Picking up the thread of an idea first broached in his discussion of baroque drama, Benjamin settles briefly on *The Arabian Nights*, itself an interesting if exotic choice in an explication of the loss of experience in modernity. Benjamin, we may recall, proposes that Scheherazade functions as a figure of distancing between then and now (and, we must note, between Europe and its Other, though this aspect is left unremarked). Remaining within his point of view for a moment, Benjamin allows us to understand that the past Scheherazade signifies is one from which we moderns have become estranged, for she belongs to a "time past in which time did not matter" (93). As we have learned from Benjamin himself, as well as influential later critics such as Benedict Anderson, the "abbreviation" of time in the present is a ubiquitous theme in the experience of modernity, seen as constantly imposing the regulative demands of the clock and calendar on the conduct of everyday life.[17] This regulation and even overregulation has correspondingly been thematized in the literature of modernity (from Dickens's or Proust's writings to Buñuel's and Dali's surrealist cinematic manifesto *Un chien andalou* to Chaplin's *Modern Times*).[18] Here, Benjamin's point about temporality is to mark the dialectical relationship between the disappearance of a world in which the full experience of life, including that of death, was comprehensible and its return in modernity as a mere trace. We now exist in a regime that, as he puts it, valorizes only "information" and has no use for the expansive sense of experience Scheherazade represents. It is in this connection that Benjamin also advances his idea about the different qualities of experience embedded in the distinction between *Erlebnis* (transient experience) and *Erfahrung* (historical experience). The consequence of temporal disjunction is that our very understanding of the real has been de-realized, though this loss keeps returning in the form of paratactic or uncanny objects and figures, frustrating the instrumental effort to shuck off the past.

For Benjamin Scheherazade serves as a dialectical image of the impoverishment of experience under capitalism. By embodying the variety of storytelling unavailable in modern times, she signals what modernity is not, conveying by this means what it can be.[19] My recourse to Benjamin's ideas about storytelling may seem tangential in the context of discussing *Ghare Baire*, but I think their applicability is more than accidental even if one only considers the preoccupation in modernist thought, be it aesthetic (as in Ray's case) or conceptual (as with Benjamin or other examples from critical theory), with the visibility of the female body and its many meanings. In their hyperbolic deployment as the object of reverence or celebration, figurations of·femininity have been seen to undermine appearances and destroy false totalities such as tradition, nation, freedom, or even love, their visibility the very mark of the superficial. In this dialectical çapacity it is not that the "woman question," as Marx characterized it, takes second place in the consideration of social equality but that it comes to stand in for its constitutive impossibility under capitalism.

Following Marx, Benjamin too relied in his writings on references to certain social types (such as the prostitute, who represents, par excellence, the substitutability of love and money) that encapsulate the essence of capitalist modernity. Illuminating the fundamental reification that life has undergone, these types elucidate the negation of the real as a result of which nothing remains other than the "reality" of exchange. Like the prostitute who must dissimulate intimacy in the context of a transaction—thereby summoning up the perversion at the core of the commodity form—Scheherazade is exemplary as one who must constantly (re)invent her attraction in order to stay alive, telling stories that will hold her lord's attention and keep him from ordering her death. In this allegorical mode she exposes not only the impossibilities of real love through her own abjection but also, and more abstractly, the limitations of modern temporality with its linear, punctual, and homogeneous logic—in which, after all, time and tide wait for none.

But it is not just that the figure of Scheherazade exposes the false appearance of love and the distemper of modernity. For, even as her own location in bygone times and a faraway place betokens complete otherness, she also obliquely signifies the catastrophe of our own moment, given that the threat of annihilation is now present everywhere, all the time, rendering storytelling and life equally tenuous as well as hollow. Nevertheless, the emphasis on the hollowing out of contemporary existence is also the means by which Benjamin formulates what Max Pensky has called a "melancholy dialectics."[20] That is, the meaning of melancholia must itself be dialecticized—to include not only the sense of mourning for a lost object and a now-disappeared zone of possibility (as Freud might suggest) but, in a crucial difference from the Freudian scheme of mourning and melancholia, also the sense of a search for redeeming those possibilities. In Benjamin's own works (from his *Trauerspiel* book to the posthumous *Passagen-Werk*, from baroque allegory to modern allegory, so to speak) the conjoining of catastrophe and utopia represents a persistent theme and is most easily evoked by the figure of the angel of history in his classic

"Theses on History." And it has now become quite common to recall that the angel's face is depicted as turned toward the past, his back to the future, but irresistibly drawn to it by the "storm blowing from Paradise."

Condensing the idea of history, ruin, and the future, Benjamin returned again and again to figures and objects that embody both the violence of the modern and, through their very disruptiveness, the possibility for remaking the future. Such an ideal also accords with the etymological derivation of catastrophe as a sudden and widespread disaster, a final event or conclusion—usually a disastrous one. Of greater interest to me is that, in Benjamin's dialecticization of this figure, a transformative power is attached to the catastrophic, a heterogeneous element that he (along with others of his ilk, such as Ernst Bloch) variously posited in terms of the concepts of trauma, spleen, shock, melancholy, distancing, and, ultimately, death.[21] From this perspective, only through a total negation of the already existent can we look forward to the not yet and not now, and it is in his specific inflection of the fatal and the futural that we rejoin the discussion of the catastrophic and the redemptive with the treatment of Bimala as a configurational form.

Once again, the most effective way to illustrate Ray's mobilization of his heroine as an emblem of futurity lies in the contrast between her and Bouthan. Ray's prismatic rendition of the contrast between these two versions of womanhood gains greater significance if we also keep in mind the radical shift of emphasis between the novel and the film in terms of the vexed relationship of their characters. In Tagore's original Bimala's sister-in-law is always alluded to formally as the "Bara Rani," and, as I have already mentioned, she never makes an unmediated appearance in the pages of the novel. In fact, nowhere does Tagore directly render any character other than Bimala, Nikhilesh (a more formalized rendering of Nikhil), or Sandip, with the effect that the novel is entirely constructed through the convergences and divergences of perspective among the principals. Given as a tripartite series of entries into a journal or diary, Tagore's literary experimentation lay in adapting into Bengali the emergent form of autobiography in order to provide a chronicle of private confession and public utterance.

As a result, the idea of *ghar* and *bahir* or home and the world is represented by Tagore in the *mise-en-abŷme* of the overlapping points of view of the three characters exclusively, each with its turns into and out of homely confession and worldly declaration, private thought and public testament. Through the artifice of molding what we know to be a very modern form (the autobiography) for expressing newly emergent sensibilities about the public and private—as these demarcations come to distinguish modern life in Bengal—Tagore emphasizes a hitherto unavailable conception of interiority and point of view belonging to the main characters. Neither the home nor the world is represented, in the sense of being designated or brought into being, by anyone else. In this fashion the tensions of the world are not only played out in the home, they are utterly encircled by it.

Given his fundamentally romantic view of the universe in a mote of dust, Tagore's stress is thus on the capacity of key relationships to conjure up the world. So, whereas Nikhilesh, Bimala, and Sandip are depicted as caught in the struggle to represent themselves along the profoundly modern lines of private subject/public citizen, the Bara Rani remains an altogether imputed presence within the space of the novel. Readers gain access to her only from another character's point of view—as, for example, in the following entry in Bimala's diary:

> My sister-in-law, the Bara Rani, was still young and had no pretensions to saintliness. Rather, her talk and jest and laugh inclined to be forward. The young maids with whom she surrounded herself were also impudent to a degree. But there was none to gainsay her—for was not this the custom of the house? It seemed to me that my good fortune in having a stainless husband was a special eyesore to her. He, however, felt more the sorrow of her lot than the defects of her character.[22]

A little later in the novel Bimala records a different encounter with her sister-in-law in her diary, one where her own feelings are really at issue:

> One day my sister-in-law remarked to my husband: "Up to now the women of this house have been kept weeping. Here comes the men's turn.
>
> "We must see that they do not miss it," she continued, turning to me. "I see that you are out for the fray, Chota Rani! Hurl your shafts straight at their hearts."
>
> Her keen eyes looked me up and down. Not one of the colours into which my toilet, my dress, my manners, my speech, had blossomed out had escaped her. I am ashamed to speak of it today, but I felt no shame then.[23]

In both instances Bimala is the narrative agent as well as the center of the problematic. The Bara Rani signifies only as a trace—whose function is to underscore the tensions of home and serve as an implicit moral contrast to her younger sister-in-law's desires, born of radically separate contingencies of desire. Nikhilesh, whose autobiographical entries also refer to the Bara Rani, provides the only counterpoint to Bimala's account of the other woman in her life, though exclusively to his companionate (as opposed to sexual) intimacy with his sister-in-law. The point is that the Bara Rani never expresses any sentiments and desires. Yet as Anita Desai has suggested in her introduction to the Penguin translation of the novel, the character of the Bara Rani was drawn on the model of Kadambari Devi, Tagore's own sister-in-law (to whom he was very close and whose suicide at a young age has been the subject of intense speculation and comment in Indian *belles-lettristic* circles). Regardless of the import of this authorial secret, the Bara Rani's shadowy and mediated existence in the novel places her in the margins of its concerns, a minor key in the overall movement of the piece. By turning away from the model of tradition, femininity, constancy, and love that might have been illuminated by representing her more fully, Tagore's formulation may well have emblematized, as Desai suggests, his unconscious desire to repress the horizon of feelings only she has the potential to symbolize. But my preference is to read her in less psychobiographical terms—as a narrative marker of the marginality of an older model of subjective existence within the novel's politics of representation.

In the lines from Bimala's diary quoted above, Tagore relays his own take on the Bara Rani from Bimala's point of view—portraying the former as petty, jealous of Bimala's privileges, and, we are told, untoward in her manners. Seen through Bimala's eyes, she embodies only *ressentiment*, historical as well as personal. Put differently, she is in the (story) world but not of it. This is because Tagore looks out onto the twentieth century from the vantage point of the nineteenth, and the Bara Rani allows him to designate a sign of the residual. If she represents a form of being no longer of interest to modern subjects, in an early twentieth-century context she is, paradoxically, even more eccentric to the dilemmas Tagore wished to explore and that were central to his pedagogic desire to bring his readers into an awareness of their incipient though alienated modernity.

By contrast, Ray's treatment emphasizes the fraughtness of the relationship between Bimala and Bouthan, departing from his source material and providing an entirely different angle on the old that is afforded, I have argued, only retroactively. Their continual and contrapuntal placement in the film marks the shift from melancholy to catastrophe, permitting us to think about a vision of the future that places its weight on the political and epistemological value on the past as ruin as well as harbinger of the new. In fact, we should recall that this is the vision underlying the aesthetic and philosophical imperatives of the historical avant-garde in Europe that Ray attempts to reactivate with his latter-day cinematic practice. One of the confusions often attending contemporary accounts of the avant-garde has to do with the (erroneous) notion that artists and writers variously associated with its movements were all equally invested in the new and the "avant."[24] Part of the reason for the prevalence of this error has to do with the well-documented desire of the avant-garde to disrupt and reject older modes of representation in order to break out of the pall over aesthetic practice imposed by traditional ideas about art. But what was key for the radical avant-garde, and what has been missed in many contemporary revaluations, is the degree to which the break with the past had far less to do with a commitment to novelty as such than with reimagining the future.

Accordingly, the avant-garde's turn to means of aesthetic *dégonflage* (deflation or hijacking) served for them to register both the alienation of experience under capitalism and the extent to which art had become deranged from the social totality in its recusal from the everyday world. Strategies of shock or chance, key devices for disrupting the ideal of the organic work of art, can thus be understood as intended to critique given conditions of society rather than as aesthetic or stylistic devices staged for the purposes of originality or novelty alone. The aesthetics of shock, perhaps exemplifying the avant-garde's most fundamental operating principle, must by this light be read alongside the politics of protest—an equally valuable motivation in the radical imperative of the avant-gardes even if it has received less notoriety in the wake of their epochal failure to lead art back into society. But this particular emphasis allows us once more to recognize that the avant-garde represents neither a set of known artists nor a historically delimited experiment in aesthetic practice that is supposed to have begun in Europe and ended predictably, if hypostatically, in the United States in the 1960s.

Those prompted by the dialectical commitment to discern and rescue the past from the ruins of the present must proceed differently and from different leads. Here we may find embodied in the paradoxical ideals of the avant-garde the catastrophic utopianism of a project guided less by celebrating the new, the singular, or the unprecedented than by reckoning with their opposites—the old and the outmoded—particularly as these bespeak the repudiation of capitalist modernity. As I argue in other chapters as well, Ray consistently displays this attitude toward reactivating the energies of the past. And although he artfully exposes the petrifaction of social relations within modernity, his effort is not to hold on to tradition for its own sake but to make available some terms for a critical cancellation of pieties, old and new. *Ghare Baire* returns to this preoccupation with the social contradictions of the modern era, and our understanding is considerably helped by situating Ray's cinematic experiment alongside earlier aesthetic and analytic emphases in the overall discourse of modernism— ranging from Louis Aragon's 1926 surrealist novel *Le paysan de Paris* and various Dada manifestations to, as I tried to establish earlier with reference to Benjamin's work, the philosophical investments of critical theory.

Placed in this context, Ray's deliberate staging of the predicament of the old in its confrontation with the modern also impels us to recognize the historiographic work the film does in signaling its distance from realities that were merely contemporary facts for Tagore. Their reactivation makes it possible for Ray—and, more important, for us—to reevaluate a mode of existence that has passed from view but whose aesthetic and political valences are part and parcel of the dialectic of history.

CONCLUSION: DETAIL AND OTHERNESS

In focusing on the inorganic nature of subjective relations in *Ghare Baire*, I hope to have established that the confrontation between old and new modes of existence staged in this film is by no means restricted to the ways that characters are depicted. In keeping with the general proposition with which I have been working—namely, that the withering of subjectivity under capitalism means that the reification of the world extends into all spheres of life—it follows that the object world is as much the domain to which the question of value must be put as any consideration of subjective enunciation. The signifying potential of objects has, as we know, provided the impetus for thinking across a number of influential approaches in cinema studies (from Sergei Eisenstein's or Lev Kuleshov's experiments with montage to Roland Barthes' explications of the "Italianicity" of Panzani pasta advertisements and Kracauer's explorations of cinema's "critical realism"). Indeed, Benjamin took his own cue from Soviet cinema, emphasizing not the agents of the destruction of the present but the "scene" of the crime, as it were, in this way calling attention to the inanimate and objective aspects of life that not only serve as its mise-en-scène but also as the ground of subjective understanding. This objectivist inflection can be found in a number of Benjamin's writings, including in the "Artwork" essay, where he draws a parallel between crime-scene photography and the emptiness of the present. Reminding us of the turn-of-the-century photographs of Eugène Atget, he points to the "evidentiary" status of the photographic image in recording what is now past—as if it were now a deserted scene where a crime had been committed, leaving behind trace evidence in the objects photographed. Similarly, in the quintessentially dialectical spin derived from Bertolt Brecht in "A Small History of Photography," he quotes Brecht: "the situation is complicated by the fact that less than ever does the mere reflection of reality reveal anything about reality. A photograph of the Krupp works or the A. E. G. factory tells us next to nothing about these institutions. Actual reality has slipped into the functional. The reification of human relations—the factory, say—means that they are no longer explicit. So something must in fact be *built up*, something artificial, posed."[25]

Cinema is the means for this new construction inasmuch as it alone betokens the technological and expressive capacity to resemble writing— what Astruc, in his turn, regarded as the camera's singularity in "relat[ing] objects to objects and characters to objects" in his theory of a new avant-garde. Less the biographical stamp of an author than "a certain tendency" *(une certaine tendance)*, to use François Truffaut's distinction, objectivism in art, including the art of cinema, has always been internal to a tradition of political critique. By this light we might reformulate Astruc's contentions about the *caméra-stylo* to say that the camera does not so much permit writing (which always depends on imaginative connections between representation and reality) so much as replaces it. This, we may recall, is very much Kracauer's emphasis on "camera reality," which, while invoking "physical reality" or the indexical dimension of film, has less to do with a metaphysical conception of the real than with immanent contingencies that bring together the filmic medium and the world of objects. As Miriam Hansen argues in her introduction to the reissue of Kracauer's book, film's medium-specific affinity with physical reality is seen as emerging *out of* the very difference between discourse and the realm of material contingency, "between," as she glosses it, "the implied horizon of our 'habits of seeing,' structured by language, narrative, identification, and intentionality, and that which perpetually eludes and confounds such structuring."[26]

To follow these insights into the filmic space of *Ghare Baire*, one cannot but be struck by the vibrancy of things, by the luminosity that they, rather than the characters, possess. As I have tried to demonstrate, if it is in the nature of commodities to seem magical in their ability to appear themselves and, at the same time, to appear otherwise, this quality is refracted on the screen in a multiplicity of ways. And, as I have also suggested, these ways depart so radically from the novel that the horizons of possibility of the source text are fundamentally altered. Nevertheless, it is worth lingering one last time over the difference between Tagore's novelistic preoccupations and Ray's cinematic strategies to clinch the argument about the aesthetics of form, particularly as it takes us into the narration of historical contradiction. The novel mounts its representational argument with words and pages that can be—and are—devoted to the slow elaboration of internal conflicts. For example, in a key segment we find Nikhil debating with himself about his uncertainty over what his appropriate moral and enlightened reaction should be to his wife's newly emergent sensibility of worldliness and its distancing effect on their relationship: "I longed to find Bimala blossoming fully in all her truth and power. But the thing I forgot to calculate was, that one must give up all claims on conventional rights, if one would find a person freely revealed in truth."[27] A little later he expresses the same dilemma, an utterly modern one about the nature of claims on another person, in the following way: "'My wife'—Does that amount to an argument, much less the truth? Can one imprison a whole personality within that name? . . . Bimala is what she is. It is preposterous to expect that she should assume the role of an angel for my pleasure. The Creator is under no obligation to supply me with angels, just because I have an avidity for imaginary perfection."[28]

These complex moral and emotional quandaries are at the heart of Tagore's worldview and expressible as such in the overwrought language of romanticism—with its fraught imagery of angels and imagination, as well as its emphasis on individual consciousness. All of this is stripped away from Ray's treatment of the same emotional predicament pared down to a single, concrete principle: the attenuation of action on the screen expressed via the image track and, equally important, the soundtrack. In this fashion the conflicts internal to the characters are miniaturized—by which I do not mean to say that are downgraded or minimized but, rather, that they are rendered as needing to be read, stretched, and even rescued from the details that signify quiddity or an objective recalcitrance. It is to this insistence on unfolding the meaning of the detail that I would attribute much of the slow pacing of shots in Ray's cinema, their lyricism but also their lingering quality. Beyond establishing a different tempo and conjuring a different pace of life, the temporality of shots, as well as what they capture, is, I suggest, less a technical preference than a dialectical commitment to the possibilities that only the detail can summon forth—much in the manner of the "spark" of the "dialectical image" that represented the bedrock of Benjamin's thinking on similar matters.

A scene that occurs about two-thirds of the way through the film, to which I turn by way of closing this chapter, will I hope substantiate my case. We come upon Nikhil, who has had his moment of self-scrutiny, melancholic though the outcome has been. The passage into this reckoning with himself is, as with other key transitions in the text, depicted with

Nikhil crossing the hallway that has by now become the bridge, as well as impasse, between home and world. The camera cuts to Nikhil as he enters the threshold of the private quarters, his hesitant footsteps muffling what the spectator is allowed to hear of the song that begins the sequence. He pauses at the doorway, and the next shot reveals a transition to the interior of his apartment, where a servant is shown hastily arranging the pillows on the bed. She pulls her veil close and averts her gaze, although he is too absorbed in his own thoughts to notice all of the silent women who inhabit his household along with his wife and sister-in-law. The camera slowly pans left, moving across the bedpost, toward the many illuminated objects in the room: first, the crystal lamp stand (before which Nikhil and the camera both pause), the candle stand and perfume bottle, and gradually, in a slow point-of-view shot of Nikhil as his gaze comes to rest on his wife's *sindurdani* (a silver box for keeping vermilion, the traditional red mark on a married woman's forehead) displayed on her dressing-table.

The eye of the camera, settling as it does on the *sindurdani*, is only retroactively understood as having functioned as an evil eye, insofar as Bimala will not be a *sadhaba* (or married woman entitled to mark her conjugal status with *sindoor* or vermilion) much longer. The *sindurdani* foreshadows that, like her other prized possessions, it will shortly be rendered useless—once Bimala becomes a widow. The portentousness of the vermilion box thus has both a denotative and connotative function: it denotes Bimala's present status even as it connotes her sterile future; all of this is evoked while allowing us (and Nikhil) to take in the scene. Another transition—this time from the brightly lit objects in the foreground to a pulled-back shot of the darkened recesses of the room, the camera panning and tracking back to recapture the stillness of the apartment with Nikhil's somber presence in it—serves to end this scene. As it comes to a close, the soundtrack punctuates the visual with the shrill whistle of a train that is heard passing by in the imputed offscreen space of the outside world, once more conjuring up other places and times, not to mention the disruptions of modernity. What we gather not only pertains to the *ghar* and *bahir* (or home and world) but present and future as well, since events unfolding in the inner quarters will have their consequences in the time that is yet to come.

This penultimate episode illustrates so much of what is also at stake in the rest of the film, filled as it is with minor presences, objects, figures, and arrangements that Ray went to great lengths to stage. It is important to see these as providing the backdrop of Bimala's destiny and Nikhil's choices, though their significance extends beyond issues of setting or mise-en-scène since they are the substance of Ray's critique of social relations as commodity relations. This, I submit, is the transformative twist he applies to Tagore's story: a new mapping of the tensions between home and world, tradition and modernity. If by dint of the disciplinary fetish of "literature," it is Tagore's rather than Ray's terms that have come to reign in interpretive contests over the meaning of the conflict between tradition and modernity in India, it is still the case that Ray offers us a filmic treatment that enables a different field of vision, one that more adequately speaks to the predicament of social and aesthetic contradictions in the present.

2 The (Un)moving Image

Visuality and the Modern in Charulata

The entire conventional approach (as exemplified by even the best American and British films) is wrong.
—SATYAJIT RAY, from a letter dated 1950

MUSICAL NEGATIONS

If the Irish critic Vivian Mercier's assessment of *Waiting for Godot* as a play in which "nothing happens, twice," has passed into the annals of the most quotable quotes in criticism, then Kenneth Tynan's allusion to *Charulata* as a film full of "unpregnant pauses" and Howard Thompson's description of it in the *New York Times* as following the pace of a "stately inchworm" or "majestic snail" should not be far behind.[1] These remarks notwithstanding, critics were mostly favorable toward the film, so the question is: What, aside from the now-standard complaint that Ray's films are slow, can explain the persistence of the spectatorial desire for something—anything—to happen so long as it corresponds to the forms of expectation peculiar to narrative cinema? I will suggest that in *Charulata* (The Lonely Wife, 1964) Ray experiments with the issue of narrative movement, overturning the conventional impulse to look for development by underscoring the propensity of narrative cinema to show without telling or, at least, telling much. Penelope Houston, writing about the film soon after its release abroad, remarked, along lines similar to Mercier's on *Godot*, that "nothing, in any direct narrative sense, has happened" (although she does not compare Ray with Samuel Beckett on the matter, only with his realist forebears from the Victorian age such as Henry James, Edith Wharton, and Anton Chekhov).[2] In marking its own passive strategies of enunciation through the inaction of the characters, the stasis of *Charulata*'s plot no less than the pacing of shots, it is as if Ray proffers his own comment on the impossibility of action or, for that matter, activism in a world where such ideals have lost their charge. It is a world drained of energy, and the challenge he takes on is to mark the temporality

63

of stasis as a hallmark, perhaps even *the* hallmark, of existence in a world devoid of experiential depth.

There is ample reason to ponder the emphasis on inaction so heightened throughout this text as to draw repeated attention to its modernist sense of deliberation, and its ironizing of modernity's incessant demand for movement, efficiency, speed, and resolution. Indeed, *Charulata* might be said to be deaf to teleological resolution in the same way that Kenneth Calhoon has drawn attention to the deafness adopted by the spectator of Chaplin's films—invoking, in the negation of speech by gesture, a utopia of possibilities embedded in the language of silent cinema that can no longer be captured *in* film but only *through* it.[3] In an analogous move the very drive to reveal a diegetic world where things are seen—and seen to happen—also enables the lesson in *Charulata* that nothing does (happen). In other words, what we are dealing with both inside and outside the story world are only the frozen antinomies of sameness and difference, tradition and modernity, blindness and insight. One might reasonably contend that the film is about the blind spot of modernity, which, paradoxically, is its own spectacularization, and we begin to glimpse this recursive sense of the visual right away in the title sequence in which Charulata, the film's heroine, is framed off-center, her figure almost entirely offscreen in the beginning, with the exception of her hands shown holding her own (embroidery) frame as she carefully threads her needle into and out of it (Figure 3).

Charulata (Charu) is embroidering the initial *B* on a handkerchief for her husband, Bhupati, the same letter of the English alphabet that will become the gesture by which the world of politics and letters that she aspires to enter as a *nabeena* (new woman) is intimated later—with references to Bengal, Bankim (Bankim Chandra Chattopadhyay, the author of the first Indian novel), *Bilet* (England), and *Black Native*.[4] This is a world only gestured at in the film, though not realized in any way, and it is in the double movement toward a larger reality whose possibilities are simultaneously betokened and foreclosed that Ray provokes the viewer to reckon with the nothing that happens.

Beginning on this note about the film might suggest that in it, like *Godot*, "nothing happens, nobody comes, nobody goes," but it is the interregnum of India's transition from feudal colonialism into the modern that drives this text, and it dramatizes a concretely historical predicament unlike Beckett's abstractly existential one. So, a summary that contextualizes the narrative circumstances underpinning the more conceptual motivations of the film may help to situate this discussion for readers unfamiliar with its plot. The story centers on the everyday life of an

FIGURE 3.   Charulata
with her embroidery.
Used by permission from
Satyajit Ray Film and
Study Center.

upper-class young woman in nineteenth-century Bengal. Charu leads a
life of bored leisure within the confines of her spacious home. Her indul-
gent, Anglicized husband, Bhupati, wishes to ameliorate Charu's growing
frustration at the constraints of her lonely existence (hence the English
translation of the title into "The Lonely Wife"), realizing that his own
preoccupation with publishing a nationalist newspaper has led to her
isolation. In keeping with his cosmopolitan sensibilities, he also wants to
encourage her into becoming a modern woman capable of independence
and autonomy. To this end Bhupati commissions his cousin, Amal, to serve
as her intellectual companion and tutor.

The film is largely devoted to elaborating the alliance of Amal and
Charulata, who discover, among other things, that they share a love of
Bengali literature and an interest in writing literary essays. With Amal's
approval as her crucible, Charu pursues a burgeoning writing career,
alongside an easy, bantering intimacy with him. Predictably, since theirs is
a relationship circumscribed by norms of propriety specific to the model of
the extended, patriarchal family in India, Charu realizes that her romantic
attachment to Amal is untenable. In the shadow of various personal and
professional betrayals leading to the shutting down of Bhupati's newspaper, Amal, too, is overwrought by his sense of confusion and guilt at the
merest hint of having violated fraternal trust—since, again, nothing really
happens between him and Charu. At any rate, like a good modernist hero,
his solution is to disavow his implication in the emotional crisis he has
provoked, and he leaves for England, renouncing his writerly ambitions in
favor of becoming a barrister. At the end of the film Charu is left to pick up
the pieces of her life and reconsolidate her relationship with Bhupati. The
ending, however, leaves the question of reconciliation ambiguous.

As the credits roll in the opening sequence, we see Charu at work, to the extent that her needlework can be said to represent labor. Part of the film's underlying imperative is to reveal the extent to which so many of modernity's demands are about the expenditure of effort in the extraction of surplus and the garnishing of labor time—from the punching of time cards, and the synchronizing of clocks to ensure being on time, to the anxiety about running out of it. But this is not a film about the laboring classes, and by situating his critique in the bourgeoisie's own wasted preoccupations, Ray makes a subtle comment about a modality of life that constitutively precludes productive action. Hence, although his portrayal of Charu is completely sympathetic, or, perhaps, because of it, a distancing note is also struck about too quickly naturalizing the bourgeoisie's own self-perceptions (which include the perception of constraints on its womenfolk) as an overall statement about "modernity" or "sovereignty."[5]

In Charu, Ray depicts a privileged housewife whose time is her own; indeed, she has nothing but time on her hands, hands that are here depicted embroidering, just as later we see them holding playing cards and, in the most self-consolidated of her actions, writing. The camera remains fixed on the embroidery frame in real time, displaying the leaves surrounding the letter B as they take shape, one stem-stitch at a time. Just as Charu has finished picking out the last leaf with her needle, the camera abruptly pulls back, presenting us with our initial view of her full presence. At this moment the scene ends, its transition signaled by the first of many temporal markers throughout the film: the chimes of a clock striking four in the background and announcing the arrival of teatime.

As she leaves the confines of her bedroom, Charu needs only to shout out to Braja, the servant, asking him to serve tea to "Dadababu" (the formal, third-person designation for Bhupati) in his office. Having performed another of her tasks for the day, she returns to her room and somewhat aimlessly picks up her embroidery again, then a book, and finally strides toward the drawing-room in another part of the house (Figure 4).

Already the opening frames have begun to stress the contrast between the density of the mise-en-scène and the lulling desuetude of the narrative. The world of objects must hold our attention because humans cannot, although they are—as in Charu's case—beautiful and decorative objects as well. This is not to say that she is only objectified; rather, her objectification is part of the problem of seeing or, to put it more drastically, part of the problem of the hypostasis of vision in a modern hierarchy of the senses. The rest of the film attempts to work out this problem. By reinforc-

FIGURE 4. Charulata
approaching the drawing
room. Used by permission
from Satyajit Ray Film
and Study Center.

ing the artifice, as well as abstraction, of vision and by using diegetic and
nondiegetic music, it introduces into the mix the sense of hearing, thereby
speaking to an aspect of cognition outside the reified register of sight.

The film begins with the strains of a sitar picking out a popular Tagore
song, "*Momo citté, niti nrityé, ke je naaché . . .* " (Who is it that dances
daily in my heart?), although its significance is likely to be missed, if not
lost, by the viewer's expectations about the action in the story. Still, the
score of *Charulata* (composed by Ray) is one of the film's most remarkable
features, and if our attention is usually solicited more by what we see
than by what we hear at the movies, this is itself part of the text's gesture
toward other modes of meaning—a gestic act, as it were, that expresses
what the image track cannot. To the attentive spectator-listener the tune
is immediately recognizable, the everyday popularity of Tagore's music
in Bengal providing an intertextual reference to the primary source of
Ray's inspiration for this film (and many others).[6] In this fashion Ray
calls out his presumptively ideal (Bengali) viewer, the one who is apt to
know that *Charulata* is an adaptation of Rabindranath Tagore's 1901
novella "Nastanirh" (Broken Nest) but at the same time likely to ignore
the musical reference to Tagore invoked in the background sound. If seeing
is the most privileged form of intelligibility, the weight placed on it is thus
remarked in the very opening, revealing the ways in which we, as moderns, are distracted by preconceived ideas about what counts as a meaningful "happening" (to allude to the reviews above). Moreover, by exposing
standard notions about plot development as constitutive of the ideology of
cinema, the title sequence also embeds in it a critique of translatability and
access to meaning. On this point Ray himself is quite instructive:

In a film like *Charulata*, which has a 19th-century liberal upper-class
background, the relationship between the characters, the web of conflicting emotions, the development of the plot and its denouement,
all fall into a pattern familiar to the western viewer. The setting is
a western-style mansion, the decor is Victorian, the dialogue strewn
with references to western literature and politics. But beneath the
veneer of familiarity the film is chock-a-block with details to which
he has no access. Snatches of song, literary allusions, domestic details,
an entire scene where Charu and her beloved Amal talk in alliterations
(thereby setting a hopeless task for the subtitler) all give the film a density missed by the western viewer in his preoccupation with plot, character, the moral and philosophical aspects of the story, and the apparent
meaning of the images.

To give an example. Early on in the film, Charulata is shown picking
out a volume from a bookshelf. As she walks away idly turning its
pages, she is heard to sing softly. Only a Bengali will know that she
has turned the name of the author—the most popular Bengali novelist
of the period—into a musical motif. Later, her brother-in-law Amal
makes a dramatic entrance during a storm reciting a well-known line
from the same author. There is no way that subtitles can convey this
fact of affinity between the two characters so crucial to what happens
later. *Charulata* has been much admired in the West . . . but this admi-
ration has been based on aspects to which response has been possible;
the other aspects being left out of the reckoning.[7]

The position Ray stakes out here is in danger of being misunderstood,
so it is worth a little consideration. In saying that visuals and subtitles
cannot, by themselves, convey the fullest range of meanings encoded in
his films, Ray is not arguing from or for a nativist perspective; nor was he
all that invested in catering exclusively to Bengali audiences who would,
presumably, have a transparent understanding of everything.[8] Rather, he
seems to emphasize the imperfect communication involved in *any* attempt
at translation, be it cinematic or linguistic. Only a Bengali viewer might
recognize the allusion to Bankim to which he refers in the quote above,
just as only the spectator trained in Tagore music might discern the song
in the opening refrain. But the important point is that this is the predicament in which his cinema finds itself more generally—caught between
a desire to make meaning and the pervasive blockages to understanding
that local knowledge can, on occasion, help to overcome. Still, the real
difficulty Ray faces is to say something by saying what it is not, since that
is in the nature of negation. What the "western viewer" he adduces would
recognize leaves a world of possibilities by the wayside. This is neither a
provincial view nor a nativist one if one accepts that linguistic complexities

necessarily preclude a fuller understanding for those who have to follow subtitles.

Indeed, to assert this is to admit the problem of translation into the cinematic equation, especially to the extent that it acknowledges the barrier that the "second skin" of the English language imposes on a critique of colonial inheritances in the first place. By the same token, that *Charulata* is not a *documentary* representation of Bengali mores in the nineteenth century is another element in Ray's attempt to foreground—as well as undercut—the notion that cinema speaks a "universal language." That is to say, one can no more "document" culturally specific ways of being than render them transparently in a universal idiom. For even if vision is a universal human attribute (except for the blind), visuality, as the institutionalization of vision in particular sociocultural settings, is not—inasmuch as it expresses specific ideologies that not only cut across East and West but also are present within India, with its complex amalgam of linguistic and sociopolitical differences. This is the larger import of Ray's agreeing to offer his ideas about his cinema and the barriers to meaning (in venues such as *Sight and Sound*). Although he formulates them somewhat more antagonistically in writing than on the screen, his cinema is the best exemplification of the ideas themselves. In both venues he scrupulously marks the dangers of appropriation and the naïveté of assuming that his films either speak for themselves or signify in the same way to all.

I belabor this point because there has been a good deal of disaffection, mostly expressed by Indian critics, about the fact that, on occasion, Ray positioned himself as a Bengali director whose films were intended for Bengali audiences. Ashish Rajadhyaksha, writing soon after the director's death (also in *Sight and Sound*), appears to bury him in the act of providing a "tribute," commenting on Ray's hypocrisy in desiring both a national and an international network of distribution for his films while claiming (once the tape recorder had been switched on for an interview) that "I make my films for a Bengali audience."[9] But there is no incompatibility between Ray's wanting bigger audiences for his films and specifying one's location, so the taint of parochialism rings hollow or, worse, resentful. "The nativist tag remained an uneasy one," opines Rajadhyaksha, qualifying this statement in the next phrase of his utterance: "and is evident less in Ray's films than in the position he was made—and in certain ways allowed himself—to represent."[10] Whatever the extrafilmic reasons for Rajadhyaksha's pronouncement, it exposes the nature of misunderstanding about what constitutes nativism, trapped as it is by its own nativizing move to detain Ray from seeking to address himself beyond national boundaries while retaining him for a nationalist project censoriously shorn of its Bengali roots.

What is curious are the quarters from which such charges are issued; no one, for example, would accuse Baudelaire of nativism for staying squarely within a limited purview of bourgeois French manners and habits, or Tolstoy for exploring the mentality of the Russian peasantry. In these cases it would be granted that the allegorical element of any representation requires, despite the "empty" character of this trope, to be bound to a configuration of place, time, and meaning. When it comes to Ray, however, critics have profoundly, if not cynically, misrecognized the import of this intertwining of particularity and generality, distrusting the simultaneous nationalism and internationalism of his vision. Formulated in the very midst of postwar socialist regeneration, Ray's cinema avoided an explicitly revolutionary stance; consequently, to the purist for whom no internationalism was worth its salt if it did not address India as a whole, his outlook seems aberrantly regionalist.

At any rate, if we return to *Charulata* and to the degree of reflexive insight in Ray's films (if not in the positions of his critics), we find a delinking of meaning from narrative anchoring or location—and, by this token, from a merely regional particularism. Instead, his effort is to relink meaning with the idea of possibility *in general* in a way that is quite distant from dominant ways of viewing film as a form that telescopes rather than expands our understanding of reality. To take just the example of the opening musical refrain, it is possible to see it as emblematizing an order of experience and meaning not accessible by emphasizing only the visuals and the plot or by relegating sound to the margins of the frame. This is because the music represents a contrast between the constraints that are to play out in the story world and an antithetical domain of possibilities—of girlhood, dancing, and unfettered action that are intimated but cannot be displayed in purely visual terms. At the same time, the spirit of the song, with its allusions to the passage from girlhood into womanhood, is undercut by the narrative itself which reveals an opposing view of the utterly routinized pace of Charu's actual existence. Signified at the end of the sequence by the chiming of a clock, the tedium of Charu's existence is multiply cued for the spectator, who is made aware of the disjunction between an idealized feminine *Bildung* and the actual measurings of life by clock time and petty duties.

As a counterpoint to Charu's (diegetic) life, the song in the background evokes the rhythms of a blossoming femininity, in this way anticipating a future outside the strict space of the story. The music thus provides an index of her incomplete subjecthood on terms that exceed what can be shown and, what is more, that negate the visual. If the song's lyrics are about being in step (*ta ta thoi thoi*—the *bols*, or beats, taught to young dancers), Charu is shown to be out of step with the person "dancing in her heart," not only because Amal has yet to arrive on the scene but also because she, like Bimala in *Ghare Baire*, outsteps her spatiotemporal placement within the narrative. Depicting her along these lines, Ray goes well beyond representing a historical model of the new Indian (or Bengali) woman into an allegorical exploration.

Of what, then, is *Charulata* an allegory? At the level of manifest content it would certainly not be incorrect to regard her as, indeed, a representation of the *nabeena* (new woman). But this is such an obvious aspect of the way that the discourse of Victorian moral education was inherited in India as to be unremarkable, particularly in a portrait of family manners set in colonial Bengal. One cannot help being surprised that this designation of the text (as an allegory of the new woman) has provided critics with as much grist for their mill as it seems to have done, as though this point were somehow new. Still, the problem is not that this reading is inaccurate but that it is both obvious and incomplete, confining itself to a fairly undeveloped notion of the allegory here as an extended metaphor for ideals of femininity and modern consciousness. To the extent that Ray adapts his narrative from Tagore's turn-of-the-century exploration, his treatment too—by virtue of this reliance—rests on exploring the dimensions of Indian womanhood as they shift from traditional to modern ways of seeing and being. But Ray's appropriation of historical and literary images of Bengali modernity—especially with regard to "the woman question"— transforms the representational issues at stake into a cinematic experiment that is as unexpected as it is unprecedented.

Colin MacCabe has observed that filmic adaptation can be read in terms of the attempt to give expression to submerged elements of source texts, a suggestion that allows one to see Ray's effort in *Charulata* as, precisely, a restaging of a historical problematic and a critique of emergence that was at best submerged in Tagore's rendition.[11] That he uses the representational forms and techniques of cinema is crucial—to the extent that his visual investments lead in directions that not only were unforeseen by his literary predecessor but that also express the problem of alienation by reconstituting the relationships between a mode of being (modern femininity) and a mode of understanding (historical consciousness). Following this idea, we can see how the formal demarcations between cinematic and literary elements transform that which is represented. This accepted, the relay between past and present, between a literary account of modern problems and its visual reconstitution on film, can be read as productive of an entirely reorganized field of vision, as well as knowledge. And it also follows that the history of nineteenth-century Bengal as realized by the film is further modified in terms of our contemporary relation to the past, though on the basis of ideas that are cortical to the present (that is, *our* present).[12] It is in this specific and cinematic sense that *Charulata* presents an allegory, one that takes up the problem of *visual* alienation in modernity.

It should by now be clear that the simple definition of allegory as an extended metaphor in which ideas largely stand in for other ideas does not do justice to the film. Rather, the text can be said to exhibit a figurative strategy that is both more disjunctive and more ekphrastic—that is, it takes on a life of its own adequate to its peculiar, formal circumstances. The best explanation of this more complex allegorical mode is to be found in Walter Benjamin's account of seventeenth-century mourning plays *(Trauerspiel)* in *The Origin of German Tragic Drama*. Benjamin argued that rather than being seen as inferior to the symbolic because of its inessential relationship to the ideas represented (the reigning view within German romanticism that still obtains), allegory is the preferred rhetorical device of modernity. Contending that this figurative mode alone captures the inorganic nature of modernity, he emphasized its peculiar adequacy under the regime of commodity fetishism—in which, we know, quality is substitutable by quantity and exchange value rules social existence. As he put it, "Any person, any object, any relationship can mean absolutely anything else."[13]

In accordance with this position Benjamin averred that, as distinct from other times, the profane world of the now is matched by a "fallen language" that no longer reaches toward a corresponding truth or reality, only a degraded and mediated one. So saying, he contrasted an earlier era of intuition and emotion, in which the symbol ruled, with the priority of allegory in the modern age, where real feelings and experiences are difficult if not impossible. In turn, this enabled him to suggest that the intellection demanded by allegory (in positing a figurative meaning that depends only on an abstract, secondary relationship with the object it represents rather than a synthetic or referential one) allows for an immanent, critical posture toward capitalist modernity. What ought to strike readers today about Benjamin's conception of a figure of speech that expresses the disunity of language and experience is that it operates within a framework quite discontinuous with the reigning model of poststructuralism (which in stressing a purely arbitrary or conventional relationship between signs and meanings would render Benjamin's position tautological). Allegory, Benjamin says, is *both* "convention and expression,"[14] proposing thereby a concrete relationship between allegory and history that was at the same time *not* about the correspondence of reality and representation. The distinction is crucial: by not touting the mere conventionality of meaning and, simultaneously, by stressing an immanent notion of its determination, Benjamin enables a materialist discussion of the technological allegory of cinema in its mediations of the real.

This approach to the problem of allegory has been taken up in important historicist work by critics such as Susan Buck-Morss and Miriam Hansen, whose specific contentions about cinema rely on juxtaposing Benjamin's extension of his positions on the seventeenth-century *Trauerspiel* with his writings on film.[15] As I see it, the peculiar resonance of his ideas in the context of discussing *Charulata* is that the form of the *Trauerspiel* (as distinct from tragedy) is, in its delineation of modern ruins and historical stasis, very much akin to the form of paralysis and lack of resolution Ray attempts to elaborate in this film. As readers familiar with it will know, *Charulata* is neither a tragic portrait nor one in which things turn out well in the end. It is, rather, an irresolute depiction of an irresolvable historical clash between a colonial past and an emergent present in which, of course, the characters—above all, Charu—are caught. Just as in the *Trauerspiel*, where time is etiolated but without a corresponding teleology, *Charulata* articulates a form that is, especially at the level of structure, episodic and arrested—where, in other words, nothing happens. This is not to say that Benjamin's theory of allegory or his notions about the mourning play are immediately relevant to our appreciation of Ray's film, but I submit that these are valuable ideas for thinking about cinema outside the terms of referential history.

Ray's film practice in general, and *Charulata* in particular, is quite resonant with Benjamin's larger arguments about sense perception in modernity, specifically when it comes to his view of the crisis of aesthetic experience (also elaborated by his younger colleague, Theodor Adorno). Ultimately, however, Benjamin's proposals about allegory are shadowed by an attendant melancholia about a profane universe no longer in contact with a prelapsarian language or experience. In this respect Ray offers a less disconsolate angle on such loss. Both here and in other chapters I try to establish that Ray's vision also points—through gesture and sound—to cultural and historical dimensions of understanding that do not rely on a Messianic (what Benjamin elsewhere calls "Adamic") or idealized horizon of meanings for its utopian yet thoroughly secular sensibilities.

As I hope to have established, in beginning with the ostensibly minor aspect of the title sequence, my stress is on the multiple modalities of signification. In this film, music expresses what the narrative or the picture cannot—namely, a conceptual and allegorical space between idea and reality. So, too, if Charu is to bear the burden of representing the relay between a character from the past and a figuration of an unfolding modernity, she also serves as an emblem of the future. In this respect she certainly resembles Bimala (which in any case is unsurprising given that *Charulata* is the model to which Ray returned in *Ghare Baire* for his treatment of futurity). Both films attest to the ways that Ray reprised Tagore's constructions of femininity, transforming them in the process. What is interesting here is that the use of Tagore's song in the opening sequence signifies, outside dialogue or action, how impossibility and constraint are articulated; how they are, as it were, embroidered not only with respect to Ray's delineation of Charu but also in terms of the overall political allegory of India's emergence. And this reflection on history can itself be contrasted with its obverse, for, as we learned from Koselleck, every meditation on the past is also a speculation about future possibilities.

The past and present—in the explicit conjoining of music and celluloid—are collocated, obviating the need to separate, more mechanistically, modern (cinematic) means of making meaning from older forms of representation and understanding. Accordingly, if, in Benjamin's scheme, allegory is to be understood less as a play for illustrative technique than as an inscription of the *contingency* of knowledge, it can be suggested that music in *Charulata* is an allegory of historical temporality as well, requiring the viewer to attend carefully to the ways that the relay between one time and another is conveyed by film music. Thus, we might say, music becomes the means by which Ray harmonizes different temporal moments: at one level he uses it to signify what Raymond Williams called "residual" elements, and at another level it enables him to formulate a statement about what is yet to be.

The place of acoustics in cinema has, as a whole, received only minor attention.[16] But as I hope the example of the first musical interlude demonstrates, it is a key concern in *Charulata*, not least as a negation of modernity's preprogrammed investment in the visual. For this reason I would also like to comment on the salience of a second musical interpolation, heard when Charu sings a song during what is possibly the most complex sequence of shots in the film. Prior to this particular scene she has been depicted humming tunes and idly fingering the piano keyboard in her

FIGURE 5. Charulata on her swing. Used by permission from Satyajit Ray Film and Study Center.

decorated, stuffy living room, indicating both her musicality (as would be expected in a story about a well-born woman's artistic training) and Ray's continued interest in soliciting more than merely a "viewing position" from his audience with the carefully constructed soundtrack. The second song not only draws attention away from the narrative by inducing an almost synesthetic effect on the viewer, it also serves as a physical counterpoint to the lack of action. Unlike the first musical refrain, rendered only instrumentally by the sitar, Charu sings this song onscreen—swaying more and more rapidly on her swing as she contemplates Amal in the garden to which the two have repaired to discuss their writing (Figure 5).

"*Phulé phulé dholé dholé*" (What gentle breeze floats in the flowers?) are the lyrics to this song, which takes up little more than one minute of screen time even though the pacing of the shots (in a sequence that lasts approximately eight minutes overall) gives the impression of a longer interlude. Later, this tune is also rendered nondiegetically, played during the scene in which Amal ponders the possibilities of marriage, adventure, and European cultural encounters—the decisive moment of the break between him and Charu. What she can only sing as a song about possibilities, Amal can actually experience in life; in this way an ironic comment is made about all that remains open to him but is closed off to Charu herself. To echo the problematic of inaction stated at the beginning, Charu's emergent self-consolidation only proceeds in the knowledge that, as far as she is concerned, nothing *can* happen.

This second song is also one of Tagore's compositions—based on a Scottish ballad he had heard on his first visit to England—denoting what is already well known about the accretive, syncretic, and cosmopolitan worldviews that he and Ray shared.[17] Later in the film there is the appearance of a classical, *dhrupad* song at the musical soirée Bhupati hosts for his effete, aristocratic friends; in contrast with its alien tonalities (for viewers unfamiliar with the *ragas* or mood schemes of Hindustani classical music), Charu's rendition here draws on conventional European tone structures, as well as on the formulaic cinematic association of music and romance. Playing to the expectation of song-and-dance numbers that are the quintessence of mainstream Indian cinema, Ray meets the generic expectations of his viewers, both native and foreign, while subverting the conventional assumption that a romance is about to follow. Consequently, in addition to serving almost a choric function in the way the lyrics comment on the heroine's predicament and the limitations on her emancipation, this song (along with the rest of the film's music) points to the disparate forms of perception and recognition synchronized by the film.[18]

TIME AND THE OTHER

What I have said thus far about musical meanings reinforces the overall sense that the narrative movement in *Charulata* is not only interlarded with them; they also have the specific effect of casting the thematic concerns of the text into a tableau of frozen history. As the subheading to this section implies,[19] we are dealing here with history's own temporality, all the more marked in this text because of the ever-present association of the non-West with timelessness. The swing sequence works to complicate further the theme of nothing happening, inserting a completely eccentric notion of temporal emergence into the mix. Ray's directorial virtuosity is fully evident in the scene, deployed to reinforce the bodily contingencies of viewership that cut across the senses of sight, hearing, and feeling. It is, of course, the case that the basic function of allegory in the film is to establish how Charu, as an emblem of the *nabeena*, represents the contradictions of Indian femininity caught between traditional and modern expectations. But in complicating the notion of the allegorical at work here, I suggest that this contradiction is not merely a metaphor of the gap between then and now. For the sequence also evokes a different configuration of temporality invoked neither through musical notation nor narrative connotation but in a metonymic displacement. In this mode an entirely new category of development associated with all things young—an idea and an ideal no less than a person or an age—is intimated. Even as the tradition-modernity couplet pits *nabeena* against *pracheena* (traditional woman) in the debate over female subjecthood introduced by Bankim into Bengali literature,[20] the swing sequence gestures to an altogether different temporal register

FIGURE 6.   Charulata's
memories. Used by
permission from Satyajit
Ray Film and Study
Center.

of feminine emergence. Earlier in the film Charu, as if in an ironic commentary on the frame narrative, was seen humming Bankim's name, as
she passed from book to book in her extensive but sterile library, pondering what to read in order to pass the time. In the present scene, that self-
referential moment is itself echoed—where, instead of being positioned
as either *nabeena* or *pracheena*, the song casts her as a *taruni* (young
woman), thereby dissociating her from Bankim's restrictive model and
associating her more explicitly with the innocence of girlhood, the idealized romance of the *Rubaiyat* (which Amal invokes at the beginning of
the swing sequence), and a model of femininity quite out of step with the
nationalist schema of the role of women.

The unseen possibilities of a carefree existence outside the political calculus of the needs of the nation make themselves visible at the moment
of their disappearance—in the rearview mirror of history no less than in
the folds of Charu's memory. A complicated temporal alignment is in this
way articulated, by means of which the spectator and Charu both glimpse
her disappearing past as she peers through her lorgnette at her desires in
the present (Figure 6). It is as if the lorgnette through which she peers
has become transformed into a bioscope—a picture show of all that is no
more. A clever reminder about the devices of memory (the camera and the
lorgnette, as well as the mind's eye), the scene also foreshadows another
technical trick, the use of the flashback sequence later in the film to reveal
Charu's recollections of growing up in the village as she writes them into
being.

The slow, deliberate movements of the swing on which Charu is seated
as she looks through her lorgnette, which she then abandons in her giddy
ride, constitute this scene's most captivating elements. Mimicking the

camera's movements, they invoke, as I have suggested, the saturated presence of the visual apparatus. The lorgnette no less than the camera is a technology of vision that mediates time (and space) though it does not disguise it. Through this expedient of reinforcing the motif of sight and instruments of seeing, Ray introduces us to his view of cinema's recursivity and its capacity to reflect on its own historicity and technological conditions of possibility, thus mirroring another of Benjamin's propositions about film.[21] And with it we are possibly offered a densely layered philosophical insight—namely, that the passage of time may have brought with it the failure of hopes and dreams about the future, but this does not negate the viability of utopian ideals; it only magnifies the limits of our vision, given our unfree times. By the same token, it also makes it possible to suggest that such a retrospective reflection is not nostalgic but, in its explicitly formal character, remains the expression of an embodied modernism that presupposes its own temporal and technological conditions of emergence.

The complexities of a reflexive time-consciousness are not just of abstract theoretical interest in this context. Rather, they have a concrete effect in our coming to terms with the swing scene, whose very intelligibility depends on spectatorial disorientation and a physical awareness of the sense of seeing in relation to movement. The shots of Charu swinging in and out of frame are literally discombobulating, the physical act of viewing once more brought to the forefront. The camera's zigzagging movements, alternately capturing and releasing Charu's figure within the frame and out of it, gradually builds a pace that renders the viewer almost dizzy. Moreover, this dizziness is provoked at the very instant that the otherwise bucolic reminder of youth embodied by the song contributes to the scene's overall sense. Music, camera movement, and Charulata thus collide in something like a parallax view. Unlike the spectators, who are trapped only temporarily in their seats at the movie theater as they undergo this disorienting experience via the action onscreen, Charu is trapped in time, the emblem of a much more thoroughgoing derangement. In the manner of Benjamin's exhortation to think of film as a medium that betokens its own failed promise to align meaning and history, Ray draws out the complicity between narrative, spectatorship, and historical experience, displaying them in a vertiginous assault on our perceptual and temporal world. Neither in time nor out of it, the figure of Charulata— through the very attenuation of her boredom and her lack of knowing quite what to do to make time go by—expresses the predicament of our own ineluctably retroactive sense of time itself.

In her 1969 essay "Bodies in Space: Film as Carnal Knowledge," Annette Michelson suggested that it might be possible to locate an "ontology of cinema" in Stanley Kubrick's *2001: A Space Odyssey*. According to her, here was a "breakthrough," a film that "perform[ed] the function of a Primary Structure, forcing the spectator back, in a reflexive gesture, upon the analytic rehearsal of his experience" (56). It was in this sense that the film (which is an allegory of knowledge via the narrative of space travel) was "carnal"; in its cinematic exploration of the limits of space, horizontality, and verticality, it forced the spectator into reckoning with a discourse of knowledge having to do with "the body's recognition of its suspended coordinates as its necessity" (57). What intrigues me about Michelson's analysis is that unlike psychoanalytic film criticism's protocol of reading through and for transference, she stresses the *formal* capacity of film to produce and elevate "doubt" to an aesthetic principle. As I understand it, Michelson contends that a film like *2001* heightens the sense of the paradox by which the "delicate dissociation" between lived reality and artistic form is reconciled by the viewing subject. Consequently, the alienation of the spectator—with respect to both bodily experience and cognitive desires—produces a restructuring of "inner" and "outer" that, finally, displaces the comfort of knowing one from the other. In opposition to a topographical mapping of the workings of the unconscious onto aspects of spectatorship, this model of reading requires attending to the experiential "dynamics of creation and perception." To quote Michelson: "the dissociative economy of film viewing heightens our perception of being physical to the level of apperception: one becomes conscious of the modes of consciousness" (59).

The point I wish to derive from Michelson relates to her insistence on the *cognitive* dimension of filmic experience, as well as of film form. At stake in the economy of film are contingencies that Michelson says are "quite beyond the luxury of identification—the occasion to gain awareness of the inner suppositions that sustain us, so that pleasure is informed with *the shock of recognition*" (59, my emphasis). I will return to the problematic of recognition as it unfolds in *Charulata*, but for now, it is worth stressing that irrespective of the purchase of psychoanalytic criticism in understanding, say, Hollywood cinema, its protocols cannot offer much in the way of a materialist reading of a film like *Charulata*. This is where the account of recognition as an ontophysical or cognitive (rather than psychic) contingency becomes useful. Not only does this allow us to understand how the film requires and produces forms of recognition "quite beyond the luxury of identification," as Michelson puts it, but it also offers a way to contend with the fact that the mechanisms by which positions of identification and disidentification are theorized within the psychoanalytic paradigm are unable to account for the historical disposition of Ray's cinema, as well as the forms of perceptual awareness it solicits from viewers.

Let me take as my last example the segment from the opening scene of *Charulata* in which she has finished with her embroidery for the moment and must now find something else to do. A lot has been said about the lengths to which Ray went to stage the details in this scene—from obsessing over the exact replication of Victorian wallpaper design, and the construction of the veranda (or balcony) surrounding the rooms, to setting up all the graphic matches and motifs in the mise-en-scène.[22] The scene proceeds from the slow, lingering shots of Charu in her bedroom, embroidering the handkerchief for Bhupati, to the mobile, tracking shots of her wandering from room to room in order to follow the insistent sounds of a monkey man drumming outside the windows of her home (Figure 7).

The visual contrast between Charu's containment within closed walls and the world outside is heightened in the medium close-ups of Charu attempting to get a glimpse of the monkey man by peering through the shutters on the windows. To help her obtain a better view of the diversions of the world, she is shown walking back quickly to her bedroom and retrieving a lorgnette, her first use of it to enhance her viewing of life beyond (quite literally) her shuttered existence and, a little later, to observe Bhupati as he walks by her studying a fat book, oblivious to her presence. Of this scene Ray himself said, "Except for one line of dialogue in its seven minutes, the scene says what it has to say *in terms that speak to the eye and the ear.*"[23]

To read his utterance on the terms provided by Michelson, this scene "forces" the spectator into recognizing the body's coordinates as necessities of comprehension, knowledge. The cues needed to "make sense" of this scene are, of course, different from the spatial sensibility heightened in *2001*, but here, too, we are attuned to the variety of "modes of consciousness" that define the limits, as well as the possibilities, of cognition.[24] What underwrites every viewer's awareness is the fact that we all see and hear (unless of course one is unable to see or hear). In this case the "we" is predicated on the universality of the perceptual apparatus, even though the "contents" of our cognition have different histories and are culturally specific. It is important to recognize that it is this formal universality of sense-perception that makes it possible for Gérard Depardieu (the producer of Ray's penultimate film), to announce, "Everybody can understand a Ray movie if they want to hear another music. Beautiful strong music. Some piece of Mozart."[25] It is perhaps unnecessary to point out that despite

FIGURE 7. Charulata peering at the world outdoors. Used by permission from Satyajit Ray Film and Study Center.

Ray's fondness for Mozart's compositions, what is given cinematically is *not* Mozart (or even *like* Mozart). But he does make it possible to engage the same kind of apperceptive contingencies that make Mozart intelligible across vast differences of time and place, and it is precisely the suturing of a universal principle (visuality, aurality) with a historical particular (the sensibility of Bengali modernity) that lends Ray's film its vivid, almost carnal, poignancy—in the sense that Michelson uses this word.[26]

As this scene unfolds, the effect of the rapid cuts and the tension they serve to build further reinforces the contrast between the stasis indoors and the dynamism of life outdoors. To this Ray adds striking graphic matches between Charu's sari; the settee in her bedroom; the patterning of the floor, doors, and railings on the balcony (encircling the inner courtyard of the house); and, finally, the window shutters through which Charu peers with her lorgnette. At one level, we may say that Charu is depicted simply as part of the mise-en-scène. She, like many of Ray's heroines, is a prop in the drama of being modern. Her historical situation, of being suspended between a Victorianism peculiar to *bhadralok* (or new middle-class) society and an emergent gendered consciousness coded as modern, is evoked with an almost fetishistic attention to shot detail and visual cues.[27] Yet these details of Charu's spatialized containment do not exhaust what can be said about this scene. For, on a different plane of signification, having to do with the apparatus rather than the narrative, Charu's inscription as a subject who surpasses her locale and location is also made palpable: as in the swing scene, it is almost as if the camera is unable to capture her movement in space and time, the zooms and reverse zooms confounding her overall image.

The sequence of shots in which Charu dashes to her study to look out of the window at the monkey man, her lorgnette swinging at her side, is marked most noticeably by a visual clash between the horizontal movement of the pendulating lorgnette, the moving folds of her striped sari as she walks by, and the vertical railings of the balcony in the background that capture her figure against their ground. The images here are blurry, almost sped up, as if to suggest that Charu's personhood is outside the reach of the camera. Once more, the limits of vision and being—hers as well as ours—are underlined. Only the lorgnette remains in focus, calling attention to the ways that technologies of representation do more than enhance sight by becoming themselves forms of intelligibility. In keeping with this idea, the lorgnette serves as more than a visual aid, acting as the sign of a compensatory investment in seeing and believing (which, not coincidentally, is a profoundly modern preoccupation).[28] From this perspective, Charu, much like Bimala after her, is recognizable as a figure that crosses over from being a nineteenth-century construct to exhibiting *our* dilemmas about the transparency of vision and modes of knowing.[29]

Despite the complexity of Ray's formal and narratological strategies, a major problem with his standing as the standard-bearer of "Indian cinema" relates precisely to the fact that little attention has been paid to his general reformulation of the question of cinematic form. He has not been given adequate credit for his conceptual accomplishments, and his directorial signature has been assessed in bland terms as vaguely "modernist," reflecting only the usual preoccupation with, and corollary subversion of, realist expectations about formal narrative.[30] To date, the annals of film scholarship do not offer much more than a ritual citing of Ray's iconic value as merely an inheritor of the realism-modernism quandary, and for this reason it is his typicality rather than his epistemological innovations that is routinely adduced. He serves, as it were, as a supplement in the tale of cinema's modernity and modernism, worthy of honorable mention but not too much scrutiny. The consequence of such a foreshortening of critical perspective is that Ray's acknowledged debts to the directorial genius of Renoir or De Sica are what is emphasized as the key to understanding his films. Tellingly, he is seen as following in the general tracks of modernist cinema (rather than entirely reshaping it); and, as is amply evident in the books and journals that mention him, the fields to which Ray is assigned, as well as the distinction he is granted, are usually conceived in narrow terms about the modernism of the standard, Euro-American moderns.[31]

By contrast, if we commit to understanding how novel ideas emerge out of paratactic or "misplaced" encounters between aesthetic models and cultural forms, then a homological model of reading—*as if* Ray's texts were (merely) modern or modernist—will not suffice. The problem lies in the fact that his films are *also* modern and modernist, but since periodizing gestures are inadequate substitutes for thinking about the social content of forms, a different protocol is required for translating the broad issue of structure into an analysis of what is at stake in historical and aesthetic terms. For we not only need to reject a mimetic view of the relationship between film and reality but also, and more importantly, we need both a cognitive outlook and an interpretive strategy that goes beyond mimicking the imperative of imperial sovereignty over all matters non-Western.

Here, too, albeit indirectly, Benjamin's propositions about allegory in an antimimetic mode can help to illuminate Ray's practice; indeed, the import of those propositions can itself be extended by this means. We know, for example, that in his much-cited artwork essay Benjamin suggested that cinema is "surgical" and has the ability to comprehend (even more than represent) "the necessities which rule our lives."[32] The specificity of film as a medium that "introduces us to unconscious optics" resides, according to Benjamin, in its historical restructuring of our understanding of the "formations of the subject."[33] Following this idea about cinema's surgical capacities, it can now be said that Ray's use of the lorgnette as metaphor and even as prosthesis serves to reinforce a larger, more general argument about allegory as the mechanism for registering the discontinuities between figurative mechanisms and historically verifiable constructions.[34] As a recurrent motif, the lorgnette continually draws attention to the contradictions of Charu's position as both subject and object of historical representation. But in addition, her attachment to this device—to peek at the world outdoors, then to scrutinize her husband, and, finally, to monitor Amal's writing from a distance—also marks the artifice of her inscription as a symbol of Indian womanhood. The lorgnette becomes the index of the ways in which her vision is in need of correction and is therefore less complete than demanded by a purely symbolic staging of the problem of representation.

As much a prop as a prosthetic subject, then, Charu's reliance on the lorgnette to render her sight and self-consciousness more adequate consistently bespeaks a crisis of vision familiar from representational debates about European modernity. She is also recouped, however, as an emergent, postcolonial figure insofar as her portrayal as a woman looking, as well as looking on, is crisscrossed by the sense that hers is not the decadent, colonizing gaze of the modern European subject, male or female. For, we might recall, the prototypical use of a lorgnette (with respect to the normative cultural resonance attached to this visual instrument) was held to occur at the scene of a spectacle—such as the opera or music hall. The baroque era ushered in the practice among spectators, especially female spectators, of wielding the lorgnette as a device to see and be seen. Thus coded in the European cultural context as a marker of class privilege, sexual subjectivity, and accoutrement of public display, the lorgnette was designed to make its owner desire and be desired, vision in this way emblematizing sexuality. The specularity that provokes and even produces this putative subject of desire is locked within an imperial problematic of vision-want-conquest that bears little resemblance to Ray's depiction. In the allegory of repetition *as* difference that *Charulata* exemplifies, the lorgnette becomes the objectified means to urge on a redirection of the symptomatic focus in contemporary forms of criticism with sexual desire and subjective agency. Charu wields her lorgnette, to be sure, but less as a ploy in the public circuit of desire and knowledge that encircles current theoretical notions about selfhood than in an appropriative gesture of sensate if private self-cognition.

Consequently, whatever power accrues to Charu's enhanced vision through her deployment of the lorgnette, it is not a view of her self as a desiring subject/desired object—the rigid paradigm for thinking about subjectivity in current discourses. Instead, the script for this particular story of the "new woman" relates to a very different understanding of sentient knowledge having to do with affective responses to the changes wrought by colonial modernity on an indigenous patriarchal arrangement. It is the woman's place as this emergent subject marked by the experience of Europeanization, but resistant to its imperative of equating self-knowledge with sexual autonomy, that is also effectively allegorized here.

In the second appearance of the lorgnette, when Charu spies on Bhupati walking past her with his nose buried in the high-minded aspirations of his nationalist newspaper (with its motto, "Truth Survives"), we are shown how the contradictions of modernity have mutually incompatible consequences for men and women. Charu can only spectate from the sidelines while Bhupati engages muscular and masculine public debates about nationalism, civic duty, and parliamentary reform in the forum of his newspaper, the *Sentinel*. That the scripts of private life and conjugality are equally at risk in the hands of a modernizing imperative as are more public domains of politics and culture is in this way signified with glancing irony. On the one hand, the desire to be an enlightened male prompts Bhupati to want to be the agent of his wife's emancipation; for this reason he becomes angry and desolate when the path of her emergence takes a form that leaves him out of her circuit of desire and action. On the other hand, the charge of being a modern wife—accomplished, literate, self-consolidated—exacts a separate toll on Charu, who finds that the returns of reciting Tennyson, Byron, and even Bankim are different for men than they are for her. Contrarily enough, it also gives the lie to Bhupati's sense of agency, since he is in the end unable to provide Charu with the affective and intellectual companionship she seeks and on which his sense of masculine authority ultimately rests.

An important dimension of the critique of colonial modernity is intimated through this tête-à-tête of private emotions and public sentiment, albeit it is neither emphasized thematically nor (as with much else in the film) does it receive much development within the narrative. Nevertheless, a whole set of ideas about romantic attachment and, more proximately, about the ways that the discourse of romance has come to dominate film narrative at large, is historicized through the interaction—and, of course, nonaction—of Charu and Bhupati. By this subtle means Ray reveals that the ideal of modern, companionate marriage—of an exclusive and dyadic partnership in emotional and social affairs—accompanying the importation of bourgeois individualism in India is of short duration and, moreover, a colonial ideology that has had a sundering effect on preexisting kinship relations. The implication is that, as with other aspects of embourgeoisement, the belated arrival of this ideal had relatively dire consequences for women, whose sense of self needed, all of a sudden, to be redefined in sexualized terms—with men in mind rather than other women, the extended family, or the community.

In this context we may recall that the Victorian ideology of bourgeois domesticity was artificially inserted into an indigenous kinship system in India, one that had previously denied the priority of conjugality over sociality. Exemplified by the relations between the film's principals, such imposition could only result in misplaced, but this time morbid, symptoms—evidenced by Charu's doomed and improper infatuation with her husband's cousin, not to mention her husband's impotence in providing her with the form of privatized, companionate affection the imported model demanded. At another level of generic expectation, the film also comments on the consititued morbidity of the ideology of conjugal love in the absurd representations of romance and marriage in mainstream films, particularly (though not exclusively) in Indian cinema. In a cultural context where sexual love can neither be avowed nor disavowed because of codes of modesty and propriety, the stereotypical resort is to sublimate it into the canned depiction of an "affair" or a "love marriage" that would still be scandalous in real life. Needless to say, perhaps, it is in these jejune guises that the modern heterosexual couple appears on the Indian screen. Ray subverts the expectation of movie audiences for such distorted narratives of love, sex, and romance (as compensation against their prohibition), offering a more self-conscious take on the vicissitudes of idealizing romantic love as the hallmark of modern marriage. This is all the more true in India though the ideology of romance is no less ideological elsewhere.

The point here is a dialectical one, and it rests on recognizing that the historical problematic of negotiating the divide between tradition and modernity is neither a fait accompli nor equivalent to the local dilemmas of East and West. On the contrary, the problem of representation is one of reckoning with the "remainder" in the historical totality—which we may in shorthand define as the emergence of a conceptual trace at the intersection of history and meaning. In other words, what is required is reading *between* "history" and "text" so that the process of translating one (what happened in history) to the other (what can be said about it) is not reduced to a matter of textual banality. The relay between the two is an active, allegorical—that is to say, inorganic—one in which the reading of a story and situation depends on a reactivation of the past in terms of the present. Accordingly, the historical specificity of the ideal of companionate marriage, for example, can only be marked retroactively as a problem conditioning our understanding of Bengali modernity. It is the ground against which the film's commentary on what is possible to say about the past proceeds: by the light of what we know in the present and refracted by the determining effects of cinema.

Only the positivity of negation, like the reminder that the moon has an invisible face, can account for the ironies and paradoxes of enunciating such a critique of nineteenth-century concerns via twentieth-century means. In fact, how could it be otherwise? By the terms of a dialectical argument, it is more appropriately the present that casts a light on the past (rather than the other way around); how else could a preoccupation either with subjective agency or the intensification of apperception signify? This contradiction of knowledge and being is also metaphorized cleverly by the film's use of the moon as a trope. In my introduction I called attention to this trope as an instance of the epistemological paradoxes Ray attempts to redeem with his critique of the image. But it is also worth alluding to it here because of its connection to the antinomy of appearance and reality explored in *Charulata*. We may recall the scene in which, in an effusive moment of fraternal sentimentality, Amal shows Bhupati one of his literary pieces, entitled "Amabasyar Aalo" (The Light of the New Moon). Bhupati, the modern rationalist, evinces surprise at the apparent meaninglessness of the essay's title and recommends that Amal put his talents to better, which is to say, more practical use. To Amal, the romantic, it does not seem so impossible that the new moon should emit its own light, only that it remains unseen. In an extension of the motif of sight and self-cognition, the film thematizes its own status as a modernist intervention, and within the terms of the narrative, the trope marks the peculiarities of the coming-to-consciousness of the Indian modern. Seen within this frame, *Charulata* is also a reflexive commentary on the fact that not all historical subjects "choose" to be modern even though that very modernity permits us to signify such (im)possibility: modernity has chosen us.

The irony of Charu's narrative existence has to do with the inevitable pitfalls accompanying the gnostic solution to the problem of consciousness (whether it be consciousness of history, nation, or womanhood). That is to say, knowledge exacts a very high price, and its value reveals itself only to those who know how much they have paid to obtain it. At the end of the film Charu is established as a figure of self-consolidation, in marked contrast to her uncomprehending and distraught husband, Bhupati, as well as the equally irresolute and disavowing Amal. Her self-knowledge is, however, bought with a certain betrayal of expectations—of the righteously saddened Bhupati, of an abject Amal, and even of herself. Still, she is reconciled to the burden of being a *nabeena* rather than *pracheena*, a choice that, at one point in the narrative, Amal facetiously offers Charu's sister-in-law, Manda as they play their parlor games. But Manda, unlike Charu, is incapable of accepting the challenge, for she does not know and cannot tell the difference embedded in the choices. As a historiographic construct, Charu's discursive predicament calls to mind Gayatri Chakravorty Spivak's much-repeated formulation of the place of the gendered subaltern in history: "Between patriarchy and imperialism, subject-constitution and object-formation, the figure of the woman disappears, not into a pristine nothingness, but into a violent shuttling which is the displaced figuration of the 'Third World woman' caught between tradition and modernization."[35]

CONCLUSION

The epistemological problem of expressing the relay between past and present, allegory and reality, has been at the heart of this discussion of *Charulata* in ways that both overlap with and depart from the previous chapter's elaboration of catastrophic emergence. Here I have attempted to deal more specifically with what might be called the ambivalent predicament of post-Kantian thought in its manifold variations. Benjamin, whose conceptual protocols I have relied on, attempted to resolve the discontinuity between appearance and reality through the construct of the "dialectical image."[36] For him dialectical images performed an anaphoric function in that they made it possible for the historian to signify the making of history along with its inscription. In this scheme the burden of representation is on intuiting "possibility" rather than establishing "truth." So, reckoning with history requires shuttling between constitutive and constituted discourses. That such a system of relays is brittle or disjunctive is evoked by the severity of Spivak's image above—of the "violent shuttling," but also the figurative tenuousness, of the Third World woman located between disappearance and presence, historical possibility and factitious objectivity.

As I have argued, the film's own metacommentary about possibility and impossibility—or what Colin MacCabe has called its metalanguage—also takes up the problem of relaying the differences between representations and social events without negating them. In the example above of Amal's essay entitled "Amabasyar Aalo" there is a subtle but telling twist in Ray's appropriation of this incident because Tagore's version gives the title of Amal's creative effort as "Asharer Chaand" or "The Moon in Monsoon." While only a minor departure from the novel, the incident again raises a more abstract point about cinema's intensification of the past-present relation. Certainly Tagore's story and Ray's film are both engagements with modernity, but since they speak to and from different historical locations, one can read the incidental difference in the title of Amal's story as a *mise-en-abŷme* of the problematic of modernity itself, understood retroactively. I suggested earlier that only the vantage point of a recent historical location makes intelligible the shifting relationship between the old and new. So, returning one last time to the trope of the new moon's illuminating powers, we can perhaps see a link between Tagore's hopeful, turn-of-the-century perspective and his rendition of the allusive remark about the moon's light; for him the matter represented by Amal's story is about its dimmed quality in the monsoon. In Ray's later, more disenchanted version, this has been transformed into an impossibility that one must nevertheless avow, the issue now being the deliberately obtuse belief that the new moon, too, sheds light. Since nineteenth-century notions of the modern were played out actively in relation to their separation from an available and even culturally dominant prior tradition, the distinction between past and present, tradition and modernity, could be characterized by Tagore—given his earlier moment—in terms of a *choice* between disruption and continuity. And given this choice, he firmly rejects modernity as a cultural betrayal; his is an absolute critique of European discourses

FIGURE 8. The broken
nest: Charulata and
Bhupati. Used by
permission from
Satyajit Ray Film
and Study Center.

that instead validates other regimes of consciousness and experience that
he regarded as possible (and preferable) in the context of India.[37]

Accordingly, from its location at the threshold of the twentieth century
Tagore's narrative casts the enterprise of being modern in quite an unde-
sirable light—at least with regard to its consequences for female subjects.
Tradition is still an available option, and the burden of representation is
to show the destructive impact of an alien and alienating modernity that,
along with British domination, must be resisted. The original title of the
story, "Nastanirh" (Broken Nest), also attests to this refusal: if the home
is a microcosm of the world, then Charulata's domestic fate can be read as
a cautionary tale against the intrusions of a maleficent modernity. No reconciliation is possible with its disruptive worldview, and this is conveyed,
above all, by the ending of the novella. In it Bhupati is unable to tolerate
his wife's betrayal and resolves to leave Calcutta to take up an editorial job
in the South, leaving Charu chained to the consequences of her presump-
tive transgressions. Only at the last moment does he relent and agree to
let her accompany him, but Charu herself demurs, realizing at this point
that the choice between home and world, husband and lover, tradition and
modernity needed to have been made much earlier. "Thaak," she says, in
the last words of the tale—"let it be"—for the nest, once broken, cannot be
repaired. As an allegorical tale about modernity, Tagore's story performs a
Newtonian split between action and reaction (Figure 8).

In contrast, Ray's filmic translation (released a little more than sixty
years after the publication of Tagore's story) is irresolute about Charu's
destiny, as well as the experience of modernity in twentieth-century India.
The modern project has consisted in a head-on encounter with disaster—
from the failed experiment with neoliberalism and the rise of religious sec-

tarianism to the channeling of individuality along exclusively bourgeois consumerist lines. Complicating these difficulties are all the indigenous and traditional regimes of discourse and experience that, although displaced, still retain a certain ideological force in the dual register of history and politics. Thus in Ray's cinematic retelling the question of an option between tradition and modernity no longer obtains, though like the new moon's light, it enforces an antinomy. Technologically, as well as discursively, modernity *preconditions* filmmaking and therefore, also, the very mode of storytelling. This is not to say that Ray's production articulates a complete descent into disenchantment but rather to stress the fatal aspects of the predicament allegorized in *Charulata*. Unlike Tagore's preference for tradition, Ray's vision permits no reversal because reversibility would ensure that we are still within sight of a resolution of historical dilemmas. Instead, the film stages its fatal narrative by conveying that that there is no turning back from the consequences of becoming modern.

Modernity is irreversible. But it is at the same time productive of the self-consolidation and discernment handed down from the past to the present. This paradox is also put to use and worked out in the film. The new moon's light, a metaphoric construction of all the impossibilities that structure the possibility of modernity, is, accordingly, an apt way to designate the present. In departing from the ending of Tagore's story, where Charu and Bhupati are definitely estranged, Ray's film leaves the question of their reconciliation unanswered. The closure implied even by an unhappy ending is thus denied to the viewer, who instead witnesses stasis—emblematized by the freeze-frames used at the end that capture, in harshly lit, grainy shots, Charu and Bhupati's immobility. Shown frozen on the threshold of their house, they will perhaps attempt to restart the action of their lives but only once the filmic action ends. This use of an expressionist montage to depict the arresting of any movement contrasts strongly with Ray's use of continuity editing throughout the rest of the film. But not only does the artifice of this mechanism draw attention to a formal strategy of disruption, it also undermines faith in the idea of historical resolution, caught as it is in the half-light of its own emergence.

The final frame of the film gives us the last word, literally: *Nastanirh*. The fact that even in the subtitled version it appears untranslated in Bengali script on the screen returns us once more to Ray's desire, referred to earlier in this discussion, to resist the seductions of translation.[38] It takes a viewer who can read the script, but who is also paying attention until the closing frame, to recognize that the film's final, writerly gesture (whether intended or not) is to intimate the broken nest; moreover, it negates the hopefulness held out in the previous frame, in which Charu holds out her hand to her husband, who, tellingly, never reaches it.

In a 1995 article in the *New York Times* Andrew Robinson questioned whether Ray should be considered "a Bengali Bergman or a Bengali Renoir." He replied to his own question by saying, "Perhaps he is more of a Bengali Renoir, both of them having been supremely intelligent artists who drew on deep reserves of feeling and humor."[39] The absurdity of posing such a choice signals the irreversibility of notions of cultural value: one cannot equally ask whether Renoir was a French Ray! Even if it is the case that Ray has been inducted into the canons of global cinema (and may thus be seen as belonging in the same company as Renoir or Bergman), the fact is that his standing is still strictly circumscribed by an utterly narrow view of the canon itself. I bring this up to remind us again that the engagement made available by his films to readers across various cultural and linguistic divides still operates on misconceived notions about artistic excellence, pure judgment, and, ultimately, reductive oppositions between meaning and difference that do not and cannot account for the aesthetics of the periphery. My effort here has been to think through the intelligibility of the visual by means of which a more adequate translation of social and political particularities is made possible in *Charulata*—on terms that cross over from their own time-boundedness (no less than our own provincialism) to offer a critique of the present.

3 Devi

Documenting the Decadent, Incarnating the Modern

Ya devi sarvabhuteshu [buddhi, nidra, ksudha, chaya, shakti,
trishna, kshanti, lajja, shanti, sraddha, kanti, lakshmi, vritti,
smriti, daya, tusti, matri] rupena samsthita
Namas tasyayi namas tasyayi namas tasyayi namo namah.
— DEVI *stuti*

The long slow passages in the epics of Dreyer and Eisenstein are
sustained only partially by their purely visual qualities, rich and
rewarding though they are: it is the emotional conviction of these
sequences, achieved through precision of interpretation, of acting
integrated to the director's total stylistic approach, that is finally
responsible for their strength, their aesthetic "rightness."
— SATYAJIT RAY, *Our Films, Their Films*

JUXTAPOSITION

In a book published in 1997 to wide acclaim, the historian of religion
Richard Davis recalls the destiny of the "Didarganj *yakshi*," an intricately
carved statue of a voluptuous female *yakshi* (spirit). Estimated as dating to the Mauryan period of the third century BCE, this spirit-statue's
existence in the Patna Museum in India today belies her past lives—from
being unearthed in a stone heap on the banks of the Ganges in the early
twentieth century to her removal to a temporary site where she was set up
by local villagers as a goddess and, subsequently, to her rescue by British
authorities in the latter days of the Raj. Only with this final move was the
Didarganj *yakshi* installed in the museum as an icon of India's antiquity;
colonial authorities renamed her "The Whisk-Bearer" to mark the distinction between her later appropriation by natives as a goddess and her
presumably original existence as the figure of an attendant in a liturgical
setting now lost. In the to-and-fro between her followers who inhabited a
different "community of response," as Davis puts it, and regional British
authorities who decided she was a museological object rather than a deity,
the fate of the *yakshi* tells the story of "two worlds collid[ing], and with

them two visions of what the newly uncovered image was and should be also came into conflict." Davis continues:

The Didarganj villagers took the appearance of the icon as (we must speculate here, thanks to Spooner's lack of ethnographic curiosity) yet another manifestation of a primordial Mother Goddess, who recurrently makes herself visible in ever new forms to her human devotees. Walsh and Spooner, on the other hand [the references are to E. H. C. Walsh, member of the provincial Board of Revenue, and D. B. Spooner, then curator of the Patna Museum] understood the object to be a specimen of ancient Indian statuary. As such, they arranged to have the statue displayed without any accoutrements in a museum for the inspection of interested students of Indian art, they assessed it in terms of the skill and success of its anonymous sculptor in realizing "correct and convincing modelling" (by which aesthetic standard Spooner judged it "primitive"), and they sought to locate it within a historical sequence of Indian sculptures through comparison with other objects.[1]

For Davis this anecdote sets the stage for an investigation of religious Indian images in terms of their value as objects over which struggles for power, authority, meaning, ownership, and identity have been waged throughout the history of India.[2] For the purposes of this chapter the Didarganj *yakshi* illustrates the complex biography of religious imagery in the imperial dispensation and, more important, the historical trajectory of mythic objects, specifically in their visual manifestations. If one of my broader objectives in this book is to establish a set of strategies for thinking about the social content of forms, the revalorization of the *yakshi* from an object of worship to a specimen of colonial art-historical discovery helps to reinforce the special place of the visual in registering the dilemmas of modern experience characterized as rational or secular, on the one hand, and superstitious or idolatrous, on the other.

By now it is widely agreed that the discourse of modernity reveals visual images and objects to have an especially charged status. More than other modes of utterance, visuality is not only the domain that has been the subject of intense speculation, normalization, and regulation, but it is also the realm of everyday practice and experience in which social existence acquires concrete shape, color, and texture, often attended by the fragile equation between seeing and believing. In the case of India the investment in the visual predates the modern per se and is deeply felt; it is also ubiquitous—evident now in everything from the iconic presence of historical objects of worship (such as the ones Davis studies) and the vibrant presence of calendar or *bazaar* art adorning both public and private spaces, to the mass popularity of cinema in a country that routinely sets the record for the number of films produced worldwide on an annual basis. Far more than has been grasped by any discussion of "the age of the world picture," the visual field thoroughly saturates modern Indian life, both sacred and profane.[3] If, in following the leads of Guy Debord's analysis of capitalism as a "society of the spectacle," contemporary critics such as Martin Jay have attempted to historicize modernity as a "scopic regime," or W. J. T. Mitchell, in representing the present moment, dubbed it a "pictorial turn," the priority of the visual tends in a twofold direction: one, a historical prioritization of the object of vision and, two, a redefinition of the subject's experience of the visual *as* image. In turn, this hypertrophy of the visual lends specificity to arguments about the pictorialization of the world or, in a more materialist vein, to an interrogation of the image as commodity. Regardless of such general pronouncements about the status of visuality within a hierarchy of senses, the problematic of the world in color and close-up traverses the various sites of Indian life in which, as Davis discusses, the meaning and being of sacred objects come into present view. More to the point, the "dialectics of seeing" (to adapt Susan Buck-Morss's phrase) also articulate the mundane—though equally mythic—discourses of advertising, cinema, and other means of technological image-making in Indian commodity culture and therefore become part of a modern critique of vision.

But while Davis refers Walter Benjamin's notion of "cult value" to the sacred images of Indian life and "exhibition value" to profane ways of seeing them, his use has the effect of thinning out the dialectical relationship Benjamin proposed with this distinction. In accounting for the different forms of "aura" that attached to objects with a ritual purpose, on the one hand, and contrasting them with mechanically reproduced works (the paradigmatic example of which is film), on the other, Benjamin's point was that *both* forms attest to the ongoing transformation of perception and experience under capitalism. The difference is that exhibition value has now overtaken cult value, thus reinforcing the degenerate, reified aura of the commodity.[4] This stress on the specificity of aesthetic experience under the regime of capitalism is lost in Davis's way of thinking about the lives of Indian objects, though he is instructive in detailing the manifold historical and administrative imperatives behind the institutionalization of religious imagery.

Staying close to Benjamin's terms would suggest that if the lives of objects bespeak a lived relationship to contestations over meaning, they also refract fundamental sociohistorical determinations not reducible to the reader-response notion of a "community of response" that Davis borrows from Stanley Fish. Indeed, the distinction between cult value and exhibition value is quite incompatible with a notion of interpretive communities since Benjamin's argument was that the work of art functions differently in the modern age given conditions of "mechanical reproducibility" *(technischen Reproduzierbarkeit)*. That is to say, interpretive differences do not matter as much in our experience of the artwork as the productive contingency of mechanical reproduction that transforms both perception *and* reception.[5] The paradox Benjamin explores thereby is how film, the medium of exhibition par excellence, becomes a ritual spectacle and a cultic attachment under fascism. So although film's transmissibility might seem to align it with the exhibition value that ordinarily destroys an art object's aura, cinema emerges as an auratic form that needs to be positioned politically for its democratizing potential to be released. Without such dialecticization the medium betokens only the phantasmagoric aspects of all cult objects. Instead, Davis renders exhibition into a necessarily pluralized and democratic value on its own; as a result, despite relying on Benjamin's ideas about the "afterlife" *(Nachleben* or *Nachgeschichte)* of objects in his examination of the relationship between art and technology, he is quite far from the former's materialist propositions given his assumptions about the essential plurality of a reader-response approach to meaning (with which Benjamin would almost certainly have disagreed).

To remind ourselves of the crucial difference between a materialist position such as Benjamin's and a pluralist line such as Davis's, we should note that the theorists of the Frankfurt School regarded the fate of art in general as symptomatic of the historical crisis of experience. This crisis is essentially a part of the reification induced by commodity existence and is, therefore, inseparable from the reprogramming of the senses that modern, particularly visual, media both enforce and externalize. In other words, there exists no separate quarter of meaning or being in which the authority of cultural objects can be independently or ethnographically secured for a particular "community" of receivers. All of it must now be understood not in terms of an opposition between ritual existence and rationalist ideology (even if Davis rightly critiques the colonial logic behind the British use of this opposition) but in the systemic dialectic of myth and enlightenment. Echoing critical theory's arguments about modernity as "eternal recurrence," we might say that the lives of Indian images are entirely pregiven by the ways that enlightenment returns as myth and vice versa. That is to say, ritual and rational modes of understanding are reflections of each other, their differences constituting the relative force of the mythic versus the modern in any given instance, with historically specific but totalizing effects.[6]

Despite indicating these differences with Davis's approach, I commenced by relating his anecdote about the *yakshi* because it does enable a meditation on the afterlife of myth. As I hope to demonstrate with reference to Ray's 1960 film *Devi* (The Goddess), the standoff between ritual and science, myth and enlightenment is at stake in our reception of this text as well. The colliding worldviews of colonial authorities and native subjects Davis narrates also allow me to distinguish Ray's messier exploration of faith from the easy dichotomy of reason and religion underlying Davis's analysis. I will argue that Ray's exploration redefines the very terms of the conventional opposition between divine and profane or goddess and object, as such categories come to define religious as well as secular idealizations of the female principle. To that end, what follows is an attempt to track the ways that the mother-goddess is taken out of her complex, habitual life in the temple or museum and into the two-dimensional, exhibition space of cinema. As we will see, her many reappearances are, in this visual treatise, established as part of the contradictions of modern life rather than extraneous to them. Ray's representation of the goddess consequently pertains as much to his understanding of the principle of divinity in profane times as it does to a conception of femininity athwart modern ideals of subjecthood.

COMBINATION

Devi is set in the 1860s and based on a story of the same name by Prabhat Kumar Mukherjee (from a theme that Rabindranath Tagore had proposed, though Tagore was hesitant to explore it given the volatility of the subject). The plot depicts the fortunes and misfortunes of Doyamoyee, the seventeen-year-old bride of Umaprasad, the younger son of Kalikinkar Roy, aristocratic *zamindar* (landowner) of Chandipur, Bengal. Kalikinkar ("servant of Kali") and his older son, Tarapada, are both great devotees of the goddess Kali, the dual embodiment of life-giving energy and destruction in the pantheon of Hindu deities. Doyamoyee (or Doya) is the jewel in the household crown. She is the favorite of her father-in-law and equally doted upon by her husband, the somewhat feckless Umaprasad, who is mostly out of the scene of action in Chandipur though there are occasional transitions to his life in Calcutta, where he attends university. In these scenes Umaprasad is shown debating the merits of the social reformist organization of the Brahmo Samaj (with which, incidentally, Tagore and

Ray were both affiliated), as well as busy remaking himself into the secular ideal of the male subject of modern Indian history. The Roy household features opulent, almost Gothic, interiors, and its members are depicted as lavishly dressed and effetely aristocratic, but the most extravagant presence is that of Devi herself, the goddess who reigns in her private temple in the mansion. She is the supernatural being to whom Kalikinkar turns at every step in order to proclaim his earthly devotion.

Early in the film Kalikinkar, who has lost his own wife, has a dream in which Doya appears as an incarnation of the goddess Kali. Patriarchal vision being law, his dream is declared as reality, and the daughter-in-law is installed in the temple as the living emblem of Devi because she is seen to possess the powers of life and death attached to Kali herself. At this turn of events Doya's sister-in-law, Harasundari, who competes with Doya for her son Khoka's affection but is also the most clear-eyed member of the household, sends for Umaprasad, alerting him to the dire situation in the household in which no one is able to distinguish between the mythic Kali and a real Doya. Doya herself has fallen into a trance, practically swooning on her seat in the temple as everyone gathers around to offer oblations and ask for blessings. Umaprasad returns from Calcutta to intervene in his father's irrationality and his wife's abjection but is helpless in the face of Doya's unwitting participation in her own deification—her confusion heightened by the miracle she has supposedly performed to save a deathly ill peasant child. Uma tries to persuade Doya to leave with him for the city, but they turn back when her uncertainty about her status (is she a woman or a goddess?) leads her to resist. He returns to Calcutta on his own, leaving Doya behind in the ancestral home even though she is by now visibly unsure of her grip on reality. Wretched consequences follow, including the death of her beloved nephew Khoka, whom she cannot cure of a high fever despite being appealed to as Ma Kali [Mother Kali]. Unable to reckon with her lack of agency as either goddess or woman, Doya goes mad, and the film closes on the ambiguous moment of her running into the sunlight, blinded as much by the unreason of all around her as she is by her predicament within a world turned upside down.

Within such a conventional story about nineteenth-century decadence and superstitious excess, what is striking are the ways that audience attention is summoned. Even as contemporary viewers we are beckoned to enter the world of the goddess, our attention solicited—and held—by the clay mask of Devi that opens the film (and that is later mirrored by the subdued and largely impassive perfection of the actress Sharmila Tagore's face in her role as Doya). The mask of Devi, like other masks elsewhere, represents

FIGURE 9.   Devi unawakened. Used by permission from Satyajit Ray Film and Study Center.

a riddle, in the process also serving as a device to estrange our expectations about solving the riddle through narrative resolution. To get at the many layers of meaning secreted by this uncanny emblem of an other world, let me turn to the film's opening. Ray uses a slow lap-dissolve to inaugurate the sequence, a choice that calls to mind Roland Barthes' proposition of "the third meaning" in cinema. We can follow Barthes in seeing this as a concrete and very specific modality of signification, a "multi-layering of meanings which always lets the previous meaning continue, as in a geological formation, saying the opposite without giving up the contrary."[7] *Devi* opens with a fade-in to a head shot of a stark white clay mask of Devi in her as-yet unadorned form. Viewers familiar with ritual Hindu practice will immediately recognize this shot of the goddess as a momentary depiction of her in a state that is not yet *jagrata* (awake, enlivened).[8] In the next frame the title "Devi" (in Bengali script) is superimposed on the white clay mask, as if to interpose the act of awakening or giving life with the act of inscription (Figures 9 and 10).

FIGURE 10.   Devi coming to life. Used by permission from Satyajit Ray Film and Study Center.

With a series of quick dissolves Devi's eyes are then shown painted in, further depicting her as coming to life. Her cosmic presence is finally established when, in a wide-angle shot of a fully decorated image of the now-awakened and vibrant visage of the mother-goddess, she is revealed in her incarnation as Durga, on her yearly visit to Earth. This is the most powerful, rousing, and awe-inspiring image of Devi circulating in India, one that would be recognized popularly as the incarnate principle of *shakti* (the principle of nature's divine feminine force) infusing earthly existence.[9] The camera pulls back from the shot of Devi in her full glory to display her ten-armed figure arrayed in the temple, where Kalikinkar and his older son, Tarapada, are depicted in medium close-up, their palms closed in prayer. An aural transition is introduced by the sounds of the *dhak*, a ceremonial drum played at religious festivals, and the scene then shifts to a shot of the drum itself.

The scene ends in a crescendo of sound that markedly contrasts with the title sequence's stillness, brought to a screaming point, as it were, with the shot of a worshipper raising a sword in the act of ritual sacrifice. With his use of a cut to pun on the idea of cinematic incision as well as depict the violent appurtenances of idol worship, Ray establishes a new scene in which fireworks are seen going off in the sky, and a child's voice is heard calling out to his uncle. With this the other major dramatis personae of the film are revealed: Umaprasad, his nephew Khoka hoisted on his shoulders, and, as the camera gradually pans, the frame expands to encompass Doya, shown taking in the celebrations hesitantly, even as her husband and nephew exult in the moment. The blasts from the fireworks are interrupted by the musical strains of a band in the background playing the "Colonel Bogey March" (a British regimental tune, we might note), and the opening episode closes by imputing the end of the festival—with long shots of the procession in which Devi is led to the river to be cast into it. The interlude terminates in a final shot of the goddess now divested of her supernatural status, and the last darkly lit frames show the icon, emptied of its divine aura, falling backward into the waters as Devi's devotees return her to the elements from which she took form. Fade to black.

It is impossible to overstate the significance of the film's opening moments as an expression of the dual crisis of sight and belief. As I hope to elaborate, the title sequence is involved in a critique that extends well beyond a conventional introduction to elements of plot and story—into the domain of what, in his film-theoretical writing, Sergei Eisenstein called "intellectual cinema."[10] His suggestion that cinema needs to be thought in conceptual rather than representational terms is taken up in exemplary manner in *Devi*, Ray's venue for pitting a political critique of the excesses of religion against an epistemological critique of the seductions of reason. Cast as a portrayal of Bengal's landed gentry at the threshold of the twentieth century, the film provides an immanent perspective on the complexities of an anachronistic historical sensibility encroached upon by a secular, rationalistic modernity. This critique is offered from a standpoint that neither castigates nor hypostasizes religiosity; at the other end, it also rejects an unrooted secularity, both of which are posed within the film's terms as problems in need of conceptualization.

The beginning of *Devi* condenses issues that are usefully illustrated along the lines Eisenstein imagined with his ideas about intellectual cinema and, as a subset of this approach, in his conception of intellectual montage. My reprise of his early arguments is prompted not by a revanchist desire to celebrate the glories of Soviet film theory, nor am I interested in labeling Ray a follower of Eisenstein. Rather, I should like to mine what remains unappreciated or, at least, underappreciated about Eisenstein's thoroughly contemporary understanding of the place of the ocular in the ideology of capitalism; more particularly, I want to demonstrate the imprint of issues originally broached by Eisenstein on Ray's practice. It also seems to me that Eisenstein's proposals for reforming the visual toward more socially transformative ends continue to be relevant in our own era despite the positivist move by a few critics to suggest that the emergence of new media technologies (such as digitalization or computer animation) have rendered such considerations moot. And it certainly is the case that in calling for a revolutionary cinema that was at the same time conceptual, Eisenstein not only anticipated many of the ideas that later came to represent the most sophisticated protocols of a left semiology; he was also understood to have done so (as Barthes elucidates when writing about his Soviet predecessor's thinking and practice). This genealogical link is regrettably absent from most anthologies in film studies, whose poststructuralist bent leads them to position Soviet cinema and film theory as old and outdated, the stuff of a hoary Marxist investment in a cinema of struggle rather than a postmodern cinema of mood or affect. By contrast, my effort will be to establish that the relay of ideas from Eisenstein to Barthes demonstrates both the contemporaneity of the former's insights and the hidden reliance of semiotics' postwar theories of the sign on a much earlier and activist mode of thinking that was concerned less with discursive than material reality. My secondary aim will be to show that Barthes was himself less interested in the ambiguities and aporias of meaning than is customarily accepted; indeed, there are important occasions, as with his reading of film stills and photographs, when he was far more invested in pursuing clarity, univocality, and even deictic fixity, based on his convictions about the quiddity of the image.

More proximately with respect to my reading of *Devi*, I would contend that only the vocabulary of cinema formulated by Eisenstein and later taken up by Barthes, as well as Siegfried Kracauer (albeit to different ends since Kracauer deemphasized montage while retaining the stress on indexicality), makes it possible to specify the radicalism of Ray's visual critique. So, to return to the construction or, more properly, to the constructedness of the opening sequence, the initial frames once more prefigure contingencies of meaning for which there is as yet no correlate in reality. At a purely nominal level, the icon of Devi-as-clay-mask conveys a potential waiting to be filled in by what is *to be* rather than what already *is*. Of his effort to imagine a new film form Eisenstein wrote that it was almost inexpressible—seeing as it was "about something that does not in fact exist."[11] His investment in such an idea had less to do with claiming aesthetic novelty for its own sake than with exploring hitherto unprecedented arenas of meaning he hoped the new form might generate, specifically, with respect to social content. For him, the main weapon in constructing a conceptual cinema was, of course, montage, which becomes more valuable as a tool the further it moves from merely juxtaposing images (associative montage) to implying a synthesis that conjures, through the sensuous magic of objects, what is otherwise inaccessible (intellectual montage). As Eisenstein put it, this was to be "a new idea, a new conception, a new image" of the objectively unrepresentable.[12]

The shift from the juxtaposed to "the copulative" represents a development in Eisenstein's attempts to formulate cinematic principles consistent with Marxist dialectics. In moving beyond existing notions (Lev Kuleshov's, for instance) that took montage to be a method for establishing correspondences between similar or dissimilar objects, Eisenstein saw himself going from associative to intellectual (or dialectical) montage. In characterizing this move as a turn from adequation or correspondence to copulation or combination, Eisenstein's stress is not on the "sum total" of objects (which would simply represent an undialectical summing up) but on their "product as a value of another dimension, another degree: each taken separately corresponds to an object but their combination corresponds to a *concept*." Attempting to voice this quintessentially Hegelian idea of sublation in imagistic terms, he says, "The combination of two 'representable' objects achieves the representation of something that cannot be graphically represented."[13] If we are now only too familiar with the notion of dialectical synthesis in Eisenstein's theory of montage, it is all the more curious that his emphasis on conceptuality and intellection—as the beyond of representation as such—has received so much less notice than the earlier, mechanical idea that image and sense are synchronized by resemblances or associations.[14]

To focus once more on the mask of Devi, as it undergoes various transpositions in the opening series, we may say that at one level it simply indexes the gap between the world of reason and that of myth or belief in its palpable embodiment of the latter. But if the viewer's attention is initially caught by Ray's deliberate use of the iconography of everyday religious practices to set up a story about the decadence of high Hinduism, this attention is also divided by everything *else* the image of Devi signifies, as well as by something that exceeds the iconic and tends toward the hieroglyphic (which is almost to say the magical). To think of this second, abstract level of ideation beyond either icon or index, we should recall that Eisenstein had himself commented on the imaginative possibilities opened up by eschewing resemblance altogether and embracing "laconicism." This was a mode that he thought captured not only the coded but also the terse nature of hieroglyphics.[15] The hieroglyph pointed the way to an ideational cinema because it depends less on similarity with the first order of the object than on a second order emerging out of the "copulation" of figurative elements and conceptual thought. In Eisenstein's thinking, all of this could operate with the brevity of grammar, now proffered specifically as a "film grammar."[16] In this manner the weight of his ideas moves from resting on the air-brushed functionality of images juxtaposed to create meaning to the very terseness of the shot, its scratched surface—very much like the calligraphic strokes required to inscribe the hieroglyph—conveying an underlying plenitude of gesture and possibility.

Lest Eisenstein's conception of cinematic hieroglyphics seem merely aestheticist or exoticist, another instance of an effete fascination with otherness, we should also recall that his thinking was spurred by his sense that the standard repertoire of European ideas about image-making was inadequate. There was, in other words, an informed understanding about the need to turn to non-European sources.[17] Moreover, his goals were clearly revolutionary, along the lines of constructivism rather than aestheticism, the ideas directed toward what he considered the "starting-point" of an intellectual and thoroughly political cinema that belonged not just to Europe but to the world. But these goals had to be established "screw by screw, brick by brick," he said, quoting Kuleshov (with whom he had studied and worked), though he distinguished his enterprise from Kuleshov's "evolutionist" approach to revolutionary filmmaking.[18]

Whether Eisenstein's suggestions about the potential of film to generate a new mode of conceptual thinking are or are not realized in his own work, they certainly permit—and even demand—reconsideration in the light of Ray's deliberate attempt to stage a new reality freed from the repertoire of meanings enabled by conventional protocols of realism. Returning to the stark opening shots of Devi in her clay mask, the initial stills gradually combine to be replaced by the vibrancy and lushness of a fully enlivened image of the goddess as Durga. This transformation indicates not only a move from the inanimate to the animate but also a shift from a benign image to a malign complex of forces that must unfold as Durga turns into Kali. That is to say, the meaning of the sign in this copulative form is not a matter of arbitrarily reading different possibilities off the surface of the image; rather, just as a hieroglyph operates (whether in Egyptian writing or in Japanese and Chinese calligraphy) by means of a very specific process of encoding and decoding, the form becomes meaningful only when the *exact* coordinates of the encoded message—inanimate icon-animate Durga-malignant Kali—are mapped onto the sense extracted from it.

Most Indian viewers (including non-Hindus) would recognize the familiar, and in that sense homely, incarnation of Devi as Durga, but this represents only one aspect of the sign of the goddess—its "referential symbolism," or what Barthes designates as the "obvious" meaning of visual, especially filmic, signifiers.[19] Somewhat less literal, though no less evident, is the sign's "historical symbolism," which is the meaning set in motion by the particular conjunction of the shots of the blank clay mask and those of Devi's decorated face—her alteration from statue into goddess.[20] For this, too, is an integral element in the demotic practices of Hinduism—in which the gods are only believed to take form once their human-made images are transformed by means of inscribing the eyes of otherwise inert icons. The volatile continuity between the natural and supernatural is marked at this auspicious and, importantly, concrete instant, when divine power overtakes human labor and, simultaneously, sentient ideas are superseded by the materiality of the spirit. Hailed as the moment of *pranapratistha* (or the initiation of life), the history of everyday Hindu religion attests to such a well-perceived continuity between profane labor and divine force, as well as to their mutual constitution. The iterations of the image thus literalize the multiple meanings of goddess worship: in the transition from blankness to decoration Devi becomes Durga (offering comfort and protection) and, at the same time, intimates that she will reappear as Kali (who avenges and punishes in her wrathful incarnation).

The initial images of Devi are not restricted, however, to delineating aspects of religious iconography alone, though the opening frames deploy the formal and graphic potential of the iconic to be anchored in specific ways. In addition, the opening shots also represent a condensation of narrative movement, gesturing toward the crisis that unfolds in the plot and terminates in the disaster that befalls the characters, particularly Doya. The emphasis Barthes places on Eisenstein's ideas about the fixed and hieroglyphic nature of the cinematic image is in this context remarkable, especially if we consider that this insistence is not only a far cry from arguments about polysemy or semiotic fluidity with which he has been associated; it also defies assumptions that have now become de rigueur within criticism about the undecidability of meaning. At least with respect to Barthes' proposition of "the third meaning," it is worth noting that he takes Eisenstein's exposition of montage as a dialectical, and almost mathematical, equation much further in the direction of *disambiguating* meaning. For although Eisenstein's conceptualization retained the sense of a precise calculus demanded by the montage principle, he left some room for interpretive autonomy. Accordingly, he proposed that at the "intersection of nature and industry stands art," which led to the corollary that "1. The logic of organic form versus 2. the logic of rational form produces in collision the dialectic of the art form." Such a formalization of the dialectic did not result in artifice or sterility because the film image ultimately derives its expressive force from "the *rhythmic relation* between law and instance, species and individual, or cause and effect."[21]

In Barthes' stringent though stunning reading of stills from *Ivan the Terrible* (1944) and *Battleship Potemkin* (1925), it is as if he calls Eisenstein's theoretical bluff, going beyond it. For his part, he underscores "a certain manner of reading 'life' and so 'reality' itself" in the "obtuse meaning" purveyed specifically by (and this is important) film stills.[22] Tellingly, moreover, Barthes proposes that a proper reading of filmic meaning requires precision, parsimony, and the stoppage of motion. With this move he draws closer to the notion that film analysis demands such disciplined scrutiny as can only be gained from decomposing motion into the fragment; but by doing so, he also distances his ideas from thematic approaches to interpretation and from the system of semiology conventionally associated with his work. For him a more penetrating analysis of filmic meaning is called for, one that is neither mere dilettantism (evident in the casual use of films to discuss historical, political, or literary themes, for example) nor the product of such ethereal theorizing that extraneous notions (for example, about the symbolic order of meaning, the unconscious, or dramaturgy) become the lever of explanation. Rather, these first- and second-order modes of semiotics have to be supplemented, according to Barthes, by an "interrogative reading" that "exceeds psychology, anecdote, function, exceeds meaning," in order to be up to the task of accounting for the punctual quality of certain representations designated as "obtuse" (54). The obtuse or third meaning makes its presence felt as a sort of "elliptic emphasis" (57) that is "at once persistent and fleeting, smooth and elusive" (54). Fully admitting to the paradox of a mode of analysis that requires the "motion picture" to be disassembled into the still, Barthes returns us to the conceptual work demanded by what both he (and Eisenstein) considered specifically filmic—although this parsing of meaning runs at a tangent from established ideas about textual ideology and the critic's metalanguage. Further endorsing the tendency of self-conscious directors to say something definite and even emphatic rather than merely illustrative, Barthes correspondingly advocates a mode of analysis that is able to follow through on the recognition that "the filmic is not the same as the film" (65) and, moreover, that "the filmic begins only where language and metalanguage end" (64).

This line of thought allows Barthes to advance a further claim about the unitary nature of the third meaning: "The obtuse meaning is a signifier without a signified, hence the difficulty in naming it" (61). Such a declaration places him much closer to Eisenstein's mathematical and programmatic conception of cinema than we might expect. Indeed, however troubled we may be by Eisenstein's so-called essentialism, his emphasis on exactness—that is to say on the coding of "emphatic" meanings in filmic form—greatly influenced Barthes' thinking, who went further than Eisenstein to propose an *identity* between "law and instance" or "cause and effect." As we can see in statements such as the following, instead of taking the relationship of signifier and signified to be exoteric and open-ended (as would be expected in a post-Saussurean scheme), Barthes reinforces Eisenstein's ideas, asserting the intrinsic and internal link between image and meaning, characterizing this in surprisingly immanent terms: "The still offers us the *inside* of the fragment. In this connection we would need to take up—displacing them—Eisenstein's own formulations when envisaging the new possibilities of audio-visual montage: ' . . . the basic centre of gravity . . . is transferred to *inside* the fragment, into the elements included in the image itself. *And the centre of gravity is no longer the element "between shots"—the shock—but the element "inside the shot"—the accentuation within the fragment'* (67, Barthes' emphasis).

The ideas condensed in this passage not only counter standard assumptions about signification but are also of great import in what they allow me to say about Ray's hieroglyphic construction of the image of Devi. So a few additional comments are in order. For one, it is worth underscoring that Barthes' nascent formulation of "a theory of the still" predicates a signifier without a signified and contends that what is specifically filmic is often, and paradoxically, not movement but an "inarticulable third meaning" (66) distributed inside and across the fragment of the still. He also asserts that even conventional and obvious imagery is not polysemic, a claim famously made with reference to Panzani pasta advertisements and somewhat less famously in terms of found footage from Mikhail Romm's *Ordinary Fascism* (1965).[23] His enlargement of Eisenstein's stills from *Potemkin* and *Ivan the Terrible* follows along similar lines: "Eisenstein's 'art' is not polysemous: it chooses the meaning, imposes it, hammers it home . . . Eisensteinian meaning devastates ambiguity. How? By the addition of an aesthetic value, emphasis. Eisenstein's 'decorativism' has an economic function: it proffers the truth" (56).

Beyond the obvious historical or referential symbolism of images lies the plane of "aberrant" signification that Barthes delegates as the obtuse or third meaning, by means of which he further illuminates the comparison between filmic structure and hieroglyphic or calligraphic writing. Importantly, in both systems meaning is seen to reside *inside* the image rather than supplementarily or polysemically. This antinomian argument about the immanent (rather than extrinsic) character of the still is one that I use as my warrant for reading the opening frames of *Devi* in terms of a similarly exact and *configurational* form of meanings—encoded, copulative, and obtuse. Doing so also allows me to maintain my distance from what has become a token of faith in interpretive criticism: the axiom about the constitutive ambiguity of signification.

SUBLATION

How, then, do we resolve the iconic and incarnate guises of Devi on the screen, if they are not to be read as polysemic signs? Part of the answer to this question resides in recognizing, as I have mentioned, that it was not always axiomatic to hold that meaning is constitutively ambiguous or polysemous. It is only since the so-called linguistic turn that the problem of signification has been assimilated, quite peremptorily, to the idea that meaning is always conventional or given only in difference. But these are neither necessary nor inevitable propositions—even if it is now unquestionably accepted that signification follows a syntagmatic chain of associations, unrolling, in the famous Derridean analogy of a carpet, along the path of *différance*. Barthes' arguments about the normative specificity of the film still unexpectedly demonstrate the contrary; to wit, that it is necessary to address the "verticality" of meaning in the cinematic image. Emphasizing contiguity and copresence rather than difference, Barthes saw this verticality in terms of "geological formations" or the "inside of the fragment" and considered the results to be the "devastation of ambiguity," gesturing in these ways toward what Eisenstein, in his turn, had conceptualized using the literary motif of a "portmanteau word." Borrowed from Lewis Carroll (whose linguistic inventiveness Eisenstein admired greatly) this coinage describes the multiple *denotatives* of the shot in relation to other shots and takes its lead from Carroll's idea that certain meanings can only be produced with help from a "portmanteau word"—defined as "two meanings packed into one word like a portmanteau."[24]

In the relay from Carroll to Eisenstein to Barthes, we are given a long-standing, comparative, and cross-cultural expanse of convictions about language and concretion. Conventional ciné-semiotics notwithstanding, it provides good reason to approach cinematic meaning as the product of synchronization and simultaneity, in the manner of objects tightly packed together yet defined in their contiguity.[25] The "portmanteau effect" is a suggestive way to think about Devi's image, spliced into component shots whose overall valence is neither polysemic nor arbitrary but definite and accretive. Each sedimented piece of this iconic sign "hammers home" (to echo Barthes) the knowing viewer's recognition that the goddess is herself one and, simultaneously, many. Clearly, this does not deny that the repertoire of concrete meanings associated with the appearances of Devi might be a closed book for some; as is the case with any reading of a cultural text, there are those who view a Ray film naively or without requisite cultural information. But my point is hardly negated by maintaining that a certain degree of specialized labor is necessary for "getting it." To the contrary, this labor must be at the heart of a conception of "intellectual cinema" and the mark of an analytic effort to distinguish "obtuse" filmic meanings from the film as a series of thematic propositions.

This may also be the place to remark that there is, in any case, no real inconsistency between thinking about montage as a principle and the film fragment as the unit of analysis. Only when montage is reduced to method does it seem pressing to locate intelligibility in the mutually exclusive terms of frame or sequence. But as Eisenstein's recourse to the image of a portmanteau suggests, it is in the packing together of images that their conceptual impact is felt. If this produces a connotative relation based on the contiguity of elements (shots), it is also a dialectical relation that rests on immanent contradictions, in the collision of what Barthes terms the "multiple denotatives," both within and across shots. In other words, recognizing that Eisenstein took montage to be the practice of dialectical theory suggests that its conceptual, philosophical ends were of far greater importance to him than were the mechanics. Certainly, the latter remain less well specified than the former, although, as I have said, the difficulties lie not in the interpretation of montage elements or sequences but in their construction. Notwithstanding his disagreements with Eisenstein, Kracauer also took the position that film's enactment of a particular historical experience is to be discerned in the principle of alienation within the shot (even as the medium is seen to capture the flow of the material contingencies of life). The unexpected convergence between Eisenstein's and Kracauer's arguments about the medium's ontology—furthered in the resonance of their respective ideas in Barthes' writings—is noted in Miriam Hansen's introduction to Kracauer's *Theory of Film*, where she, too, avers that "the single frame becomes the basis of montage because it already contains, in nuce, the disjuncture or difference that makes for montage."[26]

Ray can be said to have pursued the challenge to realize the possibilities inherent in Eisenstein's theory, and we may see in his layered construction of the image of Devi a "persistent and fleeting" sense (to borrow from Barthes) that punctures the viewer and calls into place a normative view of the icon's manifold appearances. This normativity depends on a precise textual history (that dates back some fifteen hundred years to the consolidation of two texts containing verses in praise of the goddess); that is to say, the critique mobilized here itself relies on very specific imagery and ideation that have defined a historical encounter with the goddess. Only certain ideas and certain meanings will do to "re-cognize" the goddess, and not alternative ones.[27] In fact, this is the contextual import of the first epigraph at the beginning of this chapter—which cites the Devi stuti, a classical Sanskrit verse transmitted into contemporary life through being broadcast over the radio (and now television) during the major religious festival of Durga Puja.[28] The stuti is, of course, a religious incantation, one that requires this list of the goddess's attributes to be in place for its effect. But to see it merely as mystification not only cuts off the gods from humans, it also reproduces a regressive dialectic of Enlightenment that fails to recognize the parallel mystifications of secular, modern life. As the broadcasting of the sacred via technological media implies, the production of mystified meanings occurs inside the temple as well as outside it, in the factory and the movie hall, no less than at the dinner table.[29] Thus, the image of Devi in her multiple, though definite, manifestations—as force, beauty, mother, and so on—is intended to conjure up and simultaneously call into question the implacability of the image as both sacred sign and profane representation.

In keeping with Eisenstein's theme of collocating the "objectively unrepresentable" and the "objectively represented," all of the echoes of the various names of the characters in the film—Doyamoyee, Kalikinkar, Tarapada, Umaprasad, and Harasundari—as well as the name of the town, Chandipur, in which the action is located, evoke the quiddity of the goddess and without any contradiction, the indeterminacy of belief.[30] In other words, the very recognizability and representability of the image of Devi corresponds to another layer of possibilities that expresses an unrepresentable philosophical conundrum: how to account for the contradiction of faith in modern life, easily one of the most abstract dilemmas of existence today? This is especially true in the context of India, where fundamentally incommensurable worldviews are attached to religious faith on the one hand and secular belief on the other. Instead of flattening out the terms of this incommensurability into an undialectical opposition, Ray's preference is to render it in terms that can, without exaggeration, be seen as an antinomy of consciousness. The overarching presence of the motif of Devi in the text of *Devi* thus has the function of reinforcing a caution against the dangers of belief untempered by reason—*and vice versa*. And, as I hope to have established, this is done in Eisensteinian fashion: through the concretion of form rather than via logical or expository content.

Lest my attempt to situate the opening images of *Devi* in terms of their concatenation of a religious repertoire of meanings seem like an affirmation (however indirect) of an inert Indological stance, it should be stated that this is far from my goals for this chapter or the overall study; but to take it as such would also be a profound misreading of Ray's cinematic enterprise itself. However remote the worlds adduced by this particular film, the text works to unpack both secular and religious ideals in thoroughly materialist ways. The travails of Hindu fundamentalism in contemporary India have made it difficult to think about religious belief with anything less than condemnation. So although the point may be forced, it is worth stating that to regard the sensuous display of Devi in the film as a display of mere exoticism is to fall into a historicist error. For it is a common impulse to seek the validation of certain positions and castigation of others in what one takes to be ideology critique. That is to say, a certain notion of ideological demystification proceeds from conceiving it on the sole thought that social ills need only to be exposed to disappear. This form of instrumental thinking might prompt the notion that the absence of, say, Muslims in *Devi* must mean the presence of a bias that favors Hindus or, correspondingly, that the sumptuousness with which Ray displays religious ideas and rituals must indicate his nostalgic desire to valorize them. But the logic behind such a notion replicates the idealist hope that aesthetic representations can somehow resolve the contradictions of society. Even more problematically, it assumes that critique can only proceed by means of a realist and positivist calculus.

Here we have an example of what Herbert Marcuse referred to as the banality of "affirmative culture." Its banality resides in the desire to affirm "good conscience" through the "rejection of a bad historical form of existence"; for this reason it is, in the end, counterproductive. On Marcuse's terms, an artistic or critical statement that seeks to overcome the wrongs of the world by rising above it produces less corrective than concealment. It also dissimulates the "tranquilizing" imperative of bourgeois ideology to make art or culture into "the counterimage of what occurs in social reality."[31] If, throughout this book, one of my objectives is to complicate our understanding of critique in the age of instrumental reason, not only does this presuppose that aesthetic or interpretive practices cannot resolve irresolvable aspects of reality; it also accords with Marcuse's notion that the efficacy of such practices is to the same extent only negative—existing as repudiations of given society rather than as impossibly constituted formulations of alternative worlds.

However abstract this way of conceptualizing critical practice may seem in the context of a politics of representation that looks for formulaic and identitarian solutions (is a text feminist? antiracist? anticolonial? prosubaltern?), it is the ground upon which philosophical negation is built and, as such, is invaluable for detaching ideology critique from what Marcuse bitingly referred to as the "fools' paradise" of affirmative cultural expectations.[32] Indeed, it would seem that the critical possibilities inhering in negation were recognized by the least likely candidate for such a dialectical lesson: the Indian state, which took the film's reproach against religious excess (as opposed to its affirmation of Hindu belief) to be only too legible. Andrew Robinson tells us in his biography of Ray that the Indian censor board refused to authorize *Devi*'s release abroad until Jawaharlal Nehru intervened to reverse the ban.[33] If a secular response to the film questions Ray's portrayal of a religious worldview as being insufficiently critical, the irony is that this position mirrors—which is to say, reflects in reverse image—the traditional response to the film exemplified by the Central Board of Film Certification (India's censoring authority). The thorny issue here is the parallel between an endorsement of the film for exposing oppressive religious or patriarchal traditions and the reactionary response to it for allegedly depicting India as backward and superstitious. The judgment of the censors describing the film as "Westernized" and "inflammatory" paradoxically corresponds to the other side, as it were, of the one-sided view that *Devi* is an exposé of the excesses of religion and patriarchy. Consequently, if reactions to the film rest on seeing it as a rejection of idolatry, on the one hand, or a cryptic endorsement of Hindu belief, on the other, neither comes close to Ray's complex, dialecticizing vision.

Take, for instance, the apparent perspicuity of the following statements taken from a fan appreciation Web log: "Satyajit Ray creates a harrowing and compelling portrait of idolatry, obsession, and fanaticism in *Devi*. From the opening sequence illustrating the adornment of the Kali statue, Ray presents a figurative analogy for the inevitable fate of the naive and trusting Doya as she, too, is manipulated and transformed into the image of the reincarnated goddess."[34] A more scholarly articulation of the same view can be found in Ben Nyce's early study of Ray's films in which, toward the beginning of the short chapter on the film, he opines: "Set in the middle of the nineteenth century, *Devi* is a study in religious superstition and upper-class decadence. . . . It's a study of the historical past and a comment on the present. In the conflict between Uma and his father Kalikinkar, we see the struggle of modern India to escape the suffocating traditions of the past. Uma is part of the Bengali renaissance."[35] Aside from shifting the focus from Doya to her husband, Uma(prasad), in ways unsustained at the level of form or content, Nyce betrays the kind of one-sided approach to criticism that I think leaves a lot to be desired in coming to terms with Ray's constructivist aesthetic.

My contention is that *Devi* is not only a "portrait of idolatry" (as the blog would have it) or a "study in religious superstition and upper-class decadence" (Nyce's characterization), inflections that lose sight of the dialectical lessons embedded in the film. Rather, the film is also, as the references to Eisenstein and Barthes are intended to clarify, *an experiment in configurational thinking.* By this I mean to suggest that an authoritarian reading of the film as an attack on the Hindu system of belief and a liberal interpretation of its iconoclasm converge on being undialectical: each sees Ray's portrayal of Doya as (1) an attempt to undermine the sacred or, by contrast, (2) an allegory about the female subject of Indian history whose agency is blocked by the constraints of patriarchal tradition. Neither view transcends a priori assumptions about religious or secular ideals, in the process forgoing the recognition that the overlapping construction of Doya/Devi also plays out as an immanent critique of the fate of the *goddess* in modern life—which is to say, the predicament of religious belief under the sign of a rationalizing modernity.

In reading against the grain of conventional strategies for interpreting the film's thematic content, my argument is that Ray's efforts to stage the image of Devi make visible the contradictions of a regime of understanding in which religious beliefs and secular ideals have equally been turned into instrumental, fetishistic modes of habitation. The film is as much about the fate of women as about the impasse in which belief finds itself, caught between the extremes of religious obsession and secular zeal, myth and enlightenment. Neither extreme represents a choice in Ray's schema, because the dialectic of history only attests to the wholesale petrifaction of social relations—where, as he wrote in one of his essays, "teenagers do the twist and drink Coke, while the devout Brahmin takes a dip in the Ganges and chants his mantras to the rising sun."[36]

Without giving Ray the last word in deciding what our interpretation of the film should be, I would like to remark on the concrete and wholly proximate reasons to accept the dialectical and configurational terms of his critique. Throughout *Devi* he literalizes the trope of woman-as-goddess to underscore its catastrophic extravagance. At the same time, the film presents a reflexive commentary on the magic of cinema—with respect to its ability to conjure up the fetishistic appeal of the image, be it in the form of religion or the commodity. As is the case with his films generally, Ray's interest lies in more than thematic issues; so, aside from portraying Doya's fate, the larger, conceptual implication of *Devi* is that the lessons of a vernacular Hinduism have been lost in the zeal to banish the gods from a secular conception of modernity. The tragedy is that this is a Pyrrhic victory at best since the implacability of religious ideology has simply been transplanted onto the world of the commodity fetish in its many guises—where, for instance, gods and goddesses routinely appear as brand names for commodities in the Indian market such as oil, rice, or weapons, without apparent contradiction. Exposing the extent to which an apparently enlightened rationality has lost track of the affinities between the world of gods and the world of humans, the film draws our attention to the excesses of religious superstition to be sure, but it simultaneously highlights the separation of the supernatural and the natural in secular thought.

If disallowing a conception of the divine from secular conversations about enlightenment has had deleterious effects in modern India's history, the film articulates a position that is as skeptical toward the discourse of secular cosmopolitanism as it is critical of an intolerant traditionalism. Many scenes in *Devi* present a working out of this prismatic perspective: lingering over the daily rituals of Devi *puja* (goddess worship) and familial devotion in ways that reveal a more complicated portrait of the ties that bind, ritual as well as affective (Figure 11). And it is presented, above all, in the repeated appearances of the itinerant singer whose songs of devotion to Kali provide some of the film's most lyrical statements about the presence of gods and goddesses in daily life outside the ideologically inflected version of Hinduism that currently dominates debates over secularism and its other. Whether as the natural religion of the ancients or as a residual structure of feeling within modernity, an enlightened attitude to the divine as it embodies principles of nature, force, and consciousness is not only worth preserving; it may well counter the dominant. Indeed, this insight is at the very heart of the dictum "enlightenment reverts to myth," formulated by Max Horkheimer and Theodor Adorno in their classic theorization. In the present context the intimation is that the everyday, sensual

FIGURE 11.
Doyamoyee performing
Devi *puja* (worship). Used
by permission from
Satyajit Ray Film and
Study Center.

relationship to the goddess is, precisely, that which has been disrupted in the double instrumentalization of Hinduism by a baleful fundamentalism and a peremptory secularism.

In moving from the referential and historical symbolism of the image to its negation—the "not this" or "not only this"—aspect of its obtuse meaning, Ray's ciphering of Devi throughout introduces a new configuration of ideas about the power of seeing as it expresses the will of the gods. Fully exemplified by Devi's luminous gaze, this also provides a counterpoint to the secular hypostatization of vision (which, since Descartes, has always dissimulated a belief in the omniscience of God). Complicating rationalist preconceptions about the putatively correct distance between religious belief and political accountability, the film builds a case—if not "screw by screw," to repeat Eisenstein's quotation of Kuleshov, then certainly scene by scene—against the dead end of opposing tradition and modernity, sacred and secular. In doing so, the modern is unmasked as the site of mythical belief on its own. If the overcompensation usually associated with religious fervor can be seen to extend into the forms of commodity worship purveyed by mass culture, then its fetishistic nature stands revealed in secular reason as well (which, after all, is as reified as any other form of faith).

My reading so far has centered on drawing out the implications of Ray's critique of excess, the excesses of religious belief no less than the excesses involved in the imposition of juridical ideas about freedom from religion. This is not to deny the more obvious critique of excess the film also expresses at every turn: of the oppressive effects of patriarchy on the lives of those whom it encircles. But although I do want to acknowledge the thematic, sociopolitical dimensions of Ray's representation of nineteenth-century mores, his deployment of a predictable narrative about the dominative logic of the Hindu patriarchal family is hardly the most radical statement of the film. In this respect we may once more be instructed by the distinction Barthes drew between obvious and obtuse meanings. If the obtuse meaning is "elusive" despite being contained inside the filmic fragment, the obvious meaning is, by contrast, the product of a "complete sign"; in his words, it is the kind of meaning "which comes to seek me out."[37] Barthes assesses this level of understanding to be that " 'which presents itself quite naturally to the mind' " (54), and I would contend that the representation of sexuality in *Devi* exists at this obvious level of critique, even if it has provided the bulk of the emphasis in feminist and psychoanalytic readings. As distinct from the terrain of obvious meaning, we can glean a strategic imperative that Ray consistently follows in many if not all of his films: to pursue abstract philosophical explorations by embedding them in conventional narrative and thematic structures. As he put it in one of his earliest essays on filmmaking (written in 1948): "the cinema is basically the expression of a concept or concepts in aesthetic terms."[38] In *Devi*, too, the twists and turns of the narrative serve as the device enabling an investigation of conceptual and historical problems. If Hitchcock's cleverness lay in interposing the McGuffin to distract attention from the narrative, Ray's strategy seems to be to insert the narrative as a diversion from conceptual complexities. This broader investigation extends well past the nominal predictability of plot and story elements or narrative progress, as well as beyond an "affirmative" critique in the sense that Marcuse specified.

Reading Ray's visual experiment along these lines obviates the necessity to think that the main achievement of the film lies in its representation of female subjectivity in the context of patriarchy and religious orthodoxy in Bengal. For while this is undeniably the case, it is hardly surprising. Bishnupriya Ghosh has, for example, interpreted the film in terms of the familiar paradigm of "visual pleasure" formulated by Laura Mulvey in the mid-1970s, in order to provide a "third-world feminist perspective" that sees Ray's critique as being "focused through the woman's sense of self, and her degeneration into delusion and madness."[39] According to Ghosh, "it is the ideological battle between father and son [Kalikinkar and Umaprasad] which provides the scenario within which Ray takes up the challenge of constructing a female subject" (168).[40] While the thematic concerns of the film undoubtedly center on femininity in Ray's chiasmatic treatment of Doya (the woman-goddess) and Devi (the goddess-woman), the film cannot be reduced to a statement about the ideology of sexual difference or the erotics of the cinematic/masculine gaze. But although she questions the capacity of psychoanalytic categories of sexual fetishism, castration, and identification to explain Ray's critique, Ghosh nonetheless leans on Mulvey to propose that in the film,

> male agency is passed from father to son: the father controls "woman" but the son truly "knows" her. In this sense the narrative diegesis is in keeping with Mulvey's argument about the male control of femininity on screen.
>
> Moreover, the narrative can also be read using Mulvey's paradigm of castration and lack. (168)

Ghosh then qualifies her assessment: "If we recapitulate Mulvey's notion of the tension between the diegesis or the flow of action and the eroticized image of 'woman,' then Ray's film falls outside of Mulvey's categories. It fulfils, instead, Johnston and Cook's notion of a rupture in the semiotic, a denaturalization of the means of representation that exposes the myth-making functions of patriarchal ideology" (170).[41] Trying to find a way to historicize psychoanalytic concepts, Ghosh is led in the end to the question, "can a sexual signifier, such as the mother-goddess Kali, acquire a different meaning through a perusal of its iconography, and social and religious history?" (172).

Part of my argument is, of course, that taking the visual seriously ("perusing" its iconography, if you will), precisely does lead to different meanings. Even if the designation of Kali as a "sexual signifier" misses the contextualization of "signifying practices that inscribe gender" (which Ghosh cites as Teresa de Lauretis's corrective to Mulvey's original project), a certain precision is also missing in Ghosh's own application of psychoanalytic concepts. Take, for example, the following sentence: "More telling is his [Kalikinkar's] dream upon which Doyamoyee's deification is based: in the dream, the eyes of the goddess Kali, the site that evokes castration, are replaced by those of Doyamoyee, who appears in place of the goddess" (169). It is perhaps not out of order to recall that the primary texts of psychoanalysis do not suggest that the "site" of the *eyes* "evokes the fear of castration"; a very different part of the female anatomy is supposed to induce this in the looking (male) subject! Of course, this may be only a minor misprision, the result of confusing "sight" with "site," but in any case, neither the site of Kali's eyes nor her sight is at stake in Kalikinkar's fetishistic obsession with his daughter-in-law. At best, it is *his* visual fantasy about woman-as-goddess (pleasurable or horrifying) that, in any psychoanalytic reading, must be seen as causing the displacement. One must thus insist on the inappositeness of turning to the fear-of-castration/

FIGURE 12. Kalikinkar relaxing in his easy chair. Used by permission from Satyajit Ray Film and Study Center.

fear-of-looking formula to explain the iconography of Devi's *bhayankar* (fear-inspiring) image because it functions in an entirely distinct epistemological register: as an apotropaic portent of disaster.[42]

As something of a cautionary tale, let me provide the sense of a quite different way that the discourse of fetishism in the film has been addressed in the literature. In doing so, I am less interested in rejecting the terms of existing discussions wholesale than in pointing out their limited ability to account for Ray's use of the image as a critique of reason. For this, let us consider the scene in which Kalikinkar gets a foot massage from his daughter-in-law, Doya. It opens with the shot tightening on a fur-lined easy chair that is the patriarch's preferred seat in his bedroom. As the camera moves in to capture the texture and form of the fur covering, we hear Kalikinkar offscreen, sighing, "Ma" (Mother). In the next shot he lowers himself into the chair and leans back to relax (Figure 12).

At this point a cut provides the transition to a long shot of Doya, softly padding toward her father-in-law's room, her face veiled in traditional manner by her sari. She is bringing him his nightly medication, and after delivering it, she tends to his aching legs by kneeling in front of him as she massages away the pain caused by his gout. Kalikinkar (played by the leading actor of the Bengali stage at the time, Chhabi Biswas) is shown smiling and relaxed as he compliments Doya for having "lit up the household" and for renewing his interest in the world since entering it, he says, as his mother. Doya listens to him patiently and demurely, her veil partially obscuring her face from both him and the viewer, until the short scene ends with her fully turning away as she shyly declines to answer his teasing question about whether her "Christian" husband writes to her daily from Calcutta.

Perhaps unsurprisingly, this scene produced a spate of commentary on *Devi's* release outside India. We begin to note the perception of the foot massage in Andrew Robinson's reference to it in Ray's biography: "To the non-Indian eye at least, this seems an erotic act." But Ray, he says, denied the sexual intent despite accepting the scene's Freudian connotations as follows: "I had not a shred of that [Freudian] element in my mind. *Padaseba* (foot-massage) is a conventional Hindu conception and *swasur padaseba* (foot-massage of a father-in-law) would be considered a very admirable thing for a daughter-in-law to do. You can read a sexual element there if you want to, but it wasn't in my mind. Otherwise why does he [Kalikinkar] install her as a goddess? That immediately removes that element from his life."[43]

An intricate psychoanalytic apparatus is not needed to observe that, Ray's denials notwithstanding, the erotic content of the scene is not too far below its surface. In fact, the appearance and texture of Kalikinkar's fur-lined chair literally, and obviously, install the sense that we are in the presence of a fetish—which, as the classic Freudian scenario goes, requires a displacement of the disavowed object (female genitalia) by the avowal of an acceptable, metonymic substitute—with animal fur being the most tangible and visible likeness. But this is such a completely formulaic understanding of the principle of substitution underlying sexual gratification as to require something more compelling as an explanation of the scene's workings. In this connection Pauline Kael (one of the reviewers to see the film in a favorable light upon its release in the United States) recalls her abreaction to the compression of the scene into a sexualized paradigm of understanding. "The film," she says, "has so many Freudian undertones that I was not surprised when the filmmaker sitting next to me in the empty theater muttered, 'Think what Buñuel would do with this.' I'm grateful that it's Ray, not Buñuel, and that the undertones stay where they belong—down under. Buñuel would have made it explicit."[44]

In other chapters I have drawn attention to Ray's ability to produce conceptualizations of historical and social contradictions in ways that were specific to a vocabulary of cinema or, in terms from earlier in this discussion, to a conception of cinema that is "filmic." We may recall that this refers to modes of signification that derive their meaning from what is immanently onscreen rather than through the mediation of external frameworks of understanding that require, as Barthes put it, a reduction of the image into "psychology, anecdote, function." Here, too, I would propose that Ray's success at formulating an aesthetic particular to cinema exceeded even the accomplishments of undeniably important directors as different as Ritwik Ghatak, Fritz Lang, Glauber Rocha, or, as in this case, Buñuel. It is because Ray was not Buñuel that we have more to go on. This is what Kael also implies with her expressed preference for Ray's understated and subtle directorial choices over Buñuel's overt Freudianisms. Only if we do not oversimplify his representation of the foot massage by reading it as a display of foot fetishism (thereby reducing the scene into the exclusive scheme of psychic substitutions) can we recognize a different possibility: that the scene operates as much in terms of a psychic disavowal *(Verleugnung)* as it does as a marker for preserving meanings and modes of practice that, like the disavowed object, now threaten to be lost. Even without idealizing the scene—as Penelope Gilliatt does in reviewing the film for the *New Yorker* in 1973, referring to the "strength of family feeling" it conveys[45]—one can explain the basis of this scene without relying on the hydraulics of the patriarchal family system to account for it.

To put this differently, it is not axiomatic that the latency of sexual signifiers—foot, dream, mother-goddess—necessarily translates into a content-driven interpretation of fetishism as the transference of unconscious desires onto topological forms. Rather, the imagery of the foot massage also signals its formal uncanniness, albeit less as a fetish than as the *conscious* form of fascination demanded by the presence of an anachronism.[46] On this reading the palpability with which the film thrusts anachronistic images into the viewer's field of vision—from the very first images of the clay icon, and subsequent images of Kali, to a dazed Doya installed in the temple as the living form of the goddess—speaks to Ray's attempt to rediscover a different articulation of the past and present than the one commonly given in psychoanalysis or, for that matter, in his own reference to Hindu traditions.

We might say that the viewer's position is not so much sutured as brought up short by an encounter with images that make their uncanny presence felt—in the manner that, as Ackbar Abbas has suggested, Benjamin described the logic of "fascination." Attenuating the power of the image, fascination becomes the "rebus-like" construct that represents yet another approximation of the means by which a mode of critical reflection is made possible in and through cinema. This analogy helps us to see that Ray's pursuit of the oddity of the practice of foot massage, whatever its obvious connotations, cannot be comprehended fully by thinking of it as a Freudian element, Jungian idealization, or nostalgic appropriation alone. Rather, it is the means for turning a fascinated gaze on "that third thing, the image," as Abbas quotes Benjamin (in a curious echo that presages Barthes' own usage of the "third meaning").[47] So even though Ray rejects "that element" in his conversation with Robinson, the reappearance of the erotic requires being seen, as Abbas goes on to argue with reference to Benjamin's writing on Baudelaire, as a mark of the contrary force of "dubious practices like witchcraft and the casting of spells which deprive one of any power of resistance. . . . We are reminded time and again that in the allure of fascination lies a lure."[48]

The lure of the past, its decadent rituals, its destructive attachments are all part of Ray's practice of the image, although his orientation is not just retrospective but prospective as well; on this reading his representation is not just a replaying of the discourse of fetishism but an enactment of the fascination of objects receding from view. The multiple valences of decadence are thus woven into a depiction of the very fantasy of modernity. That modernity is itself decadent can, as his cinema documents, only be understood retroactively—through the reactivation and redeployment of the wish-symbols of the past. I have tried to explore a different configuration of this argument in my discussion of *Ghare Baire*. In *Devi* it serves to challenge our notions of the transportability of meaning even as it recontextualizes it, and the foot-massage scene is one of many, social practices that can only (even thankfully!) be seen as obsolete. For if, as I suggested earlier, there is an element of the "not this" in reckoning with the ciphered image of Devi, that imperative of negation is in place in Ray's treatment of Doya as well—insofar as she cannot suffice as a model of female subjectivity.

This is to contend that it is finally not compelling to propose that Ray carves out a space for the articulation of female subjectivity in *Devi*. Such a proposition runs aground if we consider only the principal female character's muteness throughout the space of the diegesis. It is the passivity of a form of subjecthood that has not yet come into its own or acquired any agency in the face of the contrary forces that threaten to overwhelm its emergence. Rather, Doya is an emblem of the disjointed way in which the past looks back at us—whether implacably, as in the vision of Devi in her fear-inducing form, Kali, or uncomprehendingly, as we might say is the case with Doya herself. Indeed, throughout the film she is overinscribed from without: first, by the joint family system into which she is placed as a *mateer putul* (pampered doll or, equally, clay figurine); then by Kalikinkar, whose fixation betrays, as we have seen, her double displacement as a sexual and religious fetish; and finally again by Umaprasad, who attempts to transform her into the proof of his own virtuous faith in the reformism of the Brahmo Samaj. Consequently, if the depiction of Doya as the figure of struggle between religious and secular myths can be said to exemplify a "feminist attempt to create a female subject,"[49] she is at best a fascinating image, irresistibly attractive but also fatal. In this very duality lies Ray's considerable investment in painting her as a luscious appearance rather than real presence or actual model for subject constitution.[50]

In contrast to the foot massage scene, which by way of its erotic and exotic charge has solicited the all-too-predictable attention of reviewers and critics, I turn now to a final illustration from *Devi* that has garnered no interest at all, despite its visual richness and cinematic depth. This is the scene, a little over halfway through the film, in which Doya has been installed as the household's living goddess. Paralleling an earlier scene in which the itinerant singer appears to beg for alms, Ray again places him in the diegesis, devoting a significant amount of screen time to his song—this time in praise of Doya, whom the singer now professes to recognize as Kali. "*Ebar torey chinechhi Ma*" (I have recognized you this time, Mother), states the opening line of the song, in this way aligning the powers of life and death that attach to the myth of Kali with her supposedly human incarnation in the diegesis.[51]

Within the space of the narrative the beggar's faith—like Kalikinkar's vision—has been reinforced by the miracle that Doya is supposed to have performed by curing his deathly ill son. This, we know, is a foreshadowing of a miracle she will not be able to repeat when it comes to her beloved nephew, Khoka. What is so striking about this scene is its apparent marginality and yet evident centrality in both formal and narrative terms. We first observe this in the framing of the scene. The sequence unfolds with the beggar and his son appearing in the center of the frame only to be moved to the sidelines as the camera pulls back to reveal the masses of people who are on their way to beg for blessings from the mother-goddess. In this scene the scope of action shifts, almost abruptly, from the cloistered, claustrophobic interior of Kalikinkar's estate to the harsh outdoors. The song provides the lyrical yet ominous backdrop to Ray's framing of the indigent, the ill, and the disabled as they move in and out of shot. Never represented individually, they are, rather, depicted as typical of the masses who have been falsely persuaded about the magical powers of the goddess and who are likewise forced to turn to her because they have nowhere else to go. As the singer continues with his rendition of the lilting melody about Kali's extreme beneficence, the camera reverses direction from what is immediately laid out for the eye, withdrawing from the deep-focus, tightly framed shots of a disoriented Doya seated in her temple to long shots of the utterly denuded countryside. Nature, too, is revealed as sick from the depredations imposed on her by humans, reinforcing the insight that the domination of nature proceeds along the same lines as the material exploitation of humankind.

As in so many other of his films, Ray's skill at capturing the actualities of life embodied in the landscape speaks to the naturalist impulse inherent in photography and film but pursued by only the most reflexive directors like Vittorio De Sica, Federico Fellini, and, of course, Eisenstein himself—a capacity, we may recall, that Kracauer famously referred to as cinema's "redemption of physical reality."[52] Long shots of long lines of the poor, the frail, and the sick in their futile quest for the grace of the goddess are revealed in a subtle, cinematic quotation of Eisenstein's Strike (1924) and Battleship Potemkin, made a year later. If nothing else, these allusions bring home the lessons of my concerted effort to situate Ray's practice in relation to Eisenstein's. For while it is generally acknowledged that Ray's upbringing was cosmopolitan and Westernized, his own intellectual history has rarely been examined, except to try to make the case that, notwithstanding his exposure to and interest in European ideas, he was essentially an "Indian" director whose cinema exemplifies the classical theory of rasa (aesthetic mood).[53] If such exceptionalism is rendered problematic in and by the wide range of Ray's writings, sources, or directorial choices, it also reflects a glaring neglect of the enormous impact of a broadly based cinematic internationalism on his practice. To say this is to accept that neither his stature as an Indian director nor his accomplishments as a modernist need to be evaluated or qualified in mutually exclusive terms.

It bears repeating that Ray's allusion to the revolutionary imperatives of Eisenstein's cinema functions not just as a visual pun. It contains a statement, even a radical one, about the dangers of a worldview that depends on maintaining divisions in society—between rich and poor, urban and rural, worker and landlord, us and them. The series of intercuts of the singer, on the one hand, and the approaching masses, on the other, establishes an entirely different plane of reference for the spectator invested in pursuing the idea of an "intellectual cinema." For, even as the song draws to a close, the masses, who have hitherto been rendered only in long shot, appear to emerge out of the screen and into spectatorial space. The highly geometrical construction of the shots—that, almost literally, triangulate the physical relationships among nature, humans, and the supernatural—restates Ray's avant-garde commitment to a form of cinema that is less interested in realistic depiction than in mobilizing the audience's consciousness of the hidden, human tragedy that extends beyond Doya's individual destiny (Figure 13).

FIGURE 13. Doya's end.
Used by permission from
Satyajit Ray Film and
Study Center.

Accordingly, in contrast to the image track, the song (which is both diegetic and nondiegetic—in that, while the itinerant singer is a character, the percussion instrument of the *khol* and flute we hear with the second rendering of the refrain have no coordinates onscreen) once more works to reorient us to the many denotations of Devi. She is the one who can be misrecognized as mere stone or, within the narrative, as mere woman. At a different level of conceptuality, however, she is neither; this is an expressive truth that cannot be signified by cinematic means alone, only intimated in a way that simultaneously directs the eye and the ear of the spectator—exhorting her instead to think of the image as a critique of reason rather than as its lure.

CONCLUSION

The fractal qualities of the image in *Devi*—simultaneously familiar and unfamiliar, emergent and residual, as well as concrete and abstract— must be placed in a larger, institutional context of Indian cinema (with its own long history). As I suggested in my introduction, Ray's cinema only acquires its salience and intelligibility as "art house" filmmaking within a particular framework of production and reception, as well as a specific social and intellectual situation. We may recall that as early as 1948 he had speculated on the need for a different approach to film than could be found in mainstream cinema both regionally, in Bengal, and elsewhere. In his essay "What Is Wrong with Indian Films?" Ray argued that Indian films are products of a misunderstood medium.[54] In keeping with other modernists, he thought that cinema's uniqueness rested on its capacity to heighten the tensions, as well as resemblances, among technology, materiality, and the spirit world—a potential very much at the center of Eisenstein's early twentieth-century experiments and, what is more, a project that should have come easily to a culture in which the power of technology and the power of the gods are not at all at odds (since automobiles, machinery, and other technological gadgets used everyday are regularly propitiated in India as divine objects). Nonetheless, Indian cinema had, in Ray's opinion, forgone the opportunity to articulate the sensual linkage between the magic of technology and that of the divine, opting instead for "visual dissonances" that resulted from mixing Hollywood style with Indian themes. Contending that cinema in India had vacated the opportunity to create "a style, an idiom, a sort of iconography of cinema, which would be uniquely and recognisably Indian," he proposed the need for a different mode of engagement, one that also explored "the language of cinema."[55]

As such, he contended, modernity's quintessential medium needs to find its message somewhere other than in the hyperbolic dialogue, extravagant costumes, and outlandish scenarios witnessed in mainstream films. These compensatory narratives only make visible the utter variance between the medium and modern Indian life, be it rural or urban, despite or perhaps especially because most films claim to represent a timeless India. The specific status of cinema in the dialectic of reification and utopia is, therefore, an important stake for Ray, and one of the ways he formulates his own response to the formula of mass-entertainment films is to pitch his portrait of the mother-goddess against a whole slew of "mythological" films that were the consensus narratives of his day. Although his own cosmopolitanism made it unlikely for him to regard these films (with their over-the-top representations of gods and goddesses cavorting about in poorly constructed scenes supposedly depicting heavenly locales) as anything but absurd, he also understood that the popularity of the formula betokens a fascination that needs to be interrogated rather than ignored or dismissed. The heavy ornamentalism of *Devi's* mise-en-scène comports precisely with this desire to defamiliarize audiences and to distance them from their mental images of Hindu deities derived from popular films, as well as other textual forms (such as calendars, cheaply framed pictures intended for private worship, and so on).

Kalikinkar's decadent household is resplendent with luxurious objects such as his fur-covered easy chair and elaborately wrought birdcage (itself symbolic of trappings and entrapment); even the marble porticoes of the mansion in which the film's action is largely located are conspicuously excessive. To these we can add the representation of Doya's bejeweled garb and the decorations surrounding the display of the goddess. All of this bespeaks an economy of overabundance that is in marked contrast with later shots of the denuded countryside. At an intertextual level, the Victorianism of the interior, depicting the nineteenth-century penchant for all things plush and patinated, evokes as well the useless expenditure and sensationalism of mainstream Indian cinema, in which both gods and humans are given a high-gloss, "Color-by-Technicolor" appearance implicitly critiqued by the film. In contrast to the opulence of the interior, the countryside depicted in *Devi* has none of the lushness of the panoramic views that characterize the depiction of a mythical India in mainstream cinema—with their hills and dales, waterfalls and sunsets, skies and clouds through which heroes and heroines, gods and goddesses pass.

The distance between the exterior landscape and the interior of Kalikinkar's household is only too marked. For there are no elements of relief in the landscape in *Devi:* no baroque ornamentation, no carapaces or coverings that give the bourgeois nineteenth-century imagination its substance or twentieth-century escapism its content. The modern is coded—as Benjamin and Adorno both argue in their respective meditations on surrealism—as the shellacking of the private sphere in which more and more layers are added to protect the "private rooms of our prosaic understanding," to use Benjamin's phrase, from exposure to the public. In contrast, the countryside in *Devi* reveals that the poor have no such escape to withdraw into. Importantly, neither does *prakriti* (or nature) herself, stripped as she is of any signs of vegetation or plenitude.

As opposed to the superfluous ornamentalism of mainstream movies, then, Ray emphasizes cinema as a form of conceptual critique; by the same token, the medium's placement within mass culture indicates its limited efficacy, suspended as it is between reified life and critical practice. The implications of such an epistemological and political standpoint have largely been lost in approaching cinematic meaning, particularly when it comes to postwar films from outside Europe or the United States, as if the only issue of critical value is to detect "accents" of difference.[56] Accordingly, Ray's films have been studied almost exclusively as if their merit resides in the extent to which they can be said to represent, appropriately, some historical or political constituency: women, nation, India, or the Third World. Only this is seen as defining the current terms of engagement, notwithstanding the parochialism. By contrast, if we recall the reference I made earlier to Kracauer's theorization of cinema's essential ontology as a form of "redemption," we are better positioned to assess the successes and failures of this cinema as a whole and to reflect on the specific attempt made in *Devi* to revitalize the dynamics of filmic form. That this revitalization proceeds by highlighting the contradictory relationship of modern viewers to the spectacle not only redeems Devi; it also reveals the predicament of belief as a fundamental contradiction of our time. In this specific sense *Devi* retains its efficacy as a political statement—whose poignancy is only increased by the fact that the original negative of the film was lost in a fire.

4 The Music Room Revisited

Jalsaghar, *Attraction, Perception*

The task is not to compose ordinary music for unusual instruments;
it is more important to compose unusual music for ordinary
instruments.

—THEODOR W. ADORNO and HANNS EISLER, *Composing for the Films*

ATTRACTION

The term *attraction* has become something of a commonplace in film-critical discussions. It is attached, first, to Sergei Eisenstein's proposition from the 1920s that cinema be conceived as a "montage of attractions" geared toward producing an active emotional and psychological response to the synthesis of image and action on the screen.[1] From this early, revolutionary imperative to provoke spectators into action in real life through the dynamic sublation of the two-dimensional oppositions of sight and sound or shot and meaning, the term has since traveled to its more current deployment as an aspect of cinematic spectacle. This use, popularized in the 1980s by the film historian Tom Gunning, refers to "a cinema of attractions" to describe the relationship of early film audiences to the space-time of the onscreen image. Defining *attraction* as governed by an "aesthetic of astonishment," Gunning proposed that in early cinema the appeals to experience go beyond imitation and narration and relate to their sensual and psychological impact; he and other critics have, since then, expanded the idea to include later cinematic works and a variety of forms of impact on the sensorium under the rubric of attraction.[2]

As rich as the work inspired by this use has been, what is mostly forgotten is a rather different emphasis in Eisenstein's thinking (based on his collaboration with Sergei Tret'iakov from 1923) on attraction as a "unit for measuring the force of art."[3] My point in beginning this chapter on Ray's *Jalsaghar* (1958) with a look at this term has to do with the conviction that an exclusively different terrain of interpretive possibilities is opened up by returning to that submerged aspect in Eisenstein's and, more particularly, Tret'iakov's conceptions of attraction. I hope to demonstrate that such a return enables us to take better account of Ray's *theatrical* rather than cinematic intentions in this film, which is about the decadence and decline of the landed aristocracy in Bengal. These intentions are centered on and routed through two sets of "vehicles": one, the larger-than-life personality of the Bengali stage actor Chhabi Biswas (who plays the nobleman, Biswambhar Roy); the other exemplified by music—which takes on greater significance here than in any of the other films discussed in this book and, by the end, becomes the main subject or, we might say, the main attraction, of the film.

We can set out by recalling that attraction was presented as a rational and calculative means to provoke the spectator into confronting the real rather than withdrawing from it. A little later I will link this up with a consideration of Ray's use of music (and dance) in *Jalsaghar*—as offering a mode of perception that speaks to a heightened sense of the real while simultaneously undercutting the monopoly of the visual. It is worth noting that the concept of attraction has generated considerable excitement in current film scholarship precisely because it provides a way to sidestep the hegemony of psychoanalytic models of interpretation that assert the primacy of the visual (in theories of the gaze, identification, and spectatorship). But if contemporary theories of filmic experience regard cinematic attraction as bypassing a psychoanalytic emphasis, for early proponents of the principle of attraction there was no contradiction between psychic and emotional effects and affects (be they visual or otherwise). Nor were these any less important than the political—specifically revolutionary—impulses that lay behind the use value of attraction as a mechanism for the excitation of viewers.

Devin Fore has valuably historicized the distinction between "physiological criticism" (Mayakovsky's designation for the largely formulaic preoccupation with phenomenal effects) that appeared in various Soviet journals during the years 1923 to 1925 and, by contrast, the special purpose of meditations on "the theater of attractions," which sought to dismantle the illusion of art altogether. Attraction was a way to think *out* of the aesthetic realm and into a reengagement with the real in all its emergent, modern, and (in the context of the early Soviet Union) modernizing energies. In abandoning art that, as Tret'iakov puts it, "has withdrawn beyond the boundaries of reality into a ream of illusion where 'there abides not sickness, nor sadness, and especially no class war,'" a theater of attractions directed itself toward "*precise social tasks* [of converting] theater into a tool for class action."[4] In this enterprise, and quite contrary to present discussions of its psychoperceptual effects (whether on astonished, distracted, pacified, or, simply, entertained audiences), Tret'iakov affirms Eisenstein's specification of attraction in the following manner:

> Any *calculated pressure on the spectator's attention and emotions,* any combination of staged elements that is able to focus the emotion of the spectator in the direction that the performance requires. From this point of view, the performance is not at all a demonstration of events, characters, or plastic combinations, more or less true to life. It is a site for the construction of a sequence of theatrical situations that work on an audience according to a given task. The attraction seizes the audience's attention, compresses its emotion, and discharges it. In the end the performance has delivered the requisite "charging" of the spectator.[5]

We begin to glean even from these brief allusions to their complicated aspiration to use the theater and cinema for socially transformative ends that (a) the primary goal of the Tret'iakov-Eisenstein collaboration was the destruction of aesthetic illusion and a corresponding reconstruction of society, and (b) since they considered attraction to function differently in different contexts, it had to be calculated variably, according to an estimation of the form that would most sharply provoke emotion in the viewer. For, and this is also a key insight, "the attraction is not to be regarded as a new invention in the theater," which, according to Tret'iakov, "has always employed the attraction, but unconsciously."[6]

The search was thus joined in Eisenstein's experiments in the theater and cinema for the precise mechanisms by which a rational and even scientific calculation could be made to measure the unconscious elements and features of attraction. Spontaneous applause, for instance, or the reaction to tricks and stunts, both of which rely on "habitual viewer psychology," needed to be transformed into something like a neuronal response to the revolution. No more needs to be said about the fate of that revolution, though its outlooks and ends continue to be held by some of us as the hope for a better society. To that extent, what remained unrealized in the Soviet attempt to find different aesthetic correlates for cognizing historical consciousness gains a second life in Ray's project, albeit less radical, to evoke the ideals of attraction and excitation in terms of their address to the new nation. With India's independence having been declared just over a decade prior to the film's release, *Jalsaghar* unfolds like a panorama of all that is about to disappear from view in the rush to modernization. In particular, the special place of a classical music tradition in India is displayed in almost documentary fashion, with a view to prompt newly empowered citizens at the movies into a different encounter with music than was on offer in mainstream films increasingly bent on appropriating the classical tradition into a mass cultural idiom.[7]

Although Ray did not profess himself to be a follower of Eisenstein, he took many of his leads from the potentialities awakened by Soviet film, as well as from specific theoretical writings that allowed him to conceive what I referred to in chapter 3 as Eisenstein's "ideational" or "intellectual" cinema.[8] It probably goes without repeating that Ray did not consider himself a revolutionary filmmaker because he steadfastly averred that the solutions to society's irreconcilable problems could not be found in art. But with that said, and even as he distanced himself from Eisenstein's political goals, Ray held fast to the sensibilities of the avant-garde especially betokened in thinking of cinema as a means for critical reflection on the image, as well as society. Moreover, he was highly aware of the specificity of his geographical location and historical situation, responding in an interview to a comparison between himself and Eisenstein by saying, "Eisenstein aided a revolution that was already taking place. In the midst of a revolution a filmmaker has a positive role, he can do something for the revolution. But, if there is no revolution, you can do nothing."[9] In such statements we discern Ray's stance toward his own practice—which can be said to exemplify a critical negativity thoroughly imbued with the sense that, to paraphrase Antonio Gramsci, an optimism of the will is neither negated nor rendered irrelevant by pessimism of the intellect. In *Jalsaghar* the resonances of this intellection are expressed through the attraction that was of such great importance to Ray as a composer but that has been overlooked in coming to terms with his filmic statements and in examining cinema overall: music.

ELABORATION

Readers familiar with the film will know that *Jalsaghar* (The Music Room) is a film that is manifestly about music and its place in the decadent self-perception of an aging nobleman eager to hang on to his sense of importance and relevance in a world that has passed him by. It is also a text in which an immanent critique of that worldview, both of its pitfalls and its appeal, is made possible through the use of music. The contradictory force of decadence in an age whose transition to modernity has by no means eliminated the residual power of the archaic, is explored in this film through the attractions—in the specific sense of their sensuous appeal—of music and dance. The setting is, once more, the nineteenth century, and the location is the shabby grandeur of a minor *zamindar*'s (landowner's) palace in rural Bengal. Unlike *Devi*, released two years later (in 1960), in which the anachronism of the landed gentry is counterposed to the emergent, modern sensibilities of a younger generation of urbanized Indians (Kalikinkar, the father, as contrasted with his son, Umaprasad), in *Jalsaghar*, the excesses of Biswambhar Roy, the impecunious aristocrat eager to make one last, grand statement about his high birth and taste, is set against the equally excessive, though parvenu, ambitions of a petit-bourgeois, mercantile class, exemplified by the character of the usurer Mahim Ganguli.

The plot, based on a short story by one of the most accomplished contemporary writers in Bengal, Tarashankar Banerjee, is a slight one, tugging at the heartstrings with its rendition of one man's personal and familial losses accompanied by his public loss of face. The evocation of a bygone world is, in Ray's film, handled almost exclusively through musical means—based on the score written by Ustad Vilayat Khan (who, along with Ravi Shankar and Nikhil Banerjee is considered one of India's greatest sitarists). The musical counterpoint to the narrative's manifest critique of traditionalism also mirrors some of Ray's strategic choices in *Devi* and *Mahanagar* (1963). Together with them, *Jalsaghar* proffers sympathetic readings of the predicament of the old in its confrontation with the new. In the present case, notwithstanding Ray's critique of the decadent pursuits of Bengal's landowning class at the turn of the century, his portrait of Roy's melancholy existence, unmoored from the authoritative claims of blood and birth characterizing feudalism, is largely sympathetic. For he poses it as the contradiction of an existence rendered totally irrelevant in the face of an encroaching, technologized modernity—in which, as they say, only money talks. Presented in delicate strokes (in ways faithful to Banerjee's short story), the narrative does not by itself begin to account for the film's mode of drawing viewers into a world that can now only be glimpsed as it disappears from view in the seemingly magical attractions of music and dance.

Part of the documentary feel and attraction of *Jalsaghar*, then, lies in the way it introduces its primary audience of urban, middle-class viewers to the curiosity of a "music room." For the world of the aristocracy is as closed off to the ordinary citizen in India as it is elsewhere. So, although Ray stringently critiques the self-indulgent and decadent landowning class in Bengal (the *zamindars*), he was very aware of its role in preserving India's ancient and venerable music and dance traditions through the patronage system. Made roughly a decade into India's sovereign existence as a postcolonial nation, the film dramatizes how the imperatives of embourgeoisement increasingly render older traditions obsolete. What the nineteenth-century narrative setting and the film's own post-Independence moment of production have in common is that they each refer to a cultural milieu in which the special forms of appreciation required by classical practices have receded from view, as well as general comprehension. Quite apart from the cultural literacy or specialized knowledge such practices demand, and even aside from the issue of time and money needed to pursue them, lies the problem of mass culture's obdurate effect on our ability to experience pleasure. Consequently what is at stake in Ray's visual meditation are the conditions of possibility of experience itself.

Another way to pose this is to say that while the popularity of mass-cultural entertainment must surely be granted, this does not in any way obviate the need to take into account how, in the space of about half a century (that is, between the time cinema is introduced to Indian audiences and its mass-scale takeoff), popular adaptations of musical and dance traditions in mainstream cinema managed to transform both classical and folk practices into mere spectacle, parasitically deriving their attraction from earlier traditions while diluting their appeal. It is this recursive sense of the historical entanglement of real practice and ersatz product that Ray elaborates in the film., In a very particular sense, the idea of the music room evokes (not only now but also when the film was made) an aura of patrician times left behind; the film's lesson seems to be that there is as much loss attached to this disappearance as relief in escaping from the past. By bringing this aura and era to life, the film gives viewers something like a voyeuristic look at voyeurism rendered through the exotic device of the *jalsa* (performance).

Reserved only for the male members of the nobility whose households often had a public room set aside for performances of music and dance, the *jalsaghar* (music room) was the site of an aristocratic practice of voyeurism, underpinned by the exclusivity and privilege of its purveyors. This bygone modality of looking is, of course, very different from the spectatorial activities and social position of the ordinary film viewer as voyeur. In carefully staging the relay between then and now, as well as between modes of spectating, Ray offers a small history of voyeurism, as it were, intimating how its class dimensions and gendered provenance have silently reinforced prevailing ideals of refinement—albeit those notions have themselves gone underground with the rise of movies (wherein everyone is equally a peeping tom, a voyeur as much as a viewer).

The overlap between aestheticist voyeurism and consumerist viewership is also conveyed by the untutored sounds of appreciation Ganguli makes at the concert within the space of the film when he reveals his lack of knowledge about the disinterested protocol of appreciation appropriate to the event. The old retainer, Ananta, similarly displays unfettered (and uneducated) enjoyment of the *jalsa* that his master stages. Crucially, Biswambhar Roy, too, only dissimulates a contemplative appreciation that is actually at odds with his inner rage at his predicament. By contrasting their déclassé responses with Roy's languid demeanor, Ray offers a comment on the discourse of aristocratic privilege and the corresponding absence of refinement that is characteristic of the upstart Ganguli, as well as the working-class Ananta. Both of their viewing pleasures come across as unrefined though more genuine. That ways of seeing are not only gendered but also class-demarcated is thus one of the critiques proffered by the film, even if its more direct purpose is to conjure up the phantasmatic obsessions of the mandarin class to which Roy belongs.

The mechanisms of the psychic and social disruption attending this world are drawn out by placing all of them in a narrative that begins and ends, we may recall, with the gently swaying chandelier of the music room as it glows in the dark—as if inviting viewers into its hypnotic snare. As I have already suggested, *Jalsaghar* is a film in which music conveys ideas not immediately accessible at the level of narrative. It preserves for audiences some of the sense of discovery and revelation that, ever since Méliès's magical sequences of trips to the moon and infernal cakewalks, has dissociated film from its mimetic, realistic preoccupations and pushed forward other perceptual modes that recall experiences of the fairground, the circus and the dime show.[10] Indeed, Méliès's shorts, which introduced the "primitive," ethnographic, and panoramic appeal of the tableau of life laid out for the spectator's delectation, are the foundation on which the proposition of a cinema of attractions is based. Paralleling the tactile pleasures of the attraction (which needed to be laid out and displayed), early cinema relied on the device of the proscenium theater—where all action unfolds before a stationary camera. This mode of exhibition makes itself felt in Ray's deployment of the film screen as a stage, most pointedly in the latter half of the film. And it is most extravagantly in the proscenium space of the *jalsaghar* that the repository of aesthetic forms such as Hindustani classical music and dance, which once communicated more palpably but now only signify as residual, are displayed, as if for the last time—before they are, as it were, consumed by the cinema.

If one of the ways that attraction works on the spectator is through the production of the sensual or psychological impact of music (or dance), the workings of this transferal of affect, and a precise account of its channeling into the spectator's consciousness, was left unspecified in Tret'iakov's and Eisenstein's writings. This despite the latter's special efforts to incorporate musical signification into his theorizations of the dialectic of image and sound or even in musically motivated "operatic" films such as *Ivan the Terrible* (1944). Consequently, although the idea of music as a cinematic attraction is highly suggestive, its conceptualization as anything resembling "calculated pressure" or "unit of measurement of force" remains quite vague within the examples handed down by the Soviets. This gap between theory and practice (in what was an attempt to produce a "scientific" theory of filmic dialectics) is squarely addressed a few decades later in Theodor Adorno and Hanns Eisler's jointly written book *Composing for the Films*.[11] While Adorno and Eisler did not endorse the Soviet propensity to look for equivalents—either filmic or musical—that would correlate to dialectical thinking, they shared Eisenstein's antipathy toward the vulgarization of music in popular film, as well as in popular culture more broadly. Seeking to formulate a theory of musical meaning on the terms of critical theory—which for Eisler (far more than for Adorno) meant Brechtian practice—they followed in the footsteps of Eisenstein (whose *Film Sense* is credited in Eisler's preface). Much of what they have to say should be read as attempts to refine Eisenstein's foundational proposals about music as attraction and force though the inspiration Adorno and Eisler drew from Eisenstein's theory and practice is not without criticism of his failures.

It is in this dialectical exchange or, perhaps, sublation (in the sense that some of the propositions are retained, others annulled) of older critical perspectives that we may situate our own thinking about ciné-music and its attractions. The debate about sound and what it brings to cinema or, for that matter, retracts from it is joined by Adorno and Eisler, who assign a higher value to the musical soundtrack than to dialogue, averring that "the talking picture, too, is mute."[12] This is because the fundamental principle of the motion picture is not speech but motion, particularly movement in time. In this way they make clear that the challenges presented by speech and music are on an equal footing, even though the former has come to be regarded as a natural feature of the representation of characters whereas music continues to be seen as secondary to the production of cinematic meaning. Technically, however, characters are not, as they say, "talking people but speaking effigies. . . . Their bodiless mouths utter words in a way that must seem disquieting to anyone uninformed" (76). Adorno and Eisler argue that the antithetical relationship between the spoken word and the visible image needs to be mediated—and alleviated—by music (which, they remind us, has always accompanied motion pictures even if it was only synchronized with the coming of the talkie): "Music was introduced as a kind of antidote against the picture. The need was felt to spare the spectator the unpleasantness involved in seeing effigies of living, acting, and even speaking persons, who were at the same time, silent. The fact that they are living and nonliving at the same time is what constitutes their ghostly character, and music was introduced not to supply them with the life they lacked—this became its aim only in the era of total ideological planning—but to exorcise fear or help the spectator absorb the shock" (75).

What is crucial in Adorno's and Eisler's view is that music is seen to have a certain homeopathic and absorbing, as well as exorcizing, function; it allows the spectator to absorb the shock of the image and relieve his or her fear of the speaking effigy designated by the character and the attendant anxiety about being threatened by his or her own muteness. For Adorno and Eisler this threat was inseparably connected to "the decay of spoken language" (an idea they ascribe to Karl Kraus) (76). The perceptual shocks and uncanniness of everyday life in modernity are fully brought home in the movies, where the sensory overstimulation and alienation of the subject is reinforced but softened by the intervention of music.

Thus, the attraction that music embodies is more in the nature of a technical aid or a physiological corrective than an emotional or aesthetic supplement to the experience of the image. The "fraudulent" unity implied by the speech and body of the character, as well as by the simultaneity of words and pictures, is exposed by music, and their inability to produce a synthesis on their own is revealed, undermining their presumed affinity.[13] According to Adorno and Eisler speech is only superimposed on characters in films and remains both artificial and contradictory until it becomes part of the ideology of the moving picture's false totality. By this token the artifice of music not only has the potential to be less ideological but is also capable of a more constructivist, formally reflexive, and, hence, inorganic deployment.

In Adorno and Eisler's opinion the influence of Wagnerian ideas about the *Gesamtkunstwerk* (total work of art) misled Eisenstein into thinking that music in film expresses "aesthetic empathy" along a signifying trajectory whose "rhythm" has already been established by the perceived primary relationships of shots and sequences to the whole. On the contrary, they say, the function of music should be "to release, or more accurately, to justify movement" (78). The essence of music-as-attraction resides in its capacity to draw out something that was previously frozen in the image, replacing something petrified with something spontaneous. In this way the

photographing of motions, film's essential principle, is (or could be) ampli-
fied by its genuine corollary: the unfolding of the sound of music. Ciné-
music is, on these terms, much more than background sound; rather, it
"suppl[ies] momentum, muscular energy, a sense of corporeity, as it were"
(78). That its existence is quasi-independent is at the heart of the argument
for Adorno and Eisler; therefore, music in cinema is nonidentical with the
image and, paradoxically, antithetic "at the very moment when the deep-
est unity is achieved" (78). It represents the rounding out not of voice or
speech but movement and gesture and functions, as they eloquently aver,
"in the same way, good ballet music, for instance Stravinsky's, does not
express the feelings of the dancers and does not aim at any identity with
them, but only summons them to dance" (78).

These ideas make it clear that although Adorno and Eisler took many of
their leads from Eisenstein, they also regarded his efforts to find musical
equivalents for his dialectical program of cinema to have faltered on the
grounds that music remains auratic in his films. The designation of aura
as a false attempt to lend organicity is one that the authors borrow from
Benjamin, and they use it to criticize the effect of music in Eisenstein's
films as falling prey to "degenerated forms of the 'aura'" (72). These
effects, they argue, are accidental—the result of "the magic of moods,
semi-darkness and intoxication" (72)—rather than the result of precise
calculation or a montage of attractions realized by dialectical practice.

If Eisenstein's Wagnerian investments are at one end of the analytic
spectrum for Adorno's and Eisler's deliberations about music in cinema,
then the clichéd and standardized practices of classical Hollywood represent the other pole. These musical practices emblematize the false imme-
diacy, emotionalism, and bathos of mass-media experience and function to
cloak the distance between the remoteness of a mass-produced system and
audiences who have no choice but to consume its products. Conventional
movie music only underscores the illusion of closeness and of (real) experience—again installing a degenerate aura, although it is of course a different order of degradation than anything found in Eisenstein. This music
attempts, in Adorno's and Eisler's words, "to interpose a human coating
between the reeled-off pictures and the spectators. Its social function is
that of a cement, which holds together elements that otherwise would
oppose each other unrelated—the mechanical product and the spectators,
and also the spectators themselves" (59). In describing spectators as held
together by cement, Adorno and Eisler offer a position characteristic of
critical theory's overall argument about the rigidifying effects of mass
culture on subjectivity, specifying it in relation to film music by stat-

ing that it is the stuff of irrationality or, more particularly, "a rationally planned irrationality" (23).

Consider the similarity between this line of theory and Ray's view of what is known as *filmi geet* (mainstream Hindi film songs): "You have the circumstances and the basis for a formula and there is no denying that if you think in terms of tired untutored minds with undeveloped tastes needing an occasional escape through relaxation, you will have to admit that the best prescription is a well-mixed potpourri of popular entertainment. And that is exactly what is being contrived and will, I suspect, continue to be contrived for a very long time yet."[14] Nonetheless, what Ray derides as "contrivance," and what Adorno and Eisler for their part refer to as "planned irrationality," also borders on the recognition that despite the standardization and formulaic quality of music in mainstream cinema, be it Indian or Hollywood, it can (albeit not invariably) touch a chord of experience or emotion now lost to other aspects of a reified sensorium.

From this perspective, and without gainsaying the reification of perception, it can be said that music retains the capacity to soothe and evoke in ways that are not reducible to a thesis about the mere programming of the senses. Ray recognized that in the context of Indian cinema and culture more broadly, the attraction that movie music provides cannot be easily written off (as, for example, Adorno and Eisler tend to do in their distaste for "late industrial music produced by late industrial technique"). For Ray understood that "to the vast conglomerate that makes up the Indian public the cinema is the only form of available inexpensive entertainment. They have not the choice that the western public has of music halls, revues, plays, concerts, and even, sometimes, of a permanent circus. Yet the craving for spectacle, for romance, for a funny turn or two, for singing and dancing, remains and has somehow to be met. If the film does not meet it, nothing will."[15] Moreover, he recognized that Indian ciné-music is also technically innovative—especially when, as he puts it, the challenge in the song-and-dance numbers is to choreograph "each line of a lyric sung against a different scenic background."[16]

In fact, the emotive power of mass-produced music was also acknowledged by Adorno and Eisler, who provided their own historiographic take on this remainder: of music that, despite its standardization, reawakens a residual structure of feeling. Along these lines they speak to the resonance of collectivity that even preprogrammed music can activate, following Max Weber's argument that music, particularly middle-class music (given the class-configured element of all industrial forms of social organization and rationalization), has an ambivalent character. On the one hand, this music evokes what they call a "vague togetherness"; on the other, because it is a not-so-secret sharer in capitalist notions of progress, it is productive of a "sham collectivity."[17] The necessary paradox is that "the greater the drabness of . . . existence, the sweeter the melody. The underlying need expressed by this inconsistency springs from the frustrations imposed on the masses of the people by social conditions" (22). Commercial music attempts to instrumentalize this impasse between desire and reality for its own purposes by bending music "to serve regression 'psycho-technically'" (22).

If these propositions from *Composing for the Films* share more than a hint of Adorno's earlier hypotheses about fetishized music and the regression of listening, they also highlight that music—in cinema, as well as more generally—is still the outpost of rationalized processes since its very abstractness, the fact that it conjures up emotions and feelings and not objects, makes it more recalcitrant than the eye. However much ciné-music tries to "cue" the spectator into clichéd patterns of listening with "stock music"—wonderfully characterized by Adorno and Eisler as that which "transforms, for example, the *Moonlight Sonata* into a mere signpost, a sound trademark, to accompany stock dramatic events"—there is an "archaic" dimension to acoustical perception that continues, despite being degraded, to possess a greater ability to preserve "traits of long bygone, pre-individualistic collectivities than optical perception" (21).

INSTANTIATION

At this point the discussion of ciné-music along the lines I have elaborated above can be linked more concretely with Ray's practice. Unlike Adorno, for whom only music that refuses the ideal of transparent communicability was genuinely transformative, Ray takes a more expansive approach. In *Jalsaghar* (and other films) his effort is to trigger a connection with experiences and associations now submerged—that is to say, almost but not quite drowned out by the prefabricated emotional appeal of mainstream film music. But inasmuch as he explores deeper experiences and associations through the medium of cinema with music as their trigger, he nonetheless rejects (along with Adorno and Eisler) the idea of immediately communicable, prefabricated emotionality in the use of music. He is unlike them, however, in thinking that music is not validated by its own innovative, formal properties or its purely intellectual challenges. Rather, music for Ray almost plays the role of a character—as a personality with a history and now a threatened livelihood. Concurrently, the meaning of music can be said to reside in the extent to which it is emblematic of a social type and triggers associations with a distinct era. In this sense it has a content apart from itself.

In resisting the identification that the manufactured sensibility of conventional movie music imposes on audiences through the suturing of sight and sound, Ray advocated the value of a performance that has "a sustained semblance of non-reality."[18] By contrast, we know that Adorno argued that the only way to achieve critical distance from prepackaged horizons of experience sold in mainstream cinema was to eschew *all* forms of mass culture. The only avenue left was to turn inward to the autonomous composition that functions in accordance with its own formal laws, outside the dictates of utility. The different option Ray exercises is to engage the blockages to aesthetic experience by reinserting, almost paratactically, the alienation effects produced by classical and traditional forms of music into the very matrix of cinematic meanings. This turn toward reengaging now lost horizons of experience and disappearing forms of gesturality and aurality is made palpable in *Jalsaghar*.

We should recall that the articulation of filmic form and musical meaning in this film had to be advanced with the help of Vilayat Khan's score, so Ray's directorial intentions were somewhat beholden to the composer. In his later films, such as *Ghare Baire* (1984), Ray took over sole command of musical orchestration and composition, making it easier for us to read his intentions with regard to the music in its contrapuntal relation to the narrative. For this reason, referring to a musical interlude in *Ghare Baire* might help to facilitate the ensuing discussion of music in *Jalsaghar*.[19] My point is to situate the enunciative possibilities of music when it functions as its own montage cell, so to speak, against the constraints of its deployment as an attraction merely accompanying the image.

In a key scene toward the end of *Ghare Baire*, Nikhil ponders the twin disasters of his home and world—his wife Bimala's infatuation with Sandip and the public disarray of his domain caused by Sandip's demagoguery. This scene's importance rests on its articulation of narratological, technological, and musicological concerns. Ray's authorial commentary on disruption is here juxtaposed with his reflexive attention to the apparatus, but this time it is the apparatus of sound—the gramophone—that is brought into the picture. Audio technology intrudes very literally into this scene, with the gramophone appearing in the frame to provide an implicit contrast to the faux spontaneity that conventional musical interludes serve up at the movies. The disruption that the music signifies here is quite subtle, even if it is literal, and is less reflective of narrative concerns than expressive of other worlds that have disappeared but return, now and again, as uncanny reminders of their appeal.

In this connection Ray himself noted the importance of finding music that "not only sounds right but is also right for the scene for which it was meant," echoing a sentiment that Adorno and Eisler also shared, regarding music that is not subordinated to the image nor used to justify the plot but that articulates the contradiction between outward appearances and what they call its own "subjective inwardness."[20] Ironically, it is Ray the film-maker, rather than Adorno and Eisler as theorists, who seems to remember the latter's conceptual lesson that the subjectivity of the artwork and art-ist is given by the objectivity of their institutional and epochal existence. Accordingly, the contradiction between subjectivity and objectivity can only be highlighted by placing art—in this case, music—in tandem with forms that now appear either phantasmagoric or otherwise out of place, music's own unreality and inwardness registered in the oddity of its tech-nological mediation.

In *Jalsaghar*, as I will elaborate shortly, music is not simply mapped onto scenic elements but raised to the level of autonomous, dramatic expression. But in order for that discussion to become fully clear, let me again place it in relation to the gramophone scene from *Ghare Baire*. In this scene all of the tussles and conflicts internal to the characters and their situations are minimalized, which is not to say that they have been eliminated but rather that they have been distilled to the single principle of tempo: in the formal pacing of the shots and in the quality of the diegetic mood intimated through the song played over the gramophone. The slow pace of Ray's works has been noted often enough, although his orchestration of musical temporality has received little serious attention. In the example at hand the temporal link between past and present, as well as their negation by each other, is evoked through the use of a musical form that is recog-nizable in its very "pastness."

The scene unfolds as Ray intensifies the growing tension in the narra-tive by lengthening and etiolating it most obviously through movement, or to be precise, the absence thereof. There is very little by way of action in this scene, which inches forward without dialogue—if it can be said to move forward at all. The sense of stillness betokened parallels the histori-cal interregnum that the film as a whole also represents. Only the inter-polation of a song relieves (and, at the same time, reinforces) the contrast between a possible world of subjective and objective emancipation and the actual world of constraints on both personal and political freedom. We come upon these realizations as the scene fades in from black to a medium long shot of the darkened staircase in the interior of Nikhil and Bimala's residence, the darkness relieved only by dim reflections from the twin candelabras that flank the baronial staircase leading up from the public areas of the mansion to its private quarters. Nikhil's silhouetted figure is shown slowly ascending the stairs, his footsteps echoing softly, magnifying the gloom. As the camera tracks upward, a clock begins to chime, echoing the clock that had ticked in the background in the scene immediately preceding this one. This exaggerated emphasis on time draws attention not only to the lateness of the hour within the narrative's own logic but also to the distempered nature of a modernity that, in the case of India, betokens all things out of time—or, to call up Roberto Schwarz's idea from my introduction, "ill-assorted" matters.

The camera and the soundtrack are the twin points of emphasis in the exploration (also pursued in *Jalsaghar*) of the sensibility of historical decadence. Like Biswambhar's destiny in the encroaching world of modernity, *Ghare Baire* conveys the notion that there is no place for Nikhil in a milieu disrupted by anticolonial agitation and its consequences, both positive and negative. He is the embodiment of a world that has already been turned upside down, its coordinates now on the verge of disappearing into darkness (which the low-key lighting serves literally to reinforce). The scene shifts abruptly with a cut, and the camera's perspective moves from lingering over Nikhil's ascent up the stairway to a medium close-up of a gramophone, scratchily playing a Bengali song in a popular musical idiom. As an aside, we may note that the diegetic presence of the gramophone is as much an estranging move as a historical comment about the saturation of daily life by technologies of European provenance (even if the song clearly signifies as local and traditional). We should recall that many, if not most, of the modern technologies—from the gramophone, microphone, telegraph, typewriter, electric bulb, bioscope, and so on—were brought to India from Europe; by the same token, the cultural practices and ideas transmitted by them were not. What follows from this is the realization that a strict division of form and content is neither feasible nor useful in assessing the exact degree to which European cultural influences detract from a recognizably authentic Indian cultural repertoire.

In the present scene, for example, the gramophone is a prop in the representation of an indigenous style of life that fully incorporated foreign objects, a point that Ray remarks by centering it briefly in the frame, shot from a low angle. The gramophone is playing a vocal composition in the Bengali genre identifiable as a *kirtan* or devotional song, sung in the *tappa* style—a musical form that derived from Afghan and Punjabi classical styles of vocal music brought to India in earlier periods and assimilated in the nineteenth century into a popular tradition of song known as *Bangla tappa*.[21] The slightly high-pitched nasal tone of the male voice and the sibilant hiss of the recording are exploited by Ray to denote a particular time and place, as well as its lack of fit within the current staging of home and world. As I suggested a little earlier, it is not the presence of the gramophone that is anachronistic in this scene, since such technological appurtenances would be common in upper-class households of the era depicted in the film. Rather, we should note the paratactic quality of the period itself that Ray manages to evoke through his coupling of new technology and an older style of singing—replete with old-fashioned ideas that now appear out of place.

The portrayal of the convergences and divergences between European cultural or political ideals and traditional Indian modes of being is in a sense matched by the music through its very mismatched quality. It renders, in aural form, the discombobulations of a Victorianism shaded with Bengali understanding. In this way, an extracinematic set of associations is made available to those familiar with the vogue in late nineteenth- and early twentieth-century Bengal for phonograph recordings of European ballads, on the one hand, and classical and semiclassical Hindustani music, on the other. Their ill-assorted, misplaced existence together is cleverly intimated by the song, whose effect is to draw the viewer into a remembered structure of feeling expressible only through music. At the same time, the device of the song also underlines the fact that the Indian encounter with modernity has, for more than a century, been marked by media technologies, a technologization of life that the film as a whole also recapitulates.

As a final note on this example from *Ghare Baire*, it is perhaps also worth remarking that the seclusion of women exhibited in the scene (no less than in the rest of the narrative) countermands any notion that the place of technology was restricted to the public sphere or in the hands of men alone. Indeed, if the traditional women of the household are here seen to monopolize the phonograph and its magic, the Europeanized Nikhil, by contrast, is presented as both literate and more literary, with his fondness for reciting the English romantic poets. And still differently stands Bimala—who, we have learned, is attached to her English songs, often humming them as she performs her role as the manor's chatelaine. In this particular scene, when the camera pulls back to reveal to spectators the onscreen audience for the unfolding musical interlude, it shows Bouthan (Nikhil's widowed sister-in-law) accompanied by the other, subordinate women of the household gathered around the central figure of the gramophone. Its prominence in the frame is of course a self-conscious way to mark the articulation of sight and sound and, simultaneously, the very artificiality of this conjunction.

Bimala is noticeably absent from this gathering, and the songs played on the gramophone are altogether different from the ballads she is taught by her governess, Miss Gilby. The function of the music here is, at one level, to literalize nostalgia in a manner similar to the song Bimala sings in the opening moments of the film: "Tell me the tales that to me were so dear . . . long, long ago, long ago." But whereas Miss Gilby's songs hark back to English times and tales, Bouthan and her attendants listen to traditional devotional music in praise of renunciation, a mode of life that the film allegorizes through the renunciative character of Nikhil. At a second, more abstract, level the song foreshadows Bimala's fate as the sacrificed emblem of modernity, and at yet a different level of political allegory its exhortation to abjure the world is not fully apart from Sandip's call for the renunciation of British goods. Still, what the scene conveys is that such sentiments regarding renunciation are of no interest to Bimala, given her newfound passion for the ways of the world and her infatuation with Sandip. As much as Bouthan and her attendants are absorbed by the otherworldly horizons conjured up by the *kirtan*, Bimala has crossed over an entirely different threshold.

What can we say about this scene that does justice to the connection Ray draws between forgotten music and forgotten women? Ray's depiction of the phonograph and the elements of the household works to suggest the ill-fitting sense that the new and the now impose on a mode of life within which their appearance is misplaced. A variation in the overall theme of *Ghare Baire*, this scene is about that which has been discarded and made irrelevant within an epistemological and political matrix privileging change, transformation, and emergence. So it is that the gramophone playing Bouthan's *kirtan* not only signifies a world outside the main drama being staged at home and in the world, but it also evokes the role often played in conventional European musical arrangements by the minor key. The *kirtan*, with its ascetic appeal to reject worldly bonds, represents only a brief interlude in this film, but it is crucial in two ways: first, it allows Ray to introduce a critical note about the dominant parsing of the problem of the personal and political or tradition and modernity; second, it is a highly self-conscious way for him to invoke a level of reality that simply cannot be represented realistically given that it is no longer readily accessible. Ultimately, the legibility of the song depends on recognizing its provenance in a folk music tradition in Bengal dating back well over a hundred years.

In the cinematic experiment that *Ghare Baire* represents, Ray relies on popular musical practices to provide a counterpoint to what, at the level of the narrative, is an utterly conventional contrast between *ghar* (home) and *bahir* (world). Moreover, at the level of nondiegetic form, his use of such *gharoa* (homely, familiar) music also reminds the vigilant audience/reader that in Bengali, the phrase *ghare baire* would not be taken as offering a strict contrast between home and world since the terms *ghar* and *bahir* are interdependent, indeed even mutually constituted. The *tappa's* generatively "foreign" provenance, for example, or its shifting registers of meaning—ranging from private expressions of grief or devotion to earthy songs of love and pleasure—serves to disturb the narrative's domesticated emphasis on ideas of home and world, thereby conjuring up places far away from either. Only the audience can sense, in a sort of sensate intuition that the music triggers, a mood of tragedy that looms over the story world without ever being literalized in anything that actually happens in the scene.

VARIATION

In *Jalsaghar* music exemplifies an even more immediate presence. My point is not that it is unmediated here but rather that the demands of the story make the musical score the most significant element of the narrative itself. Those familiar with the film will recall that its climactic moment is a lavish musical soirée that caps Biswambhar's ruin, gesturing in this way toward the end of an era whose self-indulgence was partly to blame for the depredations caused by the British (who could blame the native aristocracy for its decadence and use this excuse to further their own ends).[22] One might say that in this film the characters mediate identification with music whereas in conventional Hollywood films music mediates identification with characters on the screen. Such a subordination of narrative movement to the relations that music introduces was in part made possible for Ray by casting the larger-than-life stage personality of Chhabi Biswas in the title role of Biswambhar Roy (Figure 14). Somewhat in the manner that Roland Barthes described "the face of Garbo," Biswas's presence gives the character a remote and figural, as opposed to fleshly, presence and renders the dynamic of tradition and modernity as frozen in an antinomy.[23]

From the audience's first glimpse of him in the opening sequence of the film, Biswambhar is portrayed as brooding and bereft though imperious—as he sits trancelike on the terrace of his dilapidated palace, his eyes unseeing, his figure as deathly still as the brick and mortar of the palace (Figure 15). Biswas, the actor-personality who plays the leading role, is

FIGURE 14. The *zamindar* (feudal landlord) Biswambhar Roy. Used by permission from Satyajit Ray Film and Study Center.

FIGURE 15. Biswambhar on the terrace of his palace. Used by permission from Satyajit Ray Film and Study Center.

always captured as an unreal person, almost as if he were part of the phan-tasmagoria of a world in which the image of the commodity has overtaken other images. One might suggest that Ray's depiction of the social type connoted by Biswambhar (with his air of rarefaction and unreality) con-tains an implicit comment on the idea of the "star" personality as a vehicle or container for deferred aspirations and ascribed desires that are beyond the reach of ordinary people and rendered unreal themselves.[24]

Indeed, the tableaulike quality of *Jalsaghar* as a whole is less alleviated than orchestrated and arranged by the musical score, which once again highlights for us how music signifies in this film and what makes its appre-ciation along conventional lines difficult. For instance, the influential film critic Stanley Kauffmann had this to say about the film on its American release in 1963: "*The Music Room* is a deeply felt, extremely tedious film. On the one hand its western derivations are patent (the Greek-revival mansion no more than the Chekhovian theme). On the other hand its chief indigenous element, the Indian music, is simply uncongenial and tiresome to our ears."[25]

Congeniality is a strange thing to be looking for in the movies though Kauffmann is perhaps right to call the Indian music "uncongenial" to "our ears" (by which he presumably means American ones, though here, too, he was largely in a minority given that *Jalsaghar* had quite a successful release outside India). But if we parse the meaning of the uncongenial as referring to that which is incompatible—in this case, with standard expec-tations about how movie music should blend in to the story—then the film's deliberate effort to hold the two apart is indeed understandable on Kauffmann's terms. Ray was, we may recall from an observation I cited earlier, invested in exploring how film music has the potential to deepen not the sense of reality but a "semblance of non-reality." By this I take it that he meant to eschew the jumpy yet unmarked ways in which films often segue into their musical numbers, instead putting in place musical and filmic segments that each represented a different point of perceptual contact—without the music sounding incidental. The music in *Jalsaghar*, then, is not merely a contrapuntal or interruptive gesture but its own thing. Eisler, to recall his and Adorno's arguments, had proposed that the primary objective of the composer was to have ciné-music speak in its own voice. Music, as is stated in the introduction to *Composing for the Films*, "must act as well as react."[26]

My main illustration of the way this objective is realized in *Jalsaghar* must, for the reason that it is absolutely central to the film, center on Ray's orchestration of Khan's score in the penultimate scene of the *jalsa* (concert) that Biswambhar hosts in his final attempt to upstage the upstart Ganguli. The scene is not lacking in pictorial depth by any means: Ray's trademark deep focus photography of the music room—with its faded, baroque grandeur and its stately though stained columns—sets up the visual parameters against which the musicians and dancer are to perform. The huge gilt mirrors that were part of the set Ray had specially built for this scene evoke an image of the past caught in its own disappearing reflection—giving what is seen a shimmering and almost reflective appearance. It is as if the vision of the singing and dancing exhibited onscreen were to present us with momentary flashes of remembrance, though any sense that such a scene might betoken an actual resemblance with the real is crucially withheld in the music room's display of its own silence and opacity throughout the rest of the film.

Into this scene of infinite regress to an era now past, of courtly life with its spectacles of music and dance, Khan's score and Roshan Kumari's *Kathak*-style dance performance are added. Conveying the sense that the film's audience is, as if magically, transported into the time of the performance itself, the dance is staged without many edits or other shot transitions (with the exception of a few reverse shots of Roy reclining against his cushion, *hukkah* in hand, and Ganguli imbibing rather indiscriminately). Most of this scene's attraction is derived from the profilmic quality of the dance, here inserted in a calculated appeal to spectators to set aside an ideological critique of feudal decadence that the film also presents in favor of a sensory appreciation of music and dance.[27] Aesthetic sensibilities lost to modernity are displayed as if on a proscenium stage, with the action that unfolds (both within the frame and in the real-time movie hall) separating the attraction from narrative meaning. The overall impression is one of distancing, given that the rarefied aura of vocal and instrumental classical Hindustani music and *Kathak* dance (in which a specialized vocabulary of rhythmic beats is spoken aloud to accompany the dancer's footwork) signals, above all, its lack of fit in the spectacle that is narrative cinema.

The attraction here is an uncanny one, for the music and dance belong to an unfamiliar experiential and temporal world that had seen its best days under a feudal social order. The unfamiliarity paradoxically reinforces the fact that although mainstream Indian cinema (which depends on and cannibalizes classical traditions) features disproportionate amounts of music and dance, the discordant blending of action, dialogue, and musical extravaganza they represent is utterly unlike what is presented here. On the contrary, it is as if Biswambhar's irrelevance in an emergent, modern order is both underscored and undermined by the reminder to the mainstream moviegoer that the sensationalism of the high-gloss, "synched" musical number in conventional Hindi cinema represents the degenerate form of aura to which this scene and its music are an antidote.

Ray himself commented on the restrictions imposed by conventions of the theater (with its implied separation of action and audience) on making films that both refuse the demarcation of the frame as a stage and, on occasion, look to subvert the frontality of the staged event through Brechtian alienation effects. He also wrote extensively about music—from the specific difficulties of using classical Indian music as background music (abohosangeet), and the special magic of European instrumental music in the *jatra* form (epic folk-theater in Bengal featuring loud music, garish costumes, and, although not invariably, male actors playing female roles), to the importance of coordinating mood music without letting it devolve into formula.[28] Over time he became convinced that classical Indian *ragas* (mood schemes) could not be used in undistorted fashion in most films because they possess an "inner integrity"[29] that is not assimilable to the demands of the image. He thought that the use of *ragas* either overwhelmed a scene with their own internal associations or hijacked it on the road to destinations unpredicted by the demands of the film. Even if this conviction was in part the result of Ray's experiences with the virtuoso musicians who wrote the scores of his early films, the question with which we are still faced in the context of *Jalsaghar* is: Why did he go to such lengths to stage a lengthy display of Hindustani classical forms? The entire film is, it would have to be said, structured around episodes that showcase performances by the *ghazal* singer Begum Akhtar, the *khayal* singer Waheed Khan, the danseuse Roshan Kumari, and the *shehnai* playing of Ustad Bismillah Khan; and their prominence rivals if not surpasses the action or drama that is the nominal subject of this text.

As I have suggested, the motivation for this is, at one level, to communicate a particular sensibility associated with courtly manners and feudal mores, connecting it with aesthetic forms that encapsulate rather than merely represent that mode of existence (Figure 16). In addition the music has an indexical function to the extent that it is itself a token of this mode of life although, of course, its presence in the filmic text serves only to mark its archaic nature. As Ray put it, "The background music in *Jalsaghar* grasped the atmosphere of the world of *zamindars* (landed gentry). There is a historical connection between classical music and this social environment with which we all are familiar; this is the worldview that Vilayat Khan was able to capture through the use of instruments like the sitar, sarod, and sarangi, that express their own aristocratic lineage."[30]

FIGURE 16.
Biswambhar descending
the staircase. Used by
permission from Satyajit
Ray Film and Study
Center.

At another level the music mobilizes a comment on the nature of cinema, depending as it does on a form of attraction that has lost out to the taken-for-granted prominence of the visual. We are all in a way forced to be deaf or, at least, tone-deaf at the movies, given our predisposition to "look beyond" the music for textual significance in just the manner that Kauffmann reveals in the review I cited above. And finally, the overarching thematic, as well as emblematic, use of music in *Jalsaghar* is a reminder of forms of pleasure and perception (from folk-theater and pantomime to the shadow play and kaleidoscope, as well as classical music) that were predicated on an audible reality, however unreal. These have been all but obliterated by the reality effects in and of film. Cinema is thus the archive of its own technological precursors—as Ray, following the paths charted by Eisenstein's reliance on folkloric and mythic associations, documents with palpable effect.

If this film is evidence of ciné-music's capacity to evoke utopian possibilities that cannot be represented realistically but only intimated in the particular nexus of vision and sound, this accomplishment derives from what Eisler, in an emphasis derived from Brecht, referred to as the *gestural* elements of music. Specifically, these are gestures that designate ideas and meanings but do not appropriate them into a whole. Whether this was an element in Ray's cinematic refutation of the bourgeois ideology of wholeness, resolution, and closure is a question that cannot be settled. Perhaps it is also not required that such settlement be seen as a matter of political intentions alone but also of Ray's directorial judgment about what can be said, what remains unsayable, and what can be said otherwise (Figure 17). From this perspective it is inescapably the case that music provides the means for registering the immanence of past and

present without recourse to a drab sentimentality or a solely reactionary nostalgia. Actually, Kauffmann's review of *Jalsaghar* is instructive in this respect, notwithstanding his dismissive tone. For if it only seemed to him to be a derivative representation of "patently" Western themes, its apparent tediousness is also a sign of his inability to recognize the specificities of cinematic attraction that, as I have tried to show, go well beyond telling stories or portraying emotions. We can safely assume that the patent on representing feeling or setting or emotion is neither exclusively Western nor an exclusive matter of narrative development and resolution. In turn, this enables us to attend to all that Kauffman missed (or, more accurately, that he missed while seeing).

What is more peculiar than Kauffman's narrow focus is the fact that his compositional virtuosity notwithstanding, Ray has been criticized by prominent Indian film critics for his alleged inability to use sound in imaginative ways. The main example of this line is Ashish Rajadhyaksha's writing in *Sight and Sound*. Commenting on Ray's career as a whole, and his filmmaking of the 1970s in particular (when it is presumed that he would have learned from his experiments of the 1950s and 1960s), Rajadhyaksha observes: "Acclaimed for his revolutionising of acting in Indian cinema, Ray was now unable to do anything in what is probably the single most powerful area of ideological manipulation in film: the soundtrack. With the Calcutta films, he started to convey more and more information through sound, with the visual illustrating what the dialogue was saying. He became increasingly embroiled in problems of naturalism—such as the accent his actors should use in their occasional English lines—even as he succumbed to the far more controversial convention of submerging effects beneath his dialogue tracks."[31]

My own focus (here and in the book as a whole) has not been on the problems of urban existence preoccupying Ray in his later films. But since my argument has been conducted on the terms of aesthetic form, I am emboldened to say that the issue about sound has less to do with a specific period in Ray's career than with whether Rajadhyaksha's assessment holds at all. For I would contend that his comments reveal a misperception of Ray's overall cinematic project. At the very least, it is certainly true in what Rajadhyaksha sees as at stake in the use of the soundtrack. Indeed, what he betrays is that fashionable ideas are often utterly conventional. I mentioned in my introduction that Rajadhyaksha is another critic for whom it has become almost de rigueur to assert that Ray's "humanism" and "utopianism" or his commitment to a "Nehruvian" vision of nation-building are outdated and jejune, subject to errors that we in the contemporary moment have been enjoined to overcome. But such thinking depends on readers assenting to the view that the culture-and-society model has outlived its utility as an analytic tool and as a mode of narration and, at the same time, agreeing that the question of the apparatus can only be addressed by a critique of ideology that announces itself thoroughly as such. Yet here the search for more sophisticated frameworks of analysis (always desirable, one supposes) is hoisted on its own petard by a residual credulousness about what constitutes sophistication. Accordingly, when it comes to sound, naturalism is professed to be bad mimeticism, while dissonance (however static) is good because it supposedly exceeds the mimetic. Likewise, conveying information through an investigation of established conventions is seen to be less preferable than an explicit subversion of the conventions themselves. Then there is the imputation that the aesthetics of protest should only take the form of didacticism, without which it can only reproduce what Rajadhyaksha impugns as "armchair liberalism."[32]

I will have occasion in the next chapter to consider the question of aesthetic standpoint and the category of political art. But in thinking about sound and music per se, it should suffice to say that no such correlation exists between, say, a naturalistic use of sound and a particular ideological effect. Nor is a more self-consciously political goal obtained through subverting conventions alone. The disjunction between art and life may at times be exposed through a deliberate avoidance of seamlessness (this goes for sound as much as it does for any other aspect of the cinematic text) but technique by itself is neither the necessary nor the sufficient criterion for evaluating whether the artwork has managed to overcome the false identifications that its origins impose on it. In the call for a more radical use of sound than Ray was supposedly able to offer, Rajadhyaksha avers that the "Ray movie" falls prey to its desire for a more authentic connection with the society from which its own position is alienated. As evidence of such sentimentality, Ray is quoted as follows: "I still believe in the individual and in personal concepts rather than in a broad ideology which keeps changing all the time."[33] Still, I would say that the suspicion of the individual as the "subject-effect" of a now-dismissed humanism is no longer as radical a statement as it has seemed to those schooled in a pre-fabricated Althusserian or Foucauldian mode of criticism. This is not least because we have yet to come up with an adequate, let alone sophisticated, substitute for the agent of cognition and action—all talk of the "posthuman" notwithstanding.

In the end, and when it comes to sound, the precipitate of the human that is the ear simply will not cede the ground of experience to anything other than itself, however much that experience is trained institutionally by our habits of listening and not listening at the movies. As the concern with music—obviously the chief element (along with dialogue) in any consideration of the soundtrack—shows, Ray does not use the acoustic aspect simply to "illustrate" the visual or vice versa. In this he was consistent with both Eisenstein and Eisler—rejecting the search for equivalents "of the purely representational elements of music."[34] In this discussion I have attempted to systematize my running interest in Ray's use of music by focusing on its conceptual and embodied aims. I also hope to have put in place a sense of the need to change the terms by which our understanding of aural perception in cinema has proceeded and, in doing so, to remark on the entirely discontinuous problem of meaning and attraction produced by the yoking together of pictorial and musical elements.

5 Take Two

Mahanagar *and Cinematic Imperfection*

In [modern] art, direct protest is reactionary.
—THEODOR ADORNO, *Aesthetic Theory*

Once in a while I feel like having a fling at a hand-held, freeze-frame, jump-cut New Wave venture; but one thing stops me short here: I know I cannot have that bedroom scene that goes with it.
—SATYAJIT RAY, *Our Films, Their Films*

References to the "lower middle class" are quite common in the English spoken in India. People routinely represent themselves as belonging to this social stratum, and others do so as well without offending the person labeled as such. To Western ears it may seem vaguely derogatory to refer to someone as lower middle class in the same way that to describe a person as petit-bourgeois always smacks more of the "petty" than the "bourgeois." But whether invoked as lower middle class or petit-bourgeois, the economic, social, and, to some extent, psychic anxieties of this class fragment are at the crux of any discussion of twentieth-century Indian cultural politics. And an understanding of the meaning of urban life, both public and private, depends on taking stock of the blockages of petit-bourgeois, lower-middle-class existence (whatever fantasies of enrichment and social mobility may circulate within the discourse of globalization).

It should be said that neither label—petit-bourgeois or lower middle class—accurately corresponds to the class disposition of the people it designates, especially in the context of India, where sociological categorizations are complicated by homegrown variables. The most one can say about the habitus of this group is that its structural ambiguity is often managed through a displacement of ever-present financial anxiety onto a concern about morals. The classic stereotype of "middle-class morality" can thus be explained in terms of the subjective need to keep objective dissolution at bay, although what then remains to be explored are the multiple dimensions of this social and psychological "crisis management."

Some of the most consequential Indian writing in the post-Independence

era has rendered the inseparability of such subjective and objective immis-
eration in fictional form—portraying the ways that economic uncertainty
is managed via a hypersensitivity to issues of propriety and its obverse,
impropriety. Caught up in lives suspended between poverty and respectability, the destiny of the Indian lower middle class provides a rich source
of material for representing the confusions and betrayals of modern social
relations. *Mahanagar* (The Big City, 1963) is a film that wades into this
terrain, exposing the tenuous existence of postwar lower-middle-class
subjects in Calcutta. It represents one of Satyajit Ray's most successful
efforts at giving cinematic form to a particular experiential predicament; I
will argue that in doing so, it also articulates a mode of political expression
appropriate to the times.

Unfolding how a moral sensibility associated with the formation of
petit-bourgeois social mores gets attached, simultaneously, to the meaning of being modern and to traditional ideals of duty and respectability,
Mahanagar is regarded as one of Ray's signature depictions of modernity
in its portrayal of life in the big city of Calcutta adduced by the film's title.[1]
My specific contention in this chapter is that although the film has largely
been interpreted in terms of its focus on women's issues—in particular, of
the contradictory effects of patriarchy and capitalism on women's lives—
Ray is more concerned with working out something like an immanent critique of the contradictions in society at large. To put this differently, one
might say that broader considerations are at stake for Ray than a purely
thematic treatment of female subjectivity. These have to do with investigating the total possibility of cinema, the extent to which its performance
involves not just technique, character, or setting but also audience and
material conditions of reception. Film is to this extent unique (at least until
the arrival of later visual technologies) in that, as a technological medium,
it is an art form that shows as much as it tells, encapsulates as much as it
represents. The multiple aspects constituting the "crisis" of capitalism as
such—of productive forces (the status of technology vs. art), life (social
relations under capitalism), and the crisis of representation itself (imitation vs. activation of reality)—are all effectively taken up in formal and
expressive terms.

Given their preoccupation with telling stories or, in the case of some
activist filmmakers, their commitment to raising political consciousness,
not all directors reflect on the special property of the filmic medium to
manifest the contradictions of its own nature. But in lingering over this
material dimension of the medium, while also heightening our awareness
of the impossibility of aesthetic autonomy, Ray demonstrates that he is in a

league of his own. To the extent that he is able to realize a politicized vision of aesthetics, he surpasses the achievements of his critically acclaimed contemporaries (such as Ritwik Ghatak in India or Glauber Rocha in Brazil). What he makes legible is the idea that aesthetic rather than agitational means are also effective persuasion. On these terms, *Mahanagar* is a paradigmatic example of Ray's contributions to a vocabulary of the cinema expressed in a self-conscious film language that at the same time expresses a specific political and cultural response to the universal predicament of reified existence.

To think along these lines is to accept that, within the broadest scheme of understanding, cinema refracts—whether reflexively or unwittingly— how things must be in all parts of the world that its own technological modernity has touched. So my ultimate goal in this chapter is to show how, far more than providing an accurate or "realistic" glimpse into lower-middle-class Indian life, *Mahanagar* presents us with an unparalleled visual critique of capitalist experience *tout court*. Ray evokes a local context and characters, to be sure, but his own text and medium also dialectically exhibit how the material bases of cinema provide the terms of engagement for a total critique of modern society. His greatest achievement in the film is to fold conceptual and representational ideas together, without romanticizing storytelling or brandishing any epistemological lessons about the necessary critical role of cinema, and so forth. I contend that Ray's directorial standpoint, taking as it does the route of an *understated* objection to existence under capitalism in general, represents the mode of aesthetic protest that Theodor Adorno considered best suited to the modern era. Insofar as critique, too, is determined by the conditions of reality it seeks to excoriate, Adorno argued there is no exoteric standpoint available from which to denounce the given world. And since capitalist modernity has made its mark globally, the question of a form of art adequate to its critique is as much a problem for conceptualizing postcolonial aesthetic practices (such as Ray's cinema) as it is for European or otherwise Western forms of critical expression.

To get closer to the subject of the film, Ray adapted his screenplay for *Mahanagar* from a story called "Abataranika" (by Narendranath Mitra). At a purely denotative level the noun *abataranika* is used in Bengali writing genres to designate a preface or an introduction.[2] In a literal sense, then, the novel presents the introduction of its heroine, Arati, into the world of the big city; but this introduction can also be seen to extend to modernity itself and to the ways that the modern world comes as something of a shock, an idea literalized in the opening moments of the film (as

I discuss later). In both short story and film the introduction shades into a lament for a form of life now lost. Quite apart from the literal, denotative meaning of *abataranika* (that most Bengali readers would associate with it), there is a further inflection to this word deriving from the Sanskrit verb *avatarana:* to descend. It connotes a woman who has climbed down from a higher sphere into a lower one, such as a heavenly maiden who, in the stuff of myth, descends to tempt mortals; or, in a very different sense, she conjures up a "good" woman lost to the demimonde. .An alternative meaning of *abataranika* consequently gives us the idea of a woman who has married beneath her social station.

That the source story describes the transformation of an unremarkable housewife into an ordinary worker suggests—in a preliminary gesture— that the subject matter relates not only to an introduction or preface but also to reversals of value persistently haunting women's existence, be it in reference to love, labor, or social standing. Neither an angel come to earth nor a fallen woman descended into depravity, the woman at the heart of the narration is simply one who leaves her private world and enters the public workplace, albeit she is tainted by this exposure. The film version pursues this problem of value further, gaining its complexity from the multiple levels at which the title's connotations are worked into the form and narrative. The ordinary difficulties of a traditional wife and daughter-in-law who must leave the security of the household and join the job force serve as the basis of Ray's exploration, although he departs from the conventional morality of his source story—which poses the dilemma of such a transition exclusively in terms of a *descent,* as if all forms of female labor outside the home hint at loss of propriety. In the original it is also the husband who is the focus of attention and around whom the narrative mostly revolves, so in a series of twists Ray redirects emphasis from the man of the household, in all his wounded and ineffectual masculinity, to the predicament of his wife, Arati.

If it is easy to see that in contrast to Mitra's male-centered narrative Ray's treatment valorizes the woman's point of view, a closer look at the film should also prompt one to guard against overly presentist readings of the idea of women's emancipation through gainful employment. Indeed, the film invites viewers to recognize that patriarchal notions about the proper place of women, on the one hand, and liberal notions of self-consolidation in the earning of wages, on the other, are twinned ideologies. If, that is, we can acknowledge that learning to labor outside the home has not produced the freedoms promised to women in modernity, it follows that middle-class feminism's solutions (exemplified, for instance, by the solicitation to become "working women") are a problem *within* capitalist social relations rather than a redoubt against them.[3] The proposition that a woman's entry into the workforce represents a descent into constraint and not an ascent into autonomy thus continues to serve as the nub of a problem that Ray adapts from the original short story—complicating rather than rejecting its terms. As a result the film's metalanguage establishes a point of view that is substantially different from the source story, shifting the locus of value from considerations of personal propriety that occupied Mitra to the intractabilities of social belonging as such.[4]

As in many of Ray's other works, *Mahanagar*'s resolution (to the degree that it has one) is neither conservative nor formulaic but ambiguous—mirroring, as it were, the sociological ambiguities he seeks to represent. Indeed, we may say that the film's entire motivation is to reveal the impossibility of effecting an aesthetic settlement of social problems and to reflect on the paradoxes inherent in their artistic reconciliation. The domestic arena, from which Arati emerges as she goes from her tattered household into the scrappier life of a door-to-door saleswoman, is filled with generational conflict, not to mention hidebound notions regarding the proper place of women.[5] Nonetheless, the *gharoa* (household) domain is one in which she is in place—like all the other props Ray goes to great effort to arrange in the mise-en-scène.[6] It is a world over which she rules, though its threadbare setting conveys that the conventional securities of this life, as well as the sensibilities that pertain to it, are no longer possible to sustain when economic insecurity is just around the corner. In tightly woven scenes of mostly unspoken nuance Ray borrows but also alters the emphases of his source material to show why a comfortingly liberal view of women's independence must be dialecticized in order to reveal its inner contradictions.

The narrative persistently advances the idea that every sphere of modern capitalist life, even the life of a woman who, as here, appears to have improved her lot by finding work, must finally be seen as a degeneration of life itself: a move downward. To be more specific, we might note that the heroine's fate represents a downfall in the sense that, despite overcoming patriarchal resistance and making some personal gains, she is no less a loser than other women who have been forced to descend in life because of circumstances. Removed from her zone of familial relationships, however troubled, Arati must encounter the moral bankruptcy of office politics, as well as negotiate the concrete difficulties of being a worker and a housewife; her predicament symbolizes both the public and private difficulties of existence in an exploitative society ruled by divisions at home and abroad.

The implication of this point extends beyond the narrative's confined and even confining vision. It conveys the larger idea that ideals such as autonomy, independence, freedom, self-consciousness, and so on are all valuably modern and part of the uneven legacy of historical emergence; but their value must ultimately be placed alongside the recognition that they come with a price, especially in an existential regime defined by the calculation of means and ends. There is, in other words, no straight line from myth to enlightenment, oppression to freedom, tradition to modernity.

By lending form to such intractable conceptual oppositions (a common motif in modernist thought), *Mahanagar* attests to a dialectical tension that, as is true of Ray's cinema generally, expresses his awareness that historical contradictions rarely admit to easy resolution. In his hands complicated issues are always rendered delicately, not in the clichéd sense of emphasizing the ambivalence of concepts such as tradition and modernity but in his detailed capturing of social relations in their quotidian complexity, as well as their structural limits. Accordingly, in this particular example he depicts women's emancipation as a mixed blessing—at least when it comes to the destiny of Indian womanhood. As the film elaborates in exquisite detail, it delivers some rewards but exacts a heavy toll on kinship and other social structures that define what makes a woman happy (to echo a question raised in the first chapter in discussing *Ghare Baire*).[7]

An important aspect of the critical possibilities opened up by the film rests on establishing that if the bourgeoisie clings to its stale worldview and the working class struggles to overcome it, the fate of those in between is more difficult, though banal. They are doomed to shuttle between the few comforts that reside in the values of familial love, responsibility, self-respect, or solvency and the futility of trying to hold on to any values at all. Unlike the working class, whose revolutionary role has, at least in theory, been predicated on having nothing to lose but its shackles, the lower middle class has but one thing to lose, albeit of incalculable value: respectability (not to be confused with the *arriviste* propriety bought by newly enriched classes). The fine line separating the "middle" from the abjectly "low" that gives the lower middle class its specificity delineates the morbidity of class society in India—morbid because it hides and reveals the self-negation that lurks beneath respectability, in turn making it impossible to hold on to any ideal of selfhood not anchored in money. To drive this lesson home as Ray does in *Mahanagar* is, I would argue, as close as it gets to a cinema of protest for contemporary times, one that can neither afford to take refuge in rousing testimonials about revolution and the working class's putative role in it nor celebrate modernity with its alleged benefits, including that of women's liberation. The habitat of the ordinary and the unheroic, the big city is a very small place for those squeezed into stuffy social spaces and even more cramped economic quarters.

As I mentioned earlier, this is exemplary of the position Adorno held on the question of political art. If there is no uncontaminated space from which to protest against the injustices of class society, then the only option left to art is an immanent criticism that fully presupposes its own reified mode of production and insertion into an unjust system. In fact, Adorno argues that to hold out for the possibility of making radical aesthetic statements that can escape their own conditions of existence is to fall prey to reactionary thinking. Along these lines he suggests: "even critical art has to surrender itself to that which it opposes." Expressing an outlook also shared by Ray, the corollary here is that critical art cannot assume that its topics or concerns are given in advance—for example, a film about revolution is not revolutionary by definition any more than a film about the bourgeoisie or petit-bourgeoisie is bourgeois—or that an exposé of the evils of society somehow ameliorates those evils. What is at stake in the idea of critical art is the rejection of given society together with the established forms of narration. Its ideal is thus to destroy the illusion of the legitimacy of artistic statements, as well as the social conditions that necessitate them. By this light neither the content nor form of art can provide the sole basis of critique since they only partially illuminate the extent to which aesthetic experience and artworks together enact the antagonisms of social existence.

If the idea of philosophical negation informing Adorno's dialectics is difficult to grasp, its concrete instantiation in a film like *Mahanagar* allows one to derive the underlying lesson: namely, that it is not possible to offer a perfect critique of imperfect life. Shared by Ray and Adorno alike, this outlook—which I take to be at some distance from mere nihilism—is at pains to insist that all critical statements issued under the sign of capitalism must reckon with the extent to which they mirror the form of the reality they refute. Otherwise, they risk lapsing into idealism or fantasy.[8]

DYSTOPIC REVISIONS

For readers unfamiliar with the film this may be the place to sketch the broad outlines of its plot. Set in Calcutta circa the mid-1950s, the film depicts a lower-middle-class family struggling to make ends meet. As would be true of extended family arrangements in India, the household consists of a husband and father, Subrata Mazumdar, a bank employee; his wife, Arati; their child, Pintu; Subrata's unmarried sister, Bani; and two aging parents—one of whom, his father, is a retired schoolteacher. Chafing under the constraints of an inadequate income, Subrata and Arati realize that she must get a job. Against the wishes of her in-laws and with the reluctant consent of her husband, Arati goes out into the world—selling electric sewing machines to the privileged housewives of Calcutta. It is a job at which she is unexpectedly successful, and, in addition to providing the family with extra resources, her employed status also gives her a new sense of confidence. Arati's independence, however, causes resentment at home, and some of the film's most powerful scenes capture the growing alienation between Arati and Subrata, as well as her in-laws' disapproval of her changed role. Before she can quit working in order to restore familial harmony, Subrata loses his job at the bank, and now the household is forced to rely entirely on her income. But her workplace, too, presents difficulties—involving Arati's friendship with her Anglo-Indian colleague, Edith, and the boss's abusive treatment of the latter. In the end Arati tenders her resignation letter to Mr. Mukherjee, the boss, whose smug manner and veiled threats make her recognize that the moral compromises he wants to extract from her are too much to make. As Arati is joined in solidarity with Edith and reconciled with her husband, the film closes on the prospect that some unspecified solution may be out there for everyone in the big city, though it resolutely defies saying more.

Should one speculate as to why—or even whether—Ray, who professed to have learned part of his craft by viewing European films, including German Expressionist cinema, chose to draw a parallel between his presentation of city life in the Third World and Fritz Lang's 1927 classic about a city of the future in a vaguely Euro-American locale? Although the word *mahanagar* translates equally as "big city" or "metropolis," it may seem to many viewers that there is nothing to link *Mahanagar* and *Metropolis* aside from this nominal similarity. On their terms it would surely be unexpected, if not unwarranted, to posit a more substantive connection. But the intertextual reference embedded in the English title Ray chose for his film (and I think it is key that he discarded the original "Abataranika" while retaining Mitra's larger meaning) is, for those interested in the shared commitments of twentieth-century cinematic internationalism, hard to overlook. *Metropolis*, Lang's Weimar-era science fiction representation, showed the parasitic nature of modern class society with its division of labor between "thinkers" and "workers."[9] As we know from the history of that tumultuous period, much of Weimar culture was uniquely geared toward exposing the hypocritical reversal of value underwriting capital-

FIGURE 18.   Daily life
in the big city. Used by
permission from Satyajit
Ray Film and Study
Center.

ism in which real, productive work is denigrated in relation to the alleged
superiority of intellectual labor. Short-lived though it was, the critique of
capitalism—with all its false conceptions—advanced by Weimar thought
in general, and Lang's film in particular, is allusively echoed in Ray's later
depiction of metropolitan vicissitudes.

In Ray's treatment, however, the big city is no longer a city of the
future—Lang's sci-fi rendition with its highly stylized mise-en-scène
(which included gigantic, architecturally detailed sets displaying a corporate city-state in 2027, accompanied by technological gadgetry, robotic
costumes, and so forth). By contrast, Ray gives us the miniaturized and
crowded inner-city space of mid-twentieth-century Calcutta (Figure 18).
This is the world of Arati and her husband, Subrata, in their straitened
daily existence. The stylistic differences between Lang and Ray notwithstanding, there are similarities that go beyond the fact that both films
are set in a metropolis, even if one looks shiny and futuristic, the other
grimy and decaying: the very relic, one might add, of the "black hole"!
Each film represents city-space as the theater wherein the urban drama of
the struggle between rich and poor, exploiters and exploited is played out.
Moreover, each provides the ground against which a certain salvational
narrative is enacted although, crucially, there is no definitive redemption
in *Mahanagar*, only an irresolute ending in which hope for a better future
is held out (but not delivered).

If *Metropolis* articulates an image of the ultimate victory of workers
both over machines and their makers, *Mahanagar* turns out to be a darker
portrayal of life in which neither technology nor humans can do more
than reinforce the daily grind. One might suggest that Ray's film serves,
almost literally, as a counterfoil to Lang's (if we refer *counterfoil* to its

etymological meaning of a record or imprint of events past). Mirroring each other's political concern with the fate of ordinary people in a corporate world and, consequently, the future of humanity, the *Mahanagar/Metropolis* couplet strikes many of the same notes about class struggle; the axis of action in both films is similarly located around the figure of a woman. But the later work does not—and cannot—reproduce the hopeful resolution of its predecessor. Read in this manner, Ray's film serves as a quotation of and a comment on the impossibility of the vision expressed by its counterpart. Indeed, the open-ended potentiality of the future evoked in *Metropolis* is resolved in the later film, albeit not in the direction of a pretty picture, still less a spectacular one. With his incomparable awareness of time and location, Ray understood that Lang's masterpiece was shaped as much by the punctual moment of Weimar, when political transformation of all sorts seemed on the horizon, as by its grand experimental impulse involving the use of architecturally complex sets, dazzling visual effects, elaborate costume design, futuristic storyline, and so on. By contrast, *Mahanagar*, in its deliberately stripped-down style, conveys its own impoverished cultural predicament and the altogether differing modalities of then and now.

As with Lang, Ray, too, represents the lives of urban workers and the fragility of petit-bourgeois existence teetering on the brink of both revolutionary and reactionary disruption. But the promise of the interwar moment Lang inhabited has in the intervening years been dashed, so history's failure to realize the transformative openings of the past marks Ray's reflexive portrait of contemporary conditions of metropolitan life. A critical perspective such as this demands that the narrative deliver something other than the formula of bourgeois storytelling, with its imperative to settle irresolvable problems of history through the device of the happy ending. Accordingly, Ray's "solution" to the crisis of everyday working life is more complicated, if more irresolute, than Lang's. Those acquainted with the film would perhaps agree that *Mahanagar* ends on an upbeat note to the extent that it portrays Arati and her husband, Subrata, walking hand-in-hand, their personal reconciliation affected amidst a mutual recognition of shared priorities. The city streets, revealed in long shot, envelop them in an anonymous embrace, betokening a friendly rather than hostile environment. In a Chaplinesque move (recalling the ending of *Modern Times* where the tramp and his lady skip off into the horizon, bound by love but with nothing else to their name) Ray conveys Arati's and Subrata's regained sense of togetherness; enfolded by the crowd, they are city-dwellers who blend in with countless others. Nonetheless, it would be a stretch to say that the film closes on a happy ending in any conventional sense, because both hero and heroine are jobless, their futures have been rendered even more uncertain, and their families are now bereft of the few material supports they had before.

The ending of the film thus magnifies the contradiction between personal happiness and economic security for ordinary denizens of any modern metropolis, be it Calcutta or New York (the city that inspired Lang's imagination). In his reflexive bid to comment on the modern urban audience's existential circumstances, as well as the narrative fate of his characters, Ray transmits an idea that Sigmund Freud made familiar, namely, that civilization's "substitute gratifications" remain only that: sublimations of the pleasure principle. Neither art (on the screen) nor love (within it) can reconcile the fundamental negation of life (outside it). In Freud, of course, "real happiness" is never more than a constitutively unattainable desire; it is itself a "narrative" rather than reality. In Ray's worldview, by contrast, the possibility and impossibility of happiness, while presented as narrative contingencies, are nonetheless held out as concretely realizable. His implication is not that we can never achieve happiness; it is rather that we need a better world in which to seek it. In this dialectical working out of the future through a negation of the present, Ray offers us a vision of personal and social fulfillment discerned in the very dregs of their current impossibility.

As in other cases, the horizon of Ray's thinking here is utopian whereas, we would have to say, Freud's is not—seeing as he would consider the idea of utopia as a dimension of wish-fulfillment. The difference, if it can be put this way, has to do with differing tendencies within modernist thought itself, embodied in the positions that Ray, Lang, and Freud each exemplify across the varied trajectory of modernism. But it is a difference in degree rather than kind. Staying with the comparison between Ray and Lang, let me suggest that if in Lang's portrayal the mediating role of the woman is the key to resolving the standoff between workers and exploiters, Ray's version offers no such romantic solution to this irreconcilable aspect of social existence. What *Metropolis* reveals is that despite Lang's avant-garde and modernist investment in portraying the world as disenchanted, romantic love is nonetheless depicted as successful in reenchanting it through the redeeming figure of Maria. As a counterpoint to her redemptive figure, Ray's Arati reinforces the antinomies governing modern life. Although circumstances enable her to gain some measure of financial independence, she is depicted as helpless in the face of structural constraints—no more able to overcome strife at home than she is to effect a transformation in her boss's ugly attitude at work.

Caught betwixt her responsibilities in the patriarchal household, her changing role in the office, and obligations to her friend Edith, whom the boss wrongly accuses of lax morals and laziness on account of her being an Anglo-Indian (the product of miscegenation), Arati's role is to mediate between the given world and an as-yet-unrealized future in which traditional prejudices, as well as postcolonial resentments, have been equally eliminated. Importantly, what is materially unrealizable is not salvaged or recuperated by the narrative, nor does the woman at its center rise to triumph over her situation. Both Arati's character and that of the other principals are shown enriched by their personal experiences over the course of the film's unfolding, but this depiction serves to mark the fundamental impasse between life and love rather than to intimate a false reconciliation of the objective universe. In the very refusal to paper over social impossibilities, Ray's cinematic vision holds out hope that they may be transcended in reality. As I think is clear, there is a distinct but subtle utopianism to this impulse and it is worth contrasting it with Lang's less-refined, albeit more celebrated, presentation of similar issues.

AESTHETICS OF DAMAGED LIFE

My reading of Ray's conception in *Mahanagar* of what, to borrow another idea from Adorno, might be called "damaged life," would not have found favor with critics who commented on the film on its first release.[10] This is especially true in the West, although it applies just as much to the reception in India, where Ray had to brook the usual flurry of protests and efforts to censor it. Pauline Kael, to take perhaps the most well-known and knowledgeable transatlantic reviewer, offered the following judgment: "The film does what it sets out to do, and it's perceptive and revealing; it stays with one. Yet it is very quiet and rather thin; it lacks the depth and richness and creative imagery of the best of Satyajit Ray."[11] "Rather thin," and lacking in "depth and richness and creative imagery . . . " One could of course point out that the absence of these attributes is also what separates—and distinguishes—Ray's scaled-down treatment from Lang's expressionist extravaganza (with its expensive models and spectacular imagery that have since defined the production values and "look" of every worthy science-fiction film—from its precursors in Méliès's shorts to subsequent "architectural" films such as *Blade Runner* [Scott, 1982] and *Brazil* [Gilliam, 1985] and, more contemporaneously, *The Matrix* trilogy

[Wachowski Brothers, 1999, 2003] or *Minority Report* [Spielberg, 2002]). So I should like to turn to the criticism of lack of depth in order to establish how it is precisely this "lack" that makes *Mahanagar* a superb cinematic statement pertaining to a regime of values simply irreducible to the logic of the spectacle Lang ushered in but that also thoroughly infuses contemporary critical judgments.

To that end let us consider the following question: what style is appropriate to a textual elaboration of "Third-World" existence? If the answer resides in something like realism (à la Lukács)—having to do with whether a text adequately corresponds to or reflects the realities of life in the global South—such correspondence, we would surely have to acknowledge, is not just a matter of content. To the contrary, it has as much to do with the total conditions of possibility of cinema, be that understood in purely monetary terms (for example, the budget for making a film) or with respect to the texture of the reality captured on celluloid, or the intentions of the director toward the audience. By this light it is hardly remarkable that Lang's early classic cost seven million Reichsmark (equivalent to about $200 million in 2005) to produce. Instead, the point is that Ray's version could not only *not* approach even one-tenth of this expense, but it *needed not to do so* in order for him to be faithful to the subject matter while experimenting with a formal aesthetic that avoided false embellishment of an impoverished reality. It is not just that Ray eschewed a big-budget film in favor of a restrained mode of enunciation pared down to the essentials; his choice also bespeaks a commitment to the kind of cinema that *materializes* the straitened circumstances of its production: a cinema of "lucidity" as well as "simplicity"—notions that must be understood as mutually given (Figure 19).

Viewed from this angle, *Mahanagar* begins to approach what Roland Barthes called "zero degree writing" *(le degré zéro de l'écriture)*: the attempt to make meaning visible through the simplicity of form and, hence, devoid of sentimental expectations. Such writing or language, in the broadest sense, is stripped of the pretense at representing something outside itself. Instead, it expresses its own impoverishment in the face of a degraded world and is thus subsumed into—and as—the "zero degree" of representation.[12] That is to say, this mode of writing concentrates less on a preexistent reality it serves only to dramatize than on the instructive possibilities of "colorlessness." Its emphasis is on what can be conveyed without adornment and without false innocence about the instrumental realities of our age. Accordingly, the very instruments of inscription—in the case of cinematic writing, aspects such as camera movement, editing, and mise-en-scène—become the "object" of the real rather than the mere

FIGURE 19.   Growing tensions between Arati and Subrata. Used by permission from Satyajit Ray Film and Study Center.

means to tell a story (which, in any case, revolves around a fairly predictable set of familial and workplace conflicts in *Mahanagar*) From this perspective, what Kael regarded as a less-than-rich film is in fact deliberately so. Ray uses the medium to impart a critique of the demand for filmic "depth" and "richness," demands that are constitutively impossible to meet or resolvable only in the terms of conventional cinema, either Hollywood or Bollywood, where a facile creativity combined with sensationalism is delivered ad infinitum.

But let us set aside for a moment the idea that Ray was preoccupied with anything so abstract as the essence of cinematic language as proposed by the likes of Barthes. It still palpably remains the case that his attention in *Mahanagar* is riveted on how to communicate the bareness of a form of social existence without caving in to conventional expectations—how, that is, one might capture the paradoxical richness of poor lives without sentimentalizing or stylizing them. And this concern is reflected in the apparent thinness of the film's form, underscoring the idea that richness and creativity lie not in *what* the film offers (as though it could construct a self-contained reality outside the actual grittiness of the real) but in *how* audiences are pressed to recognize the determining effect of external realities on what is shown or seen. In *Our Films, Their Films* Ray's own remarks along these lines are quite suggestive for taking account of his goals in *Mahanagar*. Writing in "The Odds against Us," for example, he brings up the peculiarities of being an Indian filmmaker beset with problems of money, casting, audience expectation, and the politics of censorship, all of which lead, he says, to his choice of "the field of intimate cinema: the cinema of mood and atmosphere rather than of grandeur and spectacle."[13]

While Ray writes of his directorial predicament in a manner that is certainly very different from a literary theorist like Barthes, the substance of his observations goes equally to the heart of my contentions about the necessity of thinking about cinema differently.[14] Not only does he refer to concrete constraints on his filmmaking as the particular "odds" he faced as a Third World director, but he also presents them as defining what can be said cinematically, given prevailing social and material exigencies. At the end of the essay in question he remarks on the specific risks of filmmaking in Calcutta, providing a brief glimpse into the grimy reality of his surroundings, which, I might add, could well represent the "zero degree" of life beyond fictionalization—stripped as it is of even the most basic niceties:

> The studios in Calcutta show their hallowed past in every crevice on the wall, in every tatter on the canvas that covers the ceiling. Some of the families of rodents that inhabit the rafters have lived there ever since the foundation of the industry. The floor is pitted, the camera groans as it turns, the voltage begins to drop after sundown. The general air of shabbiness is unnerving. And yet I do not mind these at all. I do not think of these as hindrances. After all, we have the essentials to make a film, and it is within us to make it badly or well. It is the bareness of means that forces us to be economical and inventive, and prevents us from turning craftsmanship into an end in itself. And there is something about creating beauty in the circumstances of shoddiness and privation that is truly exciting.
>
> Yes, I am happy to be working where I am.[15]

Quite apart from their poignancy, these observations attest to Ray's conceptual preoccupation with existential concerns as they are interwoven with his general thoughts about Third World filmmaking. In the present context they also make it possible to respond to the criticism about the putative depthlessness of imagery in *Mahanagar*. We can connect an idea raised earlier about the bareness of the form of social existence portrayed in this film with the "bareness of means" Ray speaks of in the lines above.

"Bareness" is not just a material obstacle presented by the conditions of production in a place like Calcutta; it becomes the *problematic*—that is, the sociohistorical objectivity guiding both what can be said and how to say it. Eschewing "craftsmanship [as] an end in itself," Ray thus provides an implicit riposte to the notion that *Mahanagar* lacks something his other films do not—namely, depth and richness. Whatever can be said about the other works—and there is indeed a great deal—the point here is that the viewer (or reviewer) who finds the film wanting in terms of "creative imagery" has missed Ray's highly reflexive critique of the universal impoverishment of modern life. The point, therefore, is that qualities such as richness, creativity, or depth have been rendered constitutively unavailable, and this is not just a problem of cinematic representation. On such a reading, "Calcutta"—which serves as a *mise-en-abŷme* for the degradation of life under capitalism that everywhere reinforces the schism between rich and poor—represents not just a setting for Ray's story but the crucible of all that can be said no less than experienced.

Just how the myriad conceptual stakes I have broached are captured by Ray's deployment of the cinematic image need now to be addressed. The early moments of *Mahanagar*, beginning with the title sequence, usefully set up many of the terms of his experiment in cinematic truth-telling. Such a project should, however, be distinguished from a positivist notion of factual truth in that this project centers on activating, through technological and phenomenological means, the reality of which it is itself a part, while the latter merely presents reality as positively or objectively "out there" and therefore external to the production of truth. By this token an immanent view of truth-as-activation would take it that in a film scene depicting the fluttering of leaves on a tree, a certain "camera-reality" (as Kracauer designates this), which is not just a matter of subjective creation or interpretation, concretely pressures that which can be said. From the perspective of a material aesthetics, the "truth" of such a scene depends on paying proper due to subjective and interpretive aspects, as well as to the material reality of the leaves and the tree that have left behind their imprint on celluloid. So, although not everything can be reduced to fact, it is equally the case that not everything is the result of signification—since the tree, the leaves, and the entire cinematic apparatus also mark their extradiscursive presence on the scene's meaning.

Mahanagar, shot in black-and-white, opens with a series of frames that are constructed to cast doubt on the very idea of facticity—in the way that the viewer's disorientation is deliberately elicited by the lack of establishing shots that would stabilize the meaning of what is seen. One has to *make* sense of the shots rather than be handed a frame of reference (contrary to the function of most opening scenes). The first three minutes constituting the duration of the original title sequence (the English equivalents were inserted later when the film was readied for international exhibition) are entirely taken up with medium shots of a moving pole that resolves itself into the cable of a tramcar only when the credit sequence ends and a shot transition into the tram's interior reveals Subrata, the main male character, on his commute home from work. At one level the minimalism of the shots combined with the sustained focus on a relatively undistinguished (and indistinguishable) object in the frame jar the viewer from his or her preconceived expectations about introductory material and the establishment of settings in narrative cinema; at a more abstract level, the uncertainty of all viewing experience, subject as it is to the limitations of vision itself, is also underscored by the jerkiness of a handheld camera.

Ray's use of a technique associated with cinema verité to set up a narrative film draws attention to his "documentary" intentions while simultaneously remarking on the unreliability of our experience of the really real.[16] The strobe effect of shots that zigzag into view capture the unsteady movement of the tram as it makes its way along city streets for which no coordinates are given, and all street signs are blurry in the background. Deprived of any spatial perspective by frames that are mostly blank, crisscrossed only by the grid of the tram cable, the viewer's disorientation is doubled in terms of what he or she sees, as well as how it is shown. The staccato quality of *Mahanagar*'s opening shots underlines the material precondition of all cinematic intelligibility, documentary or otherwise, in the sense that it reinforces awareness of the physical aspects of perception; how the human eye must be trained in order to make sense of what it sees is exposed with reference to the eye of the camera. What is more, this is done without any obvious breach of the cinematic illusion (differentiating the opening of *Mahanagar* from, say, a film by Jean-Luc Godard).

Through this self-referential gesture toward the camera eye Ray underscores the highly etiolated nature of the medium of film. For cinema not only depends on the prosthesis of the camera to encode a supposedly natural reality, but film's capacity to convey any meaning in the first place is also delimited by technology in the last instance of decoding or reception. So although it makes little sense to talk about spectatorship without acknowledging that all reception is predicated on the objectivity of the camera and what it does, this fact itself belies the necessity of another technological prerequisite that is equally essential to the subjective act of viewing: the artifice of projection, the device that allows the human eye to perceive a "motion picture" rather than a succession of still images. Even if most casual viewers would not stop to think about such conceptual implications behind the film's credit sequence, it remains the case that the most sensitive film directors—such as Ray—continually remind us that the discussion of what constitutes "radicalism" in art cannot proceed very far if conducted on the terms of a form/content dichotomy. The deliberate spasmodic movements of the camera in *Mahanagar*'s opening shots reverse the effect that projection at twenty-four frames per second would render seamless, reintroducing viewers to material contingencies of viewing itself, rather than to issues of form or content per se. In this way a counterpoint to the narrative is ushered in at the very beginning, one that takes the form of inducing the audience to reflect on the continuity of apparatus, viewing subject, and critique.

Our experience of the aesthetic goes beyond the artwork. This statement may appear to be a truism but its consequences are far from obvious, particularly when they bear on the slipperiness of perceptual truth and falsity. Ray's strategy in *Mahanagar* is to foreground such issues in order to establish how the problem of perception is both the subject and object of his experiment (far more than the story or situation). Our expectations, once we enter the diegetic world of the film proper, are equally subject to contravention and redefinition. But this is less a demonstration of directorial virtuosity for its own sake than a dialectical investigation of how apperception informs understanding. Subtly introducing elements of contradiction that lead out of the narrative and into the field of intelligibility, Ray conveys his insistence on the negative, on that which cannot be articulated through standard representational means because its force lies in its contrariness. Since the negative is marked by its recalcitrance to being "read off" the surface of a text either as trace or supplement (terms that belong to a different lexicon of deconstructive analysis), it must be drawn out of our material and physiological experience of the text—distilled, as it were, from all the experiential contingencies that otherwise pass by unnoticed and unrecognized in our habits of seeing.

The underlying proposition here is that the act of viewing, as part of the dialectic of art and reality, can serve as the site of a different kind of labor and engagement made present to us by cognition—in this case, thinking about what is seen and heard onscreen. And although he does not resort to gimmicks or postproduction tricks, Ray's recursive exploitation of both stylistic and narrative techniques rewards the viewer's active attention, worked out as it is within the schema of what his storytelling choices and the apparatus make possible (as opposed to the result of blindsiding the viewer with ideas or conclusions that have not been motivated through cinematic means). In other words, not only are there no surprises in a Ray film, but his deliberate, restrained shot-making is like a carefully put together puzzle or a classic ratiocinative novel that depends on critical deduction as opposed to mere contemplation.[17] Ray invites the viewer to think of spectatorship as an active dimension of the cinematic process; one is in this way exhorted to use one's cognitive skills despite being locked in a regime that demands only passivity. By baring the medium (as in the title sequence), as well as through carefully constructed narrative clues, Ray directs the canny viewer to a much broader perspective on the present, moving from intricate and highly particularized details to universal considerations of language, meaning, and history.

Many of these concerns are embedded in the scene immediately following Subrata's return home in the opening sequence. They exemplify Ray's mastery at capturing lived contradictions with a light touch. As I have mentioned, the film begins by imputing the place of technology in the crowded urban space of Calcutta, the strobing shots of the tram cable echoing the shocks in the rhythm of a daily life now seen to be transformed by modern appurtenances: mass transportation, corporate enterprise, banking, and so on. But if the place of an alien and alienating technology is marked only through the discomfort of the commuters, including Subrata, who are crammed into the streetcar, other aspects of the transformation wrought by modernity are also signified, if only fleetingly. For it is another truism to state that the most thoroughgoing changes in life occur unnoticed; indeed, to notice them would be to recall their artificiality, their out-of-place-ness within the scheme of things. The challenge that Ray sets for himself is to find a way to depict these profound though infinitesimal changes without overemphasizing them and, at the same time, remaining true to their significance.

One solution to the dilemma is embodied in the dialogue that, in the short scene after Subrata returns home (spanning about three minutes), introduces the audience to the primary cast of characters as they make do in their humble quarters. The scene typifies the living conditions of down-at-heel folk with tightly framed shots revealing small rooms separated by drab, thin curtains, and stuffed with cheap furnishings, plaster peeling from walls adorned by dirty photo frames, pointing as well to a repeated motif in many of Ray's films: the reflexive presence of visual imagery, especially photographs, to indicate the complete saturation of modern experience by technologies of vision. Subrata enters this scene and in the short exchanges he has with his father (shown poring over his crossword

FIGURE 20. Arati, Subrata, and Bani at home. Used by permission from Satyajit Ray Film and Study Center.

puzzle with his well-worn dictionary), son, sister, and wife, the dialogue betrays the curious hold of an alien presence, that of the English language, on traditional subjects desperate to cling to their ideals of cultural propriety and identity (Figure 20). But the dialogue reveals that it is too late to do so: two hundred years of British rule have rendered such resistance empty, the notion of remaining untouched by the effects of a colonial modernity made impossible even at the level of linguistic utterance.

In this scene, as well as many others, what is solicited from the audience is an awareness of historical transformations unavailable to the characters themselves. Thus, in the early context of bemoaning the change in his son Subrata (referred to by his nickname, Bhambal), the retired schoolteacher cannot help using the English word *change* at the very moment that he tries to ward off his submission to the changes being forced upon his own small world. In addition, *domestic science, pen, nursing, prestige, neglect, earning member, gossip, consider*—all key terms in the dialogue, especially given the plot's overall thematization of shifts in gender, work, propriety, and self-perception—are uttered in English by the various characters who move in and out of frame. Alien words and ideas are revealed as normalized, worked into the cadences of Bengali itself. In this fashion Ray, whose refined sensitivity toward both English and Bengali is well known, draws attention to the limits of aesthetic utterance by remarking on its linguistic counterparts; if any account of aesthetic modernism dictates contending with the permeability of its boundaries, it is equally true that language itself, particularly in the postcolonial context, has not remained impervious to outside influences in general, something that is all the more evident in the marks that the colonial experience has left on spoken Bengali.

The fate of the older generation is perhaps the most poignant emblem of the destabilizing effects of modernity and its relationship to language. With extreme sensitivity Ray captures the melancholy predicament of subjects who have been left behind in the new dispensation and must scramble to make sense of it. The early vignette of Subrata's father (whose "hobby" is to borrow what little money he can to enter crossword puzzle competitions in English) conveys his uselessness within a mode of life that passes him by at every turn while his struggle with the language betokens his loss of mastery in a world he no longer comprehends. Even with help from his trusted dictionary, he misses out on the prize money by entering the word *wife* instead of *life* in his entry, a telling mistake in the context of a narrative of the upheavals caused by the changing role of women in society.

Through the intricate, even humorous, interplay of English and Bengali in the dialogue, Ray comments on the destiny of the mother tongue, as well as the constitutive inability of everyone—both character and audience—to *be*, let alone speak, without recourse to English. Implicating his primary audience of urbanized Calcuttans (who would recognize themselves as guilty of speaking a patois Bengali), Ray urges us to comprehend that we are all translated beings, so to speak, and the contradiction this imposes on perceiving the world on inherited terms of understanding is a prime target of his cinematic elaboration. At stake is the semantic charge of a language and a worldview contaminated by the colonizer's imposition of foreign mores, ideas, and values, and yet thoroughly internalized by native subjects—who, paradoxically, still see themselves as inhabiting a completely distinct lifeworld that is in their minds authentic and traditional. In a later moment in the film Arati is shown hesitating over her application for the job she ultimately gets. Helping her to decide how to sign her married name, "Mazumdar," with a *j* or a *z* (both spellings were popularized by the British for administrative purposes), Subrata chides her for being unsure about such a basic matter: "Amaar nam?" she asks ("my name?") in response to which he scoffs, "Ta na holey ki Lady Mountbatten?" ("If not yours then should it be Lady Mountbatten's?"). Only a name uttered and a hesitation about proper conduct voiced, but an entire history of imperialism is condensed into this invocation of India's last viceregal presence. An entire panoply of experiential questions is similarly intimated by Ray's depiction of Arati's uncertainty at confronting the alien world of English and bureaucracy into which she is thrust by having to find work.

In another key scene near the end of the film Arati goes to Edith's apartment to hand over the money owed to her as commission for successful

FIGURE 21. Unlikely comrades: Arati and Edith. Used by permission from Satyajit Ray Film and Study Center.

sales. Edith has been sick for a few days, and the boss at the office intimates that she is simply malingering, as Anglo-Indians tend to do, in his view. The character of Edith, subordinate though it is, represents one of Ray's most effective attempts at depicting, in quickly drawn strokes, a charming and insouciant woman who, moreover, has also been positioned by history as an "abataranika" or degraded woman on account of her birth. Arati arrives to find Edith listening to a phonograph record, idly turning the pages of a magazine. She is in her robe, her state of deshabille discordant with Arati's conventional sari-clad form. The scene unfolds with a brilliant exchange of dialogue in which Edith describes her illness in English, and Arati responds to her in Bengali. They move from there to discuss work-related matters, all the while speaking in the distinct tongues of English and Bengali. Neither can speak the other's language, but they understand each other perfectly—both as fellow-workers and women (unlike Arati's father-in-law, who is often stumped by his crossword puzzles and the shadings of meaning in English) (Figure 21).

But even this scene of friendly intimacy points to the barriers to genuine exchange in a world where literal comprehension is less the issue than disparate worldviews and political or social differences. Arati and Edith are, however, personally simpatico, and their affinity is conveyed as much by the seamless dialogue as by Edith's simple gesture of gifting her sunglasses to Arati, saying, "You need them," when Arati resists donning such a fashionable accessory for fear that she will be seen by her family as too "forward" and Anglicized. Ray's key achievement in the scene is to have communicated the dialogic openness of their relationship with seemingly little effort. As the camera tracks across Edith's (and her mother's) dingy little apartment, it catches the fading plaster on the walls, on which

FIGURE 22.
Confronting the boss,
Mr. Mukherjee. Used by
permission from Satyajit
Ray Film and Study
Center.

are pasted torn posters of English and American film stars of yesteryear: Cary Grant and Montgomery Clift. The scene suggests that, if nothing else, the world of cinema brings everyone together only to reinforce their separation in the world of wages and work. I hope to have communicated some of the extent to which *Mahanagar* comes close to a total work of art, though not in the Wagnerian sense of closing off the real world from it.[18] Dialogue, shot composition, props, music, and lighting all function as highly precise means for conveying not just an individual story or a particular mood but a whole history of possibility and inevitability. By these means Ray advances a different program of understanding about cinematic richness in an impoverished world, as well as a protocol for thinking about the image as a dialectical expression. To look at the film in this way (and at cinema in general along these lines) is necessary in order to get beyond tepid discussions of what makes for "realistic," "satisfying," or "accurate" portrayals and into the distinct domain of thinking about aesthetic experience as an aspect of reality itself and, hence, as a trigger for its potential transformation (Figure 22).

In an era in which a postmodern sensibility of exhaustion prevails among both artists and critics, it has become fashionable if not necessary to regard any talk of political or aesthetic protest and transformation as outdated, now rendered beyond the conceptual pale, as it were. Perhaps that is reason enough to kick against the grain and resuscitate the ideal of aesthetic mobilization—not as an excuse to lapse into an "ism" of some sort (be it out of Third Worldist or other revolutionary zeal) but as a negation of a generalized complacency that seems to pervade current times. In the late 1960s the Cuban filmmaker and theorist Julio García Espinosa formulated the critical import of forging an aesthetic of emergence appropriate to the conditions of the global periphery. Today, it marks the contours of a peripheral modernism and has been very influential in conceptualizations of a "Third Cinema."[19] In several films (made well into the decade of the 1990s) and in a foundational essay entitled "For an Imperfect Cinema," García Espinosa expounded on the absolute necessity of a language of political transcendence particularly in a world dominated by elites, with their attendant ideals of aesthetic perfection.[20] This language—and practice—of transcendence, he argued, is essential to the same degree that the discourse of perfection is ideological and elitist. In his words, "We maintain that imperfect cinema must above all show the process which generates the problems. It is thus the opposite of a cinema principally dedicated to celebrating results, the opposite of a self-sufficient and contemplative cinema, the opposite of a cinema which 'beautifully illustrates' ideals or concepts which we already possess. (The narcissistic posture has nothing to do with those who struggle.)"[21]

As is clear from these statements, "technical" or "artistic" mastery was, for García Espinosa, the mark of reaction; "perfect" cinema is therefore reactionary, especially to the extent that it characterizes the high production values and commercial gloss of Hollywood and its imitations. In García Espinosa's indictment of aesthetic perfection we may hear an echo of Adorno's rejection of direct protest, although Adorno was addressing himself to the need for radical artistic practices to eschew an exoteric posture of critique rather than to the problem of bourgeois reaction as such. But both are concerned with the ways that the idealization of aesthetic beauty and complexity tends toward narcissism and is thereby implicated in what Terry Eagleton calls "the ideology of the aesthetic."[22] They suggest in different ways that, under the conditions of class society, a practice adequate to the situation of those outside the circuits of elite privilege must necessarily be in direct conflict with any theory of perfectibility. In doing so, their positions converge on a theorization of peripheral modernism that is, certainly in Adorno's case, far from what is usually attributed to his mandarin European preoccupations.

At the time of this writing, approximately four decades later, García Espinosa's contentions are no less relevant than Adorno's, even if their stridency has been muted by the passage of time. The very basis of the debate over committed or uncommitted art seems to have been voided with the fading of socialist ideals (with, to some extent, the continuing exception of Cuba). As a result the appearance of anything resembling a collective vision or action is these days viewed with disapproval or, at the very least, condescension. And Cuba itself remains largely absent from most postcolonial discussions, since it threatens to be the exception that would disprove the established rules about the smooth spaces of capital, the porosity of national boundaries, the obsolescence of socialist ideals in a postmodern world, and so on.[23] Still, even if our times are different from those of García Espinosa or Ray—both of whom shared an artistic commitment to bettering the world by intervening in it—our situation has surely not improved. So the question of the form and role of art in transforming society remains pertinent even if the idea of revolution no longer retains much traction. Another way to take up the problem of imperfect cinema, then, is to dialecticize its original formulation, overturning the value-coding of perfection and imperfection in order to point out the imperfect, not to mention inadequate, attitude of elite disaffection as opposed to the perfect necessity of a critical commitment that might in the future lead to a better society.

It is by such a subjunctive light, consistent with the idea that art expresses an *incomplete* desire for perfectibility, that one might read Ray's cinema: as an experiment in conjoining technical and aesthetic "mastery" while questioning the form of life enabling it. In fact, the connection I drew earlier between Ray and Lang underscores this point; each, in distinctive ways, was invested in the craft of cinema under given conditions of production and a given horizon of political possibility. At the same time, and in their own ways, both of them highlighted the aesthetic and political force of realizing that it is, in any case, not possible to offer a perfect critique of imperfect life. These are intertwined values and only gather meaning when their divorce is made apparent. Imperfection thus serves as a dialectical spur for both Lang and Ray (although their respective technical expertise and perfect command of their medium is unquestionable) and inserts cultural value as the relevant criterion of cinematic practice. Lang's extravagance and Ray's "lack" are, as I have argued, equally—though via very different means—directed at provoking a critical response to experiential circumstances even and especially where they fall short of conventional expectations.

On this issue I can do no better than to adduce Ray himself. In the lines that serve as my second epigraph for this chapter, he states with characteristic irrepressibility the constraints against making recognizably New Wave films as a Third World director. The "fling" at a "hand-held, freeze-frame, jump-cut" film, he says, could not work in a cultural context where codes of modesty and censorship would render the "bedroom scene that goes along with it" farcical rather than "avant-garde." Ray's comment enfolds in its apparent frivolity a deeper truth: technical gestures, be they radical or reactionary, expected or unexpected, cannot account for the variations and surprises of reality. For that, we need open-endedness: a cinema attuned not to the "perfect" or the "beautiful" (as García Espinosa decries these notions) but to the magnitude of life, which continues to require, in the obverse of Marx's famous eleventh thesis on Feuerbach, not only that we change the world but also come up with better—albeit not perfect—descriptions of it.[24]

6 Cinema and Universality

Apur Sansar *as Critique*

> It is only in a drastic simplification of style and content that hope
> for the Indian cinema resides.
>
> —RAY, *Our Films, Their Films*

In his 1953 reflections on Vittorio De Sica, André Bazin tells us that De
Sica resisted any comparison between his films and Franz Kafka's writing.
Unlike Kafka, whose heroes seem to suffer transcendentally determined
fates, De Sica emphasized that tragedy was social, not metaphysical. In a
film like *Ladri di biciclette* (Bicycle Thieves, 1948) his goal, according to
Bazin, was not to portray the evil ascribed to the "heart of man" but that
which existed in a degraded world, "somewhere in the order of things."
The lesson of *Ladri di biciclette* is that, "if there were no unemployment it
would not be a tragedy to lose one's bicycle."[1] There is an implication here
about universality as a concept and an ideal. For although the term has
come in for heavy criticism on the grounds that it dissimulates parochialism and particularity, its resuscitation may not only be in order but also
requisite because it is what best explains the enduring appeal of De Sica's
films. My reference to him in the context of a discussion of *Apur Sansar*
(The World of Apu, 1959) is, in a preliminary way, intended to gesture
toward the inspiration that Ray himself derived from De Sica's films, a
detail that biographical studies mention quite often. Aside from this, what
Bazin attributes to De Sica's tragic vision is entirely pertinent to Ray as
well: both directors considered the universality of tragedy to be of a social
rather than metaphysical character. Putting Bazin's propositions in specifically materialist terms, we may say that tragedy is given not by moralizing universalisms about the nature or destiny of humanity but by the
historical universality of commodity existence. This is also to say that the
form of social existence we all inhabit in modernity—what Marx called the
relations of production peculiar to the mode of production—is universal to
the extent that capitalism's reach is global. Only from such a standpoint
does De Sica's note about unemployment being the raison d'être of trag-

edy make sense, in the same way that only the recognition of a universal predicament allows us to collocate De Sica's and Ray's commitments. Both of them make it possible to think of the cinema as a mode of the transmissibility of meaning across particular locations, cultures, and directorial styles or, what is the same, as a site of meanings made mutually intelligible by the global articulation of apparatus, economics, and narrative.

To further a discussion of *Apur Sansar*, let me pause for another moment over Bazin's comments about De Sica because they help to shed more light on Ray's affinity with Italian neorealism than is apparent in thinking of it merely as a stylistic influence. What makes De Sica's characters and films compelling, says Bazin, is the inseparability of his depiction of "the wretched condition of the proletariat [and] the implicit and constant appeal of a human need that any society whatsoever must respect." He goes on to say, "In the universe of De Sica, there lies a latent pessimism, an unavoidable pessimism we can never be grateful enough to him for, because in it resides the appeal of the potential of man, the witness to his final and irrefutable humanity."[2] Bazin's estimation is that the aspect of De Sica's films that expresses the pathos of existence without recourse to sublime, existentialist rarefaction represents the director's greatest achievement (although he couches this in somewhat mystified terms about De Sica's "love" for his fellow beings). What Bazin allows us to suggest is that De Sica, as much as Ray, belongs in a political ontology whose coordinates are very far apart from the superstitions that rule our own moment— about the alleged irrecuperability of the ideal of universalism. Indeed, one may say that the underlying commitment of both directors was precisely to a critique of the image conducted on terms that could translate across myriad difficulties of language and understanding, based as it was on the universality of experience under capitalism itself.

This point is best illustrated by an example from Siegfried Kracauer's *Theory of Film*. Kracauer describes a scene from Ray's *Aparajito* (The Unvanquished, 1957): "The camera focuses on the ornamental bark of an old tree and then slowly tilts down to the face of Apu's sick mother who yearns for her son in the big city. In the distance a train is passing by. The mother walks heavily back to the house where she imagines she hears Apu shout 'Ma.' Is he returning to her? She gets up and looks into the empty night aglow with water reflections and dancing will-o'-the-wisps."[3] Ray's accomplishment, he suggests, was to have demonstrated cinema's unique ability to conjure up a contingency that was at the same time universal: our experience of the everyday as profound. Continuing his observations, Kracauer notes: "India is in this episode but not only India. 'What seems remarkable about *Aparajito*,' writes a reader of the *New York Times* to the editor of the film section, 'is that you see this story happening in a remote land and see these faces with their exotic beauty and still feel that the same thing is happening every day somewhere in Manhattan or Brooklyn or the Bronx.' "[4] My purpose in this final chapter is to explore the possibilities emerging from Kracauer's idea that cinema attains to universality when it is able to capture not the locality of cultural expressions but their expansiveness and generality—again, especially, when they pertain to sentiments and desires that have become ineffable. To this end I will focus on the last film in Ray's Apu trilogy, loosely adapted from the autobiographical Bengali novel of the same name by Bibhutibhushan Bandopadhyay (published in 1928).

Conventional criticism has held that Ray's films reflect both a bourgeois politics and a bourgeois aestheticism, not only in his depictions of the habits and manners of the elite but also given the redemptive "humanism" in films ostensibly about the poor. The use of the word *bourgeois* has often confounded the issues at stake in its deployment, so let us specify it by referring it to values that privilege individual mastery and agency and that correspond to aesthetic strategies that offer the consolation that even if the world is not the way it should be, artworks such as novels and films can provide the closure that life disallows. Such ideological ends are seldom served by Ray's films because even accepting that he was preoccupied by the world of the colonized bourgeoisie or aristocracy in Bengal, an emphasis on formal aspects of filmmaking or a thematic focus on the Victorianism of Bengali culture is hardly sufficient to render his artistic or political vision bourgeois. To the contrary, most Ray films embody a refusal to settle questions in a comforting fashion (excepting his children's films such as *Goopy Gyne Bagha Byne* [The Adventures of Goopy and Bagha, 1968] or *Sonar Kella* [The Golden Fort, 1974], where unambiguously happy endings are demanded by the genre). Indeed, Ray's vision of the Bengali bourgeoisie—caught between an increasingly anachronistic historical sensibility and political impotence—is more the stuff of an immanent critique of this class and its pretensions than an endorsement of them. *Apur Sansar*, like *Mahanagar*, departs from the somewhat mannerist portraits of the upper classes in the other films I have discussed, but it is consistent with them on the issue of directorial stance. Its structure of feeling is altogether negative, even though it (also like *Mahanagar*) ends on a nominally positive note. As a result, the overall sense with which the viewer is left is one of narrative doubt and a corollary awareness of Ray's nuanced handling of the medium.

Speaking of medium-specific concerns, Kracauer's insights are once more instructive in allowing us to see how film, as a constitutively open-ended form, draws its subjects from matter that continues its existence before and after it has been captured in the "snapshots" that the film strip comprises. Unlike other modes of storytelling, the raw materials of life are, as Kracauer puts it, not *consumed* in their representation by the camera, only *exhibited* by it. Ray understood this constitution of his chosen medium, and rarely did he seek to fulfill the expectation of the "happily ever after," any more than he sought to reconcile, through aesthetic means, the unresolved problems of life and history. An understanding of the formal resistance of the cinematic medium to the requirements of narrative closure is at the core of Ray's self-conscious effort to show how, in its very presentation of nature (the ripple of leaves, for instance), film reveals, in a way that other art forms cannot, the transcendence of a world not enclosed within representation. As viewers we are never in doubt that well after the camera has stopped focusing on rippling leaves, they continue to exist, as well as to ripple. This is, ultimately, a philosophical as well as aesthetic "take," to pun on a film term that also expresses an obdurately Kantian problem: the relationship of representation to reality. What a text like *Apur Sansar* demonstrates is Ray's modernist, though not bourgeois, perspective on the matter (and this is irrespective of the film's subject, which focuses squarely on the vicissitudes of ordinary life).

It needs to be said that it is less Kracauer's ideas that help to illuminate the cinema-reality-universality nexus than Ray's films that inspired Kracauer to propose them in the first place. *Theory of Film* was, we should recall, first published in 1960, although Kracauer had taken copious notes on the project for twenty years prior to its appearance. Films like the Apu trilogy enabled Kracauer to clinch his arguments about the medium's expansive capacities and, although this influence may come as a surprise to critics used to decrying the Eurocentrism of theory, what he derived from Ray (along with Fellini, De Sica, and others) is the prospect of a mode of expression that could capture the continuities between art and life without mystifying them. For Kracauer, the film theorist and historian, the search was for a conceptual language adequate to "the cinema's pull toward material contingency," as Miriam Hansen notes suggestively in her introduction to the reissue of *Theory of Film*.[5] And in this respect his theoretical outlook matched Ray's directorial efforts to avoid the comforts of realist storytelling, with its pragmatist tendencies and idealization of individual subjectivity. But more than a nominally shared outlook about film style, what brings together the divergent figures of Ray, the Bengali director, and Kracauer, the Weimar-era émigré, is their respective investment in a political conception of film. Both were witness to the cold war culture in the decades following World War II and participants in a broadly internationalist movement in which progressive thinkers and artists around the globe sought to put in place a counterculture that could refute the ideological style and substance of American realism and realpolitik.

Ray's main interest over the course of his filmmaking career was to illustrate the myriad ways that people live in the world without necessarily being in command of it. Accordingly, I want to suggest that Ray's standpoint belongs in a materialist conception of cultural practice that presupposes that aesthetics no less than politics provides general terms for a struggle against purely formalistic and particularistic stories or histories, even though (and perhaps especially because) people experience those stories and histories as uniquely their own. If Kracauer had proposed an immanent relationship between film and reality, it was also the case that he thought that "the world of film is a flow of random events involving both humans and inanimate objects."[6] *Apur Sansar* gives us an opportunity to think about how such open-endedness can be captured cinematically. It also reveals how the camera's fundamental indifference to animate and inanimate objects can be folded in as an element of the story. For the film is as much about a character, Apu, as it is about the city in which he lives and the countryside to which his destiny takes him.

The story picks up where it left off in *Aparajito*, with Apu's emergence as an adult who, like so many other men in Calcutta, exists in circumstances of gray but genteel poverty, eking out his living as a white-collar worker (Figure 23). The drabness of Apu's material existence, completed by his dingy, rented apartment and snooping neighbor, is relieved by his two joys in life: his talent for playing the flute and, a short way into the film, the arrival of the beautiful Aparna, to whom he is married in a somewhat accidental arrangement. Apu and Aparna's conjugal happiness is only a passing thing because, soon pregnant, she goes to her father's house in a rural part of Bengal to give birth, only to die from complications. Grief-stricken and unable to contemplate his now-empty life, Apu abandons his newborn son, Kajol, leaving him with his dead wife's parents. His wanderings over the next few years (condensed into a few shots to indicate the passage of time), accompanied only by a shoulder bag in which he carries the manuscript of a novel he has been writing, is finally interrupted

FIGURE 23.   Pulu visits Apu's apartment. Used by permission from Satyajit Ray Film and Study Center.

by his friend Pulu, who travels to the North to persuade Apu to return and take responsibility for his little son. The last part of the film gives us Ray's utterly charming portrait of the mischievous little waif Kajol and the gradual establishment of the relationship between Apu and his son, with the film ending on a lingering shot of the father carrying his son on his shoulder to (potentially) a new life together.

THE CAMERA EYE: TRAGEDY VS. THE EVERYDAY

The line of thought I wish to pursue here returns us to the notion of tragedy introduced earlier and has to do with Kracauer's argument that "film and tragedy are incompatible with each other." The world of tragedy, however much it evokes death, disappointment, or sadness, pertains to a different cosmos (what Bazin described as Kafka's rather than De Sica's universe), where "destiny defeats chance and all the light falls on human interaction."[7] Kracauer and Bazin thus both consider the tragic vision to be a conservative one in the end; it preserves order by giving life's trials an individualist cast, and it instructs by affirming a resolution, however unhappy. Kracauer's point is not that no films can be called tragic (Orson Welles's *Othello* [1952] is an example he gives of a tragedy) but that such films derive their tragic elements from elsewhere and not from what he terms camera-reality: "the stories which they impart do not grow out of the material life they picture but are imposed on its potentially coherent fabric from without."[8] By this light, to experience a film as a tragedy is to bring an orientation to it in which inanimate objects are not equal partners in human affairs; they only supplement the "inner event" of the tragic—which is experienced less as a cinematic event than a providential one, belonging to an ordered world in which death and destruction have a moral purpose or are predestined. However, since life does not follow in ordered fashion but results from chance and random occurrences, the most self-conscious film directors—for example, Chaplin, De Sica, Ray—with their understanding of the medium's recursive relationship to the real, work toward exploring a more indeterminate universe.

So it is that Aparna's death is not given a grand motivation in this text, nor for that matter were the deaths of Apu's sister, Durga, or his parents in the two earlier films in the trilogy. All these characters die, but their deaths do not embody a tragic purpose or signify the punctual ends of the respective films in which they occur. Instead, they serve merely to mark the contingencies of life amidst its retellings. We might say that this insight into life's essential contingency is what gives *Apur Sansar* its universal appeal, though this risks awakening the demons of antiuniversalism I mentioned earlier. But if the suspicion of universality has led to multicultural celebrations of the local and the situated, a less fortunate consequence of rejecting any notion of universals has been to make it difficult for us to speak of a shared human predicament or the entanglements between the local and the global. Not only does this keep in place the hoary dichotomy of the universal and the particular, but it also reinforces the West's normative claims while locking the non-West into relativisms about the particular and the primitive. It seems to me that a more careful evaluation of the claim to universality is in order, so that the decision about whether or not an idea or ideal aspires to the universal—like all judgments of value—can only be premised on the actual case. In the example of *Apur Sansar* contemporary viewers will readily recognize that the circumstances befalling a poor, unemployed young man from Calcutta are both different and far from life in the West; similarly, the story contains elements with which all viewers would not identify—including, especially, the depiction of a suddenly arranged marriage between the hero and his unknown wife. Nonetheless, as Andrew Robinson comments, "It is a film one virtually cannot avoid being moved by."[9] I would submit that the viewer's—any viewer's—response to this film is sparked by Ray's use of details to signify Apu's (and, by extension, their own) immersion in a daily world pregnant with chance occurrences and possibilities, even though those occurrences are far from uniform across the board.

The most poignant scenes in the film revolve around carefully constructed depictions of such quotidian plenitude: a shot of a street glistening after an evening rain, a naked child running across a railway track, a sound-image of a conch shell blown ceremonially to usher in the dusk, an interior shot of a crowded bus in which every face tells a different story. The point is not that Ray is the only director to turn to such everyday-ness, particularly given the inspiration he derived from the likes of De Sica, who used similar techniques to evoke the realities of street life. It is rather that the moving force for "what happens in the story," always a consideration even in the most formalist films, derives from a sense of expectation that only the camera can produce through its ability to puncture the ordinary and transform it into an object of wonder. With characteristic acuity, Ray himself commented eloquently on the quest to capture the physical world—or, to use Kracauer's term, to "redeem" it: "How to catch the hushed stillness of dusk in a Bengali village when the wind drops and turns the ponds into sheets of glass, dappled by the leaves of *shaluk* and *shapla*, and the smoke from the ovens settles in wispy trails over the landscape and the plaintive blows on conch shells from homes far and near are joined by the chorus of crickets which rises as the light falls, until all one sees are the stars in the sky, and the stars that blink and swirl in the thickets."[10] Along these lines Ray also wrote of the challenges in "fathom[ing] the mysteries of 'atmosphere.' Does it consist in the sights or in the sounds? How to catch the subtle difference between dawn and dusk, or convey the grey humid stillness that precedes the first monsoon shower? Is sunlight in spring the same as sunlight in autumn?"[11] In such meditations we can discern Ray's investment in coming to terms with camera-reality: film's ability to discover what Kracauer called "physical existence in its endlessness."[12]

Ever since a Paris journalist, Henri de Parville, described the early films of Louis Lumière as "nature caught in the act,"[13] what is quintessentially cinematic has always been associated with the capacity of film to render the atmospherics of objects in place (as opposed to the theatrics of people and events). Moreover, cinema heightens the randomness of life's little actions and impediments with which we all have to contend, irrespective of the variations within them. Ray's statements above can be compared with the following observations from Kracauer to reveal their shared sensitivity toward the everyday:

> If you disregard for a moment articulate beliefs, ideological objectives, special undertakings, and the like, there still remain the sorrows and satisfactions, discords and feasts, wants and pursuits, which mark the ordinary business of living. Products of habit and microscopic interac-tion, they form a resilient texture which changes slowly and survives wars, epidemics, earthquakes and revolutions. Films tend to explore

this texture of everyday life, whose composition varies according to place, people, and time. So they help us not only appreciate our given material environment but to extend it in all directions. They virtually make the world our home.[14]

APU'S WORLD, RAY'S WORLDLINESS

Apur Sansar was critically acclaimed in the West soon after it was released, despite its poor performance at the box office. But the praise that the film (and the trilogy as a whole) garnered was based either on a parochial reading, which took it to be a literal portrayal of the brute realities of the Third World, or the sentimental idea that Apu's life is a tragic allegory of life's meaninglessness. Aside from this sort of superficial valorization, there were also more serious misunderstandings about the film's import and Ray's intent. For instance, Dwight Macdonald's liberal New York *Partisan Review*–style politics did not prevent the cultural critic from proclaiming the following: "*Pather Panchali* was about a family in a village. *Apu* is about a young writer in a city, a more complex theme, and I'm not sure Ray is up to it."[15] Macdonald's sentiments are similar to his counterpart across the Atlantic, Kingsley Amis, who, in writing about a younger Apu in *Aparajito* opined that "Satyajit Ray, the director, seems to have set out with the idea of photographing without rearrangement the life of a poor Indian family, of reporting reality in as unshaped a form as possible."[16]

The charge that Ray was not up to the "complex" theme of life in a city, or that his films simply "reported" reality without being able to shape and rearrange it in an artful manner, reveals the extent to which both Macdonald and Amis failed to recognize that it was Ray's uncommon grasp of the cinema's potential to "exhibit" the little movements in life informing its larger schemas, catastrophic or comic, that allowed him to eschew the pretenses of "complexity."[17] Ray's commitment to depicting the details surrounding the givenness of life accompanies a corollary avoidance of rococo ornamentation in his texts and a spareness in the mise-en-scène. This, in addition to being an aesthetic constraint forced on a Third World director with limited resources at his command, was (as I have argued was also the reason for his choices in *Mahanagar*) a political statement that served as a reproof against the high kitsch of conventional filmmaking in India and the West. Contrary to Amis's shortsighted view, Ray's most well-wrought films (which the Apu trilogy certainly exemplifies) reveal his intricate rearrangements of detail that, far from "reporting reality in an unshaped form," enhance our appreciation of it. Elements that in another director's hands might go unnoticed are highlighted and given a luminous prominence. Moreover, Ray's understanding of the cinema's affinity with the visible world allowed him to tell a story without grand maneuverings of character and motivation, a climactic denouement, or an Aristotelian catharsis—the stock-in-trade of filmmaking, as well as formulaic storytelling in other media.

As I hope to have made clear throughout, filmmaking that merely adapts novelistic or theatrical conventions misses the medium's specificity and its photographic capacity to capture the moment, relying instead on familiar plot strategies, the predictable appeal of the content of stories, or the illusion of continuity editing.[18] Had Ray chosen to follow only these paths, it probably would have led to the provincialism with which Amis and Macdonald charge him. But like photography, which reveals the everyday world at the same time as estranging it (for instance, in the ways in which photographs of ourselves always look strange to us), cinema does more than repeat the literary emphasis on plot complications and narrative technique. The best cinematic moments reside not in rearranging life to make it appear more significant or coherent but in reminding us of the tremulousness within which we live by holding it at a distance. Ray understood this, even if his critics did not, and took his cues from the parallel—rather than simple identity—between his medium and his milieu, between the open-endedness of film and the randomness of life itself.

There is, in *Apur Sansar*, a depiction of the unsettlements amid which we all exist: the shiftless character type embodied by Apu with whom we are all familiar (no less than the other social types wandering the streets of Manhattan, Brooklyn, or the Bronx mentioned by the *New York Times* reader Kracauer quotes). There is more to be said, however, about Ray's depiction of Apu as a type because, although this film is the last in a trilogy that follows him from boyhood to fatherhood, it is not really "about" Apu, except in the most literal sense. The actions through which we see him, from his college days to his short-lived but happy marriage to Aparna, to his wanderings as a lost soul in the latter half of this film undoubtedly all pertain to the presentation of a life lived; nonetheless, the impact of these episodes is greater if we appreciate the extent to which the figure of Apu is, like Bimala and Charu after him, an object among objects. Just as other objects in the physical world are commonly deployed by the cinema to signify states of being, the passage of time, conflicts between people and forces, and so on, Apu's personal plight becomes the means for a reflection on the larger issues of responsibility, obligation, and happiness in a hostile world (Figure 24).

FIGURE 24. Apu on his wanderings. Used by permission from Satyajit Ray Film and Study Center.

Likewise, the camera's focus on things—window shutters, alleyways, railroad tracks, a stray dog, Apu's tattered shirt hanging on the wall—serve as physical counterparts to psychological states, but they also go beyond this standard metonymic relationship in order to suggest that objects do not completely capture the subjective world. In their very objectivity they evoke the flow *between* the organic and inorganic worlds depicted. The "microscopic interactions," to echo Kracauer, between Apu the individual and the world around him do not magnify his subjective character or destiny but, on the contrary, evoke the actuality of the universe with its indifference to individual psychology and subjectivity.

This emphasis on the objective and the corollary subordination of subjective motivations in Ray's treatment of his hero continue to be misperceived by commentators. In John W. Hood's recent book on major filmmakers of Indian "art cinema," for instance, the author attempts a reading that seeks to avoid hagiography in favor of a critical assessment. Hood's project is undoubtedly worthy, especially considering that Ray's canonical status has elsewhere produced celebratory rather than perceptive accounts of his artistry. But the terms of his assessment turn out to be quite simplistic and off-target because they fall back on the tired scheme of contextual analysis that has reigned for decades in literary criticism: to wit, the individual is to society as character is to setting, a scheme that most values the degree to which an author (in this case, Ray) can faithfully draw relationships between text and context. For instance, Hood maintains that the film "gets into difficulties" in its final section: "Apu goes away and takes up menial labor in his endeavor to escape the tragedy of the past. Perhaps there is an element of melodrama in this, but what is difficult to accept is his imma-ture foot-stamping in dramatically scattering the pages of his novel to the winds and his steadfast refusal to see the little boy whom he blames for his wife's death." Arguing that "wordiness, a weakness that would mar a number of Ray's films, challenges the visual image for dominance" in the last part of *Apur Sansar,* Hood nevertheless concedes, "what is particu-larly notable about Ray's affinity with the cinema as a primarily visual medium is his exceptionally effective economy of expression, a strength that is evident in all of his better films."[19]

While it is true that some of Ray's later films (*Pratidwandi* [1970], *Nayak* [1966]) betray the sort of wordiness Hood criticizes, it is difficult to see how the ending of *Apu* is guilty of this error. Rather than "immature foot-stamping," the film ends by a very economic marking of Apu's pas-sage from immaturity and anger at his fate to a maturity in which he does not understand why things happen as they do but is prepared to accept them. His novel, the writing of which had provided him an alibi and a security blanket for years, represents, as Ray shows, the outpourings of a resentful man—its romantic gesture of private protest leading nowhere. But by having his hero consign the manuscript to the winds, Ray is at pains to show him overcoming this self-indulgence (even if one were to read the gesture as melodramatic). From this point in the film, instead of continuing to bemoan the disruption of his happiness, Apu is depicted as resolute in the recognition that his obligation is not to the past but to the future—in the form of his son, Kajol, whom he had abandoned following Aparna's death. Quite obviously, my interpretation differs from Hood's, and judged by this token alone, his reading would be as valid as any other, including mine. But whether the film's ending is wordy is a less ambiguous matter that can be resolved by taking a closer look at how the final scene brings the film to closure with the rapprochement between father and son. Let me provide a quick sketch to note some of its details:

The sequence begins with a medium long shot of a portico in an old house, the camera lingering on a scene in which the only moving objects are the rustling pages of a newspaper lying on a table. Ambient sounds provide the sole disturbance to the stillness of the frame, into which Apu

FIGURE 25. Kajol sleeping. Used by permission from Satyajit Ray Film and Study Center.

enters from the bottom right, announcing himself to his father-in-law, who is shown standing at the center. Stonily skeptical at this belated arrival of a son-in-law whom he initially fails even to recognize, the father-in-law tells Apu that the boy, Kajol, is asleep upstairs. The scene then cuts to a shot of a dusty wall as Apu comes into the picture from behind it; the camera pans slowly to let him (and viewers) look into the room, and in the next shot we see the small figure of the sleeping child, his face turned away from view as he lies on the large ornamental bed amid crumpled sheets (Figure 25).

The mindful spectator will recall that this was the same room and the same bed (shown earlier in the film), once decorated with elaborate garlands of flowers, that had loomed large between the young bridegroom, Apu, and his bride, Aparna, on their wedding night. Aparna has been dead for as many years as Kajol has lived, but Ray makes no maudlin gesture, provides no hackneyed flashback to that previous scene with its very different evocation of an unanticipated romance. In fact, no words are spoken as the current scene unfolds, and nothing explicit reinforces the loss of love and the passage of time. Only the strains of a passing boatman's song can be heard in the background, as Apu takes in the moment and tries to come to terms with this first glimpse of his son. The camera then pushes in slowly and tracks around the bed, revealing the child's face in repose. Apu moves toward the window, the boatman's song now grows louder as we see, in a shot that frames both Apu and the world beyond the bars of the window, the outlines of a boat passing on the nearby river, rendering the song diegetic while also providing the sole note of pathos. Apu rouses the sleeping child by ruffling his hair; the boy wakes up, his face crinkled with sleep, only to run out of the house, away from this unfamiliar and disturbing presence. At this key moment when the focus shifts from Apu to Kajol, the latter is presented simply—a small figure against the stark landscape of late autumn on the banks of the river Khulna. Apu runs after his son, and we see the two in a long shot, separated from each other, a dawning comprehension on Apu's face and a studied but reproachful indifference in the little boy's rebellious stance toward the stranger.

The scene then cuts to a shot of a different day in the same locale: Apu calls out to Kajol, who is standing outside the gates of the house, but Kajol's response is to pick up a large stone and throw it at him, unappeased by his father's attempts to win him over. Meanwhile, the grandfather has come out to witness this exchange, and his angry response (which hints at the little fellow's ongoing treatment at the hands of his grandfather) is to raise his walking stick to strike the boy. In a medium close-up next, we see Apu preventing his father-in-law from meting out this physical punishment, and only this move communicates to Kajol that his father is now there for him. The soundtrack signifies that the wind has picked up during this interaction, as if to signal the shifts in Apu's emotions from indifference to a longing to be accepted by the son he has abjured until now. None of this is belabored, and the next few shots, in quick succession, portray Apu's continuing efforts to claim his son's attention and affection, although the boy is not quite ready to hand himself over to a father who has returned so recently to ply him with promises of stories and the lure of a toy engine.

Ray's intuitive understanding of children has been commented on elsewhere, and here we see it touchingly elaborated, with very few words and the artless gestures of the child-actor playing Kajol. Only in the final minutes of this sequence do we see the reconciliation between the adult who has so long behaved like a child and the motherless child whom circumstances have forced to grow up alone and unloved, left to his own devices and to his make-believe world. For, even before Apu becomes acquainted with his son, the film's audience was introduced to the little boy with a bird mask on his face, running around in the woods shooting real birds with his slingshot.

That earlier scene, complete with the insouciance of its soundtrack

FIGURE 26.   Apu reunited with his son. Used by permission from Satyajit Ray
Film and Study Center.

(produced by the single-stringed instrument of the *ektara*) echoing Kajol's
pranks, marks Ray's consistent interest in showing the correspondences
between the world of nature and that of children. His depiction of Kajol is
entirely sympathetic; so although the boy is shown to be a menace to those
around him, the logic of Ray's portrayal is to emphasize that the world
of children, filled with its own dark motivations and mischief, is, like the
physical world: oblivious to categorical separations between human and
animal, good and bad, subject and object. Like the natural world, children
are indifferent to the reasons for their lot in life (as is Kajol), inhabiting
only its givenness—making it possible for us to recognize that the distinction between tragedy and happenstance is very often imposed from without, through our expectations of what should or should not happen, rather
than from any essential momentousness of actions or events. Whatever
one may want to make of such metacritical implications, the fact remains
that all of it is merely suggested, never stated (let alone overstated) by Ray.
A less wordy ending to *Apur Sansar* cannot, I think, be imagined, with
the film closing on a shot of Apu walking away from the past with his son
on his shoulders, a smile on both faces, and no other reassurance given to
viewers about their future together (Figure 26).

If I have expanded at such length on the film's culmination, it is less to refute Hood's account of it than to convey to readers a sense of the economy with which Ray conveys the depth of sentiment that informs something as important and universal as filial ties, however fraught they are and however differently they unfold. I also want to suggest that the details of shot and sequence, and the texture of the cinematic image, contribute as well to our appreciation of Kracauer's idea of a material aesthetics.

Throughout this book I have pursued the idea that cinema can be thought of as a mode of expression that tries to avoid the formulaic transpositions of psychological and social motivations. As my references to Kracauer have aimed to buttress, a material aesthetics privileges, somewhat literally, the *material* of the cinema itself—what Kracauer simply calls its "content," which, crucially for him, did not mean the physiognomy of plot and story but the physiognomy of film in its structural affinities with the world. More than other modes of talking about film culture, a material aesthetics usefully describes Ray's particular experiments with avant-garde principles for the purpose of transforming them to render his own subject matter. The term underscores, as well, his synthesis of "our films" and "their films," a synthesis resulting as much from his local, cultural milieu as from his European sources. When it comes to discussing independent cinema in India, only nativism could make us resist recognizing that part of the very inspiration for doing something different was, in Ray's historical moment, drawn from a much broader germination of ideas about technology (such as film), culture, and social development.

The paradigm for debating cultural issues in India may not be internationalism, as Geeta Kapur has argued, although it is difficult to sustain this view given the historical facts.[20] When it comes to movements in the visual arts, there is certainly room for disagreement on this score, as the art historian Partha Mitter's recent work has amply shown.[21] Moreover, Kapur's argument that Ray's vision is reformist because it does not avow a socialist or programmatically revolutionary perspective can also be seen as misguided if one agrees, as I do, with Kracauer's point that it is untenable to postulate an inherent link between cinema and any form of socialism or collectivism.[22] What the record shows, in fact, is that various New Wave film movements in Europe and India, with their mutual commitments to internationalist politics in the postwar period, were not only in conversation with each other; they were also involved in some of the same debates that are still under way about the role of art and the place of philosophical criticism in conceptualizing the world. Indeed, we would be remiss in not recognizing that many of the ideas that have emerged as foundational to film theory and method overall (attached to names such as Bazin, Susan Sontag, Béla Balázs, or Kracauer) were very much at issue from the 1950s to the 1980s within Indian ciné circles in which Ray was undoubtedly a central presence. I should also add that this was well before the moment that contemporary postcolonial studies has asserted is the one when Euro-American theory finally had to come to terms with Empire striking back. Venues such as the Calcutta Film Society—founded by Ray, along with other cinephiles such as fellow artist Chidananda Das Gupta, in 1947 (the year of India's independence)—amply testify to a much more lively and frankly internationalist conversation that took place decades ago in the spirit of a serious and seriously politicized engagement with cinema as the paradigmatic medium for a critique of modernity.

Ray's stature as one of the great modernist directors was firmly established with the Apu trilogy, especially after the films were exhibited outside India and received numerous international awards. So a discussion of his work does not need to be premised on vindicating a lost or unappreciated genius in the language of subalternity. But, despite his widespread fame both during his lifetime and since his death in 1992 (witness the number of Ray retrospectives that have been staged in the United States alone), I think that he has been less well understood with regard to his commitment to an avant-garde mode of storytelling. On this point I am once more in disagreement with Kapur's characterization of Ray's style as realist and, hence, reformist because I take his impulse to reside in a mediation of realism predicated not only on the constitutive place of the technology of film (which is both modern and modernist) but also because there is simply no warrant to equate, as she does, Ray's humanism with the values of liberal reformism. Any number of examples from Frantz Fanon to C. L. R. James, Walter Benjamin, and Jürgen Habermas, not to mention Marx's own writings, would attest to this. In other words one can be a humanist without falling prey to liberalism's pieties about reform.

What is more to the point, Ray did not regard his cinema only as an "art" but as a mode of intervening in politics and philosophy. Like the European avant-gardes of the early twentieth century, his effort was not only to disrupt accepted ways of making films but also to question the very institutions of art and political practice in their separate relations to other sociocultural realities. Unlike the European avant-garde artists, however, who, as Peter Bürger has argued, were epochally conscious of their failed mission to lead art back into life, Ray's historical location and personal convictions took him out of an exclusively intellectual engagement with the visual image into a political questioning of the historical and social contradictions that govern the production of art.[23]

This is not to say that Ray's conceptual take on the world was realized or realizable; neither do its limitations render his vision romantic or naively optimistic. So I do not want to leave the impression that there was, somehow, a perfect coherence between Ray's aspirations regarding cinema's redemptive potential and his achievements. Ultimately, the issue of redemption is less discursive than material. But his refusal to submit to the realist demand that he document the approved story of the Indian nation or, equally, that he reject storytelling for aesthetic strategies of estrangement should be seen as his own remark on the impossibility of leading art back into social life and, at the same time, of the necessity of doing so. *Apur Sansar* is a film in which authenticity of atmosphere and emotion, so much a hallmark of Ray's practice, works in conjunction with his awareness about cinema's capacity to penetrate the surface of reality. In this way it remains faithful to what would recognizably be Indian (or Bengali) themes, manners, and artistic models even as it departs from the pieties and sentimentalities that have come to characterize contemporary Indian cinema's effort to transcend the entertainment/politics divide.[24]

The risks of being accused of a naive aestheticism, an equally naive apolitical attitude, and so on, were ones that Ray confronted directly. As he put it in one of his reflections, " 'Classical' and 'humanist' are epithets often used by western critics to describe my films. They are generally used as compliments, and occasionally, one suspects, as euphemisms for old-fashioned, a further insinuation being that my films are not innovative."[25] It might be added that Western critics were not alone in their charges though the more significant point is that the question of politics or protest could not, for him, be settled easily through the seductions of narrative; neither did he set off to deploy purely formal strategies to disorient or alienate his audiences and thereby elevate his films to a "properly" avant-garde aesthetic. Instead, what we get in the best Ray films is the working out of a different challenge: how to use the image as an approach to the world, a mode of human communication.

Conclusion

Lateness and Cinema

Thinking is not the intellectual reproduction of what already
exists anyway.
—THEODOR W. ADORNO, "Resignation"

A new age does not begin all of a sudden.
My grandfather was already living in the new age
My grandson will probably still be living in the old one.
The new meat is eaten with the old forks.
—BERTOLT BRECHT, *Die Neuen Zeitalter*

Our memory of the twentieth century has already begun to fade as we
move forward into the twenty-first; by that very token, we confront our
thoroughly belated entry into the debates about modernism and the avant-
garde. As I have tried to demonstrate, this delayed recognition does not
render those debates irrelevant or represent an overcoming of the problems they made visible (a comment that returns us to my reference to
Raymond Williams in the introduction). Indeed, as Williams suggested,
the question of modernism remains of value even now because we have
yet to emerge fully from the period associated with it or outlive the need
to think about the aesthetic, political, or philosophical issues within its
purview. The manner in which Ray faced this sense of a general rather
than specifically "Third World" belatedness can be discerned pointedly,
for example, in the movement from a work like *Charulata* to one such as
Ghare Baire—films with similar themes that marked a radical scission
between his early and late career, a journey from low-budget black-and-
white realism to stylized Technicolor and, despite this, from optimism to
a darker, brooding vision.

Taking up the question of his overall project in an interview with
Cineaste magazine, Ray stated, "the one film that I would make the same
way, if I had to do it again, is *Charulata*."[1] He did, of course, return to
many of its themes and motifs in *Ghare Baire*, released two decades later,
so even if it is not a literal remake of the earlier film, the turn-of-the-
century worlds depicted in both echo each other in more than passing
manner. In the use of similar props and interior sets and, of course, with

197

the subject matter of a love triangle captured from a woman's point of view, Ray reprises in *Ghare Baire* the structures and sensibilities he had depicted in *Charulata* to a degree that makes it reasonable to consider the stakes of this repetition, particularly as a meditation on endings.[2]

Aside from exchanging the black-and-white of *Charulata* for color in *Ghare Baire*, Ray also chose a different actress (Swatilekha Chatterjee) to play the heroine, Bimala, in *Ghare Baire*, though he had apparently considered casting Madhabi Mukherjee, who had acted as Charu, in this role as well. The later film ends more tragically than *Charulata*—which hints at a rapprochement between the principal characters—the finality of Nikhil's death marking the denouement of *Ghare Baire*. In each film Ray reverses course with respect to his adaptation of source materials: Tagore's short story "Nastanirh" (Broken Nest), from which *Charulata* is taken, ends on a note of discord as Bhupati leaves Calcutta, as well as Charu, who is left home to contend with her renewed isolation. By contrast, the screen version closes on the gesture, albeit stilled by a freeze-frame, of her inviting Bhupati back into her life. Ray thus intimates reconciliation, whereas Tagore's story has an unambiguously unhappy ending. *Ghare Baire* similarly departs from Tagore's 1915 novel (of the same name); the film's ending reinforces the dissolution of the world with Bimala's tragedy at home, whereas Tagore's story ends by implying that Nikhilesh survives his attempt to put out the religious riots on his estate. Ray's filmic rendition of this final episode closes with a slow-paced, long shot of the village elders approaching the household with news of Nikhil's death. This shot is then replaced with a series of dissolving close-ups of Bimala as she is transformed from decorative wife into colorless widow.

Of his choice of Swatilekha rather than Madhabi to play Bimala, Ray apparently reported wanting an actress who conveyed depth rather than beauty as a way to subvert audience expectations about femininity.[3] Above all, the lyricism of *Charulata* is replaced by the somber mood of *Ghare Baire*, even down to its self-referential allusions to the earlier film. In the most memorable of such allusions, the shots of Bimala's first glimpse of Sandip from behind a screen (deliberately evoking the picture of Charu peering through the shuttered windows at the outside world) are now presented with shadows striping across the window screen and Bimala's face, thus rendering her a shaded presence in contrast with Charu's vibrant one. It is as if the excitements of the world have now been replaced by the restrictions of existence. (Figure 27; cf. Figure 7).

If *Charulata* exhibits an interiorized world that remains largely restricted to household locations and concerns, in *Ghare Baire* the outside

FIGURE 27. Bimala
and the world beyond.
Used by permission from
Satyajit Ray Film and
Study Center.

world is shown to force its way into the household, disrupting in the process the demarcations between inner and outer, interior and exterior. This also attests to a shift in Ray's emphasis, despite echoes of the earlier film in the later one. The gentle disappointments of Charu's affection for Amal and the constraints on her personal emergence give way to the greater tragedy of Bimala's widowhood and the even larger failure of the nationalist movement to extricate India from the grip of the world market.

Two decades intervened between the making of these films, and when Ray does return to a portrayal of the life of an upper-class woman along the lines established in *Charulata,* he gives us a portrait of unproductive, unabated tension without the earlier film's cinematic élan. Unlike *Charulata, Ghare Baire* is full of foreboding: "you know everything is going to fall apart," as Ray himself described it.[4] Yet he was unwilling or, perhaps, unable to narrate it otherwise. What marks *Ghare Baire* far more than *Charulata* is a sense of modernity as the experience in which instead of the unexpected, it is the inexorability of the expected that must be suffered and narrativized.[5] I take this less as a sign of Ray's investment in depictions of a bygone world than a paradoxical mark of his general resistance to a seamless take on historical unfolding. History does indeed unfold though it does so "retrocessively," as Hegel put it, rather than in unilinear or teleological fashion.

By most estimates, the later film is not as effective or as affecting as the former, its rough edges continually revealed by mismatched sound edits and the unrelieved ponderousness of the shots. When judged by conventional criteria, Ray's "remake" seems to be less of a filmic accomplishment than evident in the apparently "intuitive" command of the medium he displayed in *Charulata.*[6] So, although by the time *Ghare Baire* was released, Ray was in the mature phase of his filmmaking career, his solution to the problem of representation is, we may say, an intransigent rather than virtuosically developed one.[7]

In the same *Cineaste* interview that I cited earlier, when asked why he had not taken more narrative and political risks (in the manner of Fellini or Bergman), Ray's words attest to this intransigence:

> I can't do all that Bergman and Fellini do. I don't have their audiences and I don't work in that kind of context. I have to contend with an audience that is used to dross. I have worked with an Indian audience for thirty years and, in that time, the general look of cinema hasn't changed. Certainly not in Bengal. You'll find directors there are so backward, so stupid, and so trashy that you'll find it difficult to believe that their works exist alongside my films. I am forced by circumstances to keep my stories on an innocuous level. What I can do, however, is to pack my films with meaning and psychological inflections and shades, and make a whole which will communicate a lot of things to many people.[8]

Ray was obviously very discerning about the constraints on the production and reception of his cinema. He was also unabashedly critical of the banality of Bengali (and other regional) film industries, though his disapprobation goes against the reigning consensus that regards mass entertainment forms as expressions of an authentic populism; anything more substantial is often waved off as elitist by both critics and audiences. But any conversation about aesthetics grinds to a halt without a regime of value in place, so despite anticipating that his vision—isolated, alienated, and aloof—would attract the reverse snobbery of mass culture enthusiasts, Ray continued to experiment with ideas formulated in an earlier moment of high modernism. His was not a stance of generalized disenchantment or "ironic disillusion," to echo Georg Lukács's characterization of modernist literature, but the standpoint of someone who understood the paradox of making aesthetic statements under the reified sign of the contemporary.

Staying with the contrast between *Charulata* and *Ghare Baire*, we may say that in retelling another one of Tagore's stories, as well as in revisiting his own portrait of betrayal in the earlier film, Ray resurrects a familiar theme in *Ghare Baire*. But this film shows signs of aging—of itself as a cinematic statement and, although less important, of its author. Concretely, the disappointments of political culture in India, a degraded mass-entertainment system, and, more abstractly, the continuing betrayal of the promise of a better society after the departure of the British are all enacted dialectically in the film's form—though not in the simple calculus of parody or indifference, both of which presuppose the inevitability of growth and decline. Instead, *Ghare Baire* articulates its critique of the present with deliberation and emphasis, through technical means such as the tone of its color. One of few color films Ray made, it is nevertheless darkly lit, giving it a drab appearance and saturating its vision with a loss of vitality (with the key exception of the passageway between the inner and outer quarters which is almost garishly lit, the artificial brightness of its stained-glass windows appearing as if in a kaleidoscope).

What is more, by repeating patterns in the mise-en-scène that he had used twenty years earlier in *Charulata*, Ray modifies attention from resting on signs of privilege to those of exhaustion, along the same lines that Bimala's presence, when compared with Charu's, betokens understanding rather than piquancy. Still, as I suggested above, Ray does not parody the past but re-cites it, the recitation giving his later portrayal the sense of being after the fact and too late, though urgent nonetheless. In its epistemological strategy we may say that *Ghare Baire* evokes the past while revoking it, intimating that the promises held out for its future, our present, have been rendered dissolute. Through a series of relays that structure the differences between the two films both in formal and narrative terms, Ray reminds us not only of the continuing necessity of returning to the past but also of doing so when it seems as though the questions it raises have all been settled in final, if unsatisfactory, ways.

PARATAXIS: RAY AND ADORNO

The problem of melancholia as the form in which historical consciousness comes into its own in modernity is one that Theodor Adorno explored extensively. Interestingly, he did so not only in his philosophical writings (with their markedly Hegelian commitments) but also in his aesthetic criticism. In particular, he turned his prodigious mind to the problems of a disappointing present—the betrayer of its own past—in drafts of a book on Beethoven's music. For Adorno, no other composer so perfectly exemplified "Hegelian philosophy" as Beethoven, and his "projected philosophical work" was to be a critical response to the master, though he died before completing it.[9] According to Adorno a naive faith in development, be it of artistic style or the autonomy of music as a form, will not do; indeed, this is the lesson he derives from Hegel (even if speed readers of Hegel have associated him with a banal teleologism or mistaken Adorno for being anti-Hegelian). In proposing an affinity between Beethoven's music and Hegel's thought, Adorno took the idea that the inseparability of form and content required recognizing the "objectivity" of music with respect to its time. Resisting the hypostatization of an artist's "development" as a matter of individual growth, Adorno called Beethoven "the stenographer of the objectified composition," implying with this locution that music is both independent of its composer—"something existing in itself, not originally made by him"—and recorded by him like a "clerk."[10] This surprising statement is meant not only to point toward the objective quality of the music but also to suggest that the idea of "Beethoven" is legible only as a sign of the artifice and reification of the individual.

In a dense formulation (among other elusive pronouncements in his *Beethoven* drafts), Adorno also refers to the "*shame* of the accidental subject before a truth that has been granted him as the whole." But this density is meant to underscore the determinate relationship of music to objectified history and contains the dialectical idea that only against the backdrop of rationalized processes that have led to the "end of the individual" does the category of subjectivity become meaningful.[11] Or, to put it differently, the false appearance of wholeness disguises the truth of inessential, accidental existence. For Adorno Beethoven's mature works embody the discontinuities of the history of which they are a record. In this manner they come to represent signs of intransigence and alienation, their very maturity the mark of a critical, negative relationship to organic elaboration. This nexus of ideas, positioned with reference to the concept of "late style" *(Spätstil)*, represents Adorno's attempt to capture the expressivity of music in the vocabulary of a "late Marxism" *(Spätmarxismus)*, a term that Fredric Jameson tells us was already in broad use in Adorno's time.[12]

The discussion of Beethoven's oeuvre—not as an unmediated movement from his early to late works but as a colliding, at times antithetical, emergence of an unharmonious whole—provides the terms for a different look at Ray's cinema as well, the lack of harmony across his filmmaking project expressing a similar preoccupation with the derangements of history Adorno attributed to Beethoven. I hasten to add that it is not that Beethoven and Ray are essentially alike in any way but that they can both be seen as symbols of a historical predicament. On these terms Ray's recapitulation of issues portrayed in *Charulata* as they are reshaped in *Ghare Baire* gives us a concrete, though radically different, illustration of the idea of lateness Adorno promulgates in relation to Beethoven. As an example it also illuminates the possibilities of and constraints on Ray's entire filmmaking project, a necessarily late entry into a critique of history as the unfolding movement of progress and civilization that the modernist experiment overall had attempted to counter. Hence, even if Adorno's concerns in the *Beethoven* book initially seem to be about completely different and distant matters, they allow me to bring the arguments of this book to a close: First, by highlighting Ray's own idiolect, his cinematic signature on the problem of cognition and recognition that modernism opens up (and which Adorno, in his own fashion, thematized). Second, they make it possible to speculate on the relevance of Ray's midcentury moment of cinematic experimentation to the present time, recursively serving as a diagnosis of lateness along the lines of Adorno's theory.

Adorno's dialectical contentions about Beethoven, although obviously pertaining to quite disparate aesthetic problems and cultural settings, throw a kind of paratactic light on Ray's cinema and permit a different kind of theorization of his practice. In much the same manner as Beethoven's late style embodied, for Adorno, the hollowing out of content as an aesthetic protest against the vicissitudes of history, Ray's cinematic vision presents us with its own version of temporal disintegration. The landscape of modernity is the landscape of catastrophe, and Ray's cinema represents this catastrophe anew in and through the materiality of the image. But catastrophe has less to do with doom and disaster (though there is that, as well, in films such as *Ashani Sanket* [Distant Thunder], 1973) than with history itself, which in the case of India is also a history of domination, neglect, and misunderstanding.

Our view of Ray's belated encounter with the panoply of issues associated with the emergence of an avant-garde centers precisely on this problem of historical consciousness and is thus sharpened with reference to Adorno, who saw the avant-garde as taking up the crisis of art as an institution as opposed to being about strategies of experimentation alone. In both of them we find a conviction about the inextricability of the aesthetic and the historical and a corresponding need to think of their mutuality in terms of the rules that govern the making as well as experience of the artwork. There are, of course, key differences between Ray and Adorno when it comes to their registers of thinking: one opaquely philosophical, the other expansively imagistic. Then there are the fundamental disparities in their location, self-formation, and political experience. As if this were not enough to deter comparison, Adorno also did not expend much effort in writing about film,[13] and he certainly did not know much about Indian culture. All of this requires us to tread carefully in attempting to cross the distance between his European sensibilities and Ray's situation both as a director and a subject from a part of the world that was, in the 1950s, only emerging from the shadow of two hundred years of British colonialism. Nonetheless, I would contend that the conceptual affinities that bind their thinking—as exemplary instances of what modernism has to offer us today—legitimate putting them together in a conversation. Moreover, one would be justified in pointing out that the connections between Adorno and Ray are also determined in part by the historical similarities between the short-lived moment of the Weimar Republic (the formative milieu of Adorno's thinking), with its parliamentary, republican experiment with a "controlled revolution" against empire, and the early decades of India's independence from the British that formed the crucible of Ray's practice.[14]

But the affinities extend beyond purely historical resemblances. If we consider the problem of modernism as it advances in late modernity, Adorno's formulations about Beethoven's late work illustrate the overall parallels between the development of art and the contradictions of society. For, regardless of its sense of completion or telos, all art betokens its estrangement under capitalism, and in this respect, Ray's cinema, like any other artistic endeavor, is a refracted expression of what Adorno called a "lost totality." In saying that "in the history of art, late works are the catastrophes," Adorno emphasized the late as a generative aspect of both art and the present stage of capitalism.[15] He thereby conceived the category of totality not as a "comprehensive principle of explanation" or an "ontologized" and "primeval reality" but a diffuse notion, as the late Gillian Rose argued, of "lost perspective."[16] This was Adorno's way of extricating an understanding of greatness in art from the bourgeois conception of progress and, similarly, from the immortalization of great works rendered as "timeless." By being regarded as late, art makes visible the materiality of time and with its constitution marks the illusion of a harmonious totality that the experience of capitalism forecloses in reality. Adorno's commitment to deciphering the ways that the modern continually reveals itself as the primitive is one that Ray can be said to share so concretely as to shine a more congenial light on the former's difficult pronouncements, enlivening them for an understanding of our own late predicament decades down the road from either of them.

It should be clear from my earlier references to *Charulata* and *Ghare Baire* that the question of Ray's late style has less to do with showing that the cracks in the seams of his filmmaking result from the passage of time or a loss of mastery than with recognizing that the passage of time is itself, in as reflexive a filmmaker like him, marked as a sign of the times themselves. Ashish Rajadhyaksha has, on the other hand, opined that by the time of the 1970s, Ray betrayed "growing frustration [about] a reality too complicated to handle" in his aesthetic choices, implying thereby a decline in his cinematic vision.[17] Adorno's criticisms of an approach that emphasizes growth or decline allows us to see that Ray's career does not need to be examined by the retrospective logic of Rajadhyaksha's assessment. For it only reveals what it sets out to look for in developmentalist terms, albeit in reverse—finding the shift from the hopeful realism of early Ray films to the uncontrolled and frustrated vision of the 1970s and 1980s to be a diminution of insight.[18] Instead, what is required is, as I have tried to demonstrate, a more dialectical view of how historical contradictions are registered within aesthetic experience, particularly by forms that self-consciously emit their sense of placement within history.

The analytic and political standpoint enabled by critical theory and, in the particular context of this closing discussion, Adorno, works against the overvaluing of subjectivity in contemporary theory, highlighting instead the ways that to be involved in cultural talk these days is to overcome somehow the snare of self-preservation (be it in the guise of the subaltern, the postcolonial exotic or ethnic, or the other of the West). This is the import of Adorno's conceptualization of lateness as a moment in the history of modern culture that not only parts company with biographical notions of the individual but is also only intelligible as a by-product of the very traditions whose exceptionalism and provincialism it has now survived. To propose this in a book on a single director's films is to acknowledge that my approach may be altogether heterodox. But it is driven by the Frankfurt School's insistence on a critical negativity toward matters of culture and aesthetics and an accompanying conviction about its relevance for postcolonial criticism in general. This is in spite of the fact that the Frankfurt School's emphases largely confront us today with their dated Eurocentrism—rather like the aging works of Beethoven themselves, which, as Adorno put it, sound "as if someone alone, were gesticulating and mumbling to himself."[19]

Nonetheless, if Adorno's most radical insight was to pit the idea of the negative against the positivity of culture (in which we would now have to include the work of interpretation as well), the effect of his insight is deadened to the extent that it is rendered into a matter of theoretical difficulty and distance, on the one hand, and pithy sloganeering, on the other. What remains to be pursued are the implications of the epigraph from Adorno, that what must be thought cannot signal its self-evident appropriateness—or timeliness—less because it has not been thought before (in this sense, it bears no resemblance to Michel Foucault's notion of thinking the unthought) than that it cannot be thought otherwise. By the same token, as Brecht reminds us, if the new meat is always eaten with the old forks, we are in danger of mistaking our staleness or, at least, the staleness of our implements (forks no less than frameworks) for a new and exclusive understanding only now made possible. It is by this light that Ray also serves as an exemplar of lateness, the very originality of his cinematic conceptions marking their alienation from all that goes in the name of the now and the new.

LATENESS AND RENEWAL

The continuing purchase of the worldview and expressive modalities of modernism has been importantly asserted by Fredric Jameson and Edward Said, and it is relevant for my purposes that they too take many of their leads from Adorno, albeit to different ends. Jameson, for instance, has addressed cinema more directly than Said, writing about it as the specific "cognitive mapping" or unconscious of the world system of capitalism in the present moment. In his preface to Jameson's book on the subject, Colin MacCabe avers that Jameson's conceptualization of cinema's "geopolitical aesthetic" is another take on the "attempt, after a loss of innocence about representation, to invent forms which will determine their own audiences, to project an interiority onto a future unmediated by any form of commodity. It is for this reason that the history of modernism is marked by new forms of sponsorship and above all by an avant-garde ethic which, be it of an aesthetic or political form, looks into the future for an ideal Joycean or proletarian reader."[20]

For his part Said argued that "many of the most prominent characteristics of modernist culture, which we have tended to derive from purely internal dynamics in Western society and culture, include a response to the external pressures on culture from the *imperium*."[21] What we see emerging in Jameson's and Said's respective ideas is, on the one hand, an emphasis on cinema as the form that best articulates the dilemmas of contemporary modernism and, on the other, an emphasis on the priority of the non-West for an understanding of modernism's possibilities as a whole. Accordingly, Jameson offers a theoretical argument about the role of cinema in mapping the cognitive, social, and political delineations of modernist thought within the totality of capitalism, while Said suggests that modernism represents, even "prominently," an aesthetic response to the pressures on European culture from the colonies, though his references are exclusively to the role of fiction. On his reading, the strategies of "self-consciousness, discontinuity, self-referentiality, and corrosive irony, whose formal patterns we have come to recognize as the hallmarks of modernist culture," become retroactive procedures to manage the anxiety about European vulnerability, functioning as a "re-take," as it were, on the historical destiny of Europe's culture.[22]

Their differing inflections notwithstanding, Jameson and Said make it possible for us to conclude that cinema and modernism are, perhaps more than ever, involved in the challenges of the present—which we might characterize as the world system of capitalism for the former and a broadly postcolonial zone for the latter. But this understanding remains incomplete to the extent that neither of them gives full credence to the other's terms. Accordingly, if Jameson is unable to contend with Third World cinema except on the terms of national allegory or "art naïf," Said ignores the diversity of cultural expression, including cinema, emerging in the wake of the decolonization and nationalist movements of the twentieth century. This is by no means to suggest that Jameson's propositions about allegory (misunderstood by his critics) are inimical to the positions I have advanced in this book. On the contrary, I find his idea that allegory as a form is appropriate for telling the tale of the Third World nation to be suggestive and theoretically sound, taking as he did the leads of Walter Benjamin and Ernst Bloch for his conception of national allegory.[23] Likewise, Jameson's arguments about contemporary Third World cinema, found largely in his discussion of Kidlat Tahimik's *The Perfumed Nightmare* (1977), remain useful for thinking about forms of collective expression after the moment of "imperfect cinema" as conceived (as I related in chapter 5) by Julio García Espinosa in the 1960s and 1970s. If the challenge of Third World cinema as "art naïf" can be said to rest on the continuing search for alternative modes of film practice (alternative to mainstream narrative, that is), Jameson provides a robust account of its relevance as political art for the present.[24]

Nonetheless, there is something rushed about Jameson's arguments when it comes to modernist experimentation in the Third World, as if merely citing its "extrinsic," as well as "intrinsic," qualities will do. His reliance on the model of cognitive mapping—a necessary and sufficient axiomatic for him—is, in the end, unsatisfying, just as Said's lack of interest in anything outside the literary (or musical) comes across as inadequate for a full account of expressivity. It can hardly be denied that at its most influential, modernism as a mode of thought has been most palpably conveyed and radicalized in extraliterary genres, especially in the Third World, with cinema accounting for some of the most compelling ways in which the cultures of the former colonies have erupted into metropolitan consciousness. A great deal of the variety of contemporary modernist expression has been missed because of a general lack of attention to this fact (regardless of the claims about "world literature" advanced by the modeling efforts of Franco Moretti, for example, or even Said's interventions on behalf of postcolonial writing).[25] It is in accounting for the cinematic component of modernism's historic challenge that Ray's project gains its full significance as a reworking of the "old order," though its late encounter with that history necessarily means that it cannot overcome the contradictions it exposes.

The apocalyptic aspect of Adorno's modernist vision or, more precisely, its lateness, is one that Said also identified, referring to Adorno "as lateness itself."[26] But it is worth noting that Said did not relate his arguments about postcolonial issues to his readings of Adorno, preferring instead to deploy his intimate familiarity with Adorno's aesthetic theory exclusively in his literary and musical elaborations of European texts and authors.[27] Still, by folding Adorno into his conception of lateness, Said emphasized the contrary predicament of criticism at large, a predicament he evoked via Adorno as *the* model: about criticism's still regnant deictic capacities, its compulsion to disturb the pieties of the day, together with its sense of loss and an almost catastrophic attitude that persists in saying no, this is not it at all. For Said, not all theory or practice exemplifies such negativity, only that which operates with an acute and modernist sense of "intransigence, difficulty, and unresolved contradiction."[28]

At the same time, such criticism is aware of the needs in the present for a consciousness that refuses to give up the authority to "stir up more anxiety, tamper irrevocably with the possibility of closure, and leave the audience more perplexed and unsettled than before."[29] Said's understanding of the problem of lateness, specifically in its manifestation as late style, centers on the situation of the engaged critic (as exemplified by Beethoven, Adorno, and, by extension, Said himself) confronted with the impending sense of ending—of work and life. This is undoubtedly a highly poignant bit of self-positioning by perhaps the most important literary critic of the last century, then, too, about one of its most important philosophical figures, and, as if this were not enough, about arguably the most important musical genius in the European tradition. That said, it is not the way I would wish to position an understanding of Ray or his cinema—as another, but this time non-Western and postcolonial, embodiment of late-artist-cum-late-style par excellence. In my estimation such a reading detracts from Adorno's dialectical rather than "contrapuntal" form of criticism (the adjective with which Said most closely associated his own method). It also renders problematic my efforts to conceive Ray's cinema along the lines of a material aesthetics that invests less in subjective affiliations between the world, the text, and the critic (to echo the title of one of Said's earlier works) than in conjunctions between the formal, compositional dimensions of the aging work of art and the historical moment of its emergence and experience.[30]

Shierry Weber Nicholsen has usefully reminded us that Adorno's aesthetic theory cannot be understood except in terms of his dialectical interest in creating "a theory of 'musical materialism,' "[31] a phrase, she points out, he used to express the concrete "material" available to individual composers with respect to their relationship to history and to the ways that it both constrains and enables what can be uttered in musical form. In other words neither late work nor late style has, in Adorno's thought, to do with the aging or senescence of the artist (contra Said). Rather, as Nicholsen suggests, "it reflects the Hegelian aspect of his aesthetics in its concern with the 'end of art.' "[32] Only this perspective in elucidating the dialectic of subject and object through music allows Adorno's ideas about lateness to acquire their meaning because, as Nicholsen again points out, they center on "late music in general rather than an individual composer's later period."[33] She clarifies the argument as follows:

> The popular view holds that in Beethoven's late style we see subjectivity given free rein to ignore form and contemplate death, fate, and mortality. But for Adorno, mortality is part of human beings' life as natural creatures, and it cannot enter into the inorganic work of art as such. Hence, although what we see in Beethoven's late style is indeed a response to human mortality, it is not an expression of subjective feeling about impending death. *Rather what we in fact see in the music is the return of musical conventions,* such as the extensive trills in the late piano sonatas, now untampered with by the compositorial subjectivity that subordinated all elements of musical form to itself in the middle-period works.[34]

It is in the emphasis on form as a coding of experience—invoking the processes of reification that all human expression necessarily undergoes within capitalism—that Adorno's propositions about late style gain focus and, more to the point, aid in our reading of Ray's cinema. It also links up Adorno's musical preoccupations with my own interest in Ray's films since both are premised on investigating how the truth of existence is ciphered in aesthetic forms. The category of the "late," as it underpins Adorno's thinking, stresses the visibility of conventions (in music), the laying bare of formal strategies in unharmonious, uncompromising ways that refer not to psychological or biographical elements in a composer's life but to the mediation of that subjectivity by the objective landscape that forces all art to cast off its illusions. Referring to late work as dead fruit and, perhaps for that reason, also as the fruit of dead labor, Adorno says: "The maturity of the late works of important artists is not like the ripeness of fruits. As a rule, these works are not well rounded, but wrinkled, even fissured. They are apt to lack sweetness, fending off with prickly tartness those interested merely in sampling them. They lack all that harmony which the classicist aesthetic is accustomed to demand from the work of art, showing more traces of history than of growth."[35]

Within this perspective the aging artist, expending his or her labor in protest against art, no less than the aging artwork and the historical moment in which it is experienced, all refract the universal character of the commodity. Given this view, we might say that Beethoven's late work becomes, for Adorno, paradigmatic of the predicament of historical subjectivity itself: it is not merely the abstract rendition of the problems of an individual composer's "style" but also a dialectical image of damaged life. Indeed, the desire to read Beethoven's music as an encapsulation of the problem of modern existence is quite explicitly stated in one of the notes Adorno took in planning his proposed study: "The task of the book will be to resolve the riddle of humanity as a dialectical image."[36]

I should like to submit that Ray's films also be approached as dialectical images of the socially alienated existence of cultural forms in modernity. Precisely to the degree that the very idea of an Indian or Third World modernism is outré or eccentric, it becomes the spur for gaining insight into the problems of modern existence that European versions of modernist theory and avant-garde experimentation undertook to explore but failed to realize fully. For this argument to succeed, it *does* matter whether the genre of exploration employs self-evident strategies of defamiliarization and aesthetic estrangement or reinforces a more naturalist or realist take on the issues at stake, but it matters only to the extent that in an overall sense artworks are seen to encrypt social contradictions that they self-consciously work to expose through various formal, conceptual, and narrative means. Accordingly, to think of Ray as betokening his own late style is to regard his imagistic critique of a rationalized reality (as well as rationalized and escapist cinema) as representing a particularly uninhibited comment on his historical predicament that comes across throughout his filmic works irrespective of the precise moment of their making. To the instrumentalities that characterize mainstream life, mainstream cinema, and mainstream thinking, his critique seems, along with Adorno, to say: no, not this.

By this light, Ray's modernism is not only a belated one—arriving on the scene well after the historical avant-gardes had evacuated it—but the take he offers on problems of modernity is also configured disjunctively. Accordingly, he is less hostile to the possibilities of modernization in post-Independence India (in its moment of nation-building) until much later in his career, while his efforts to reveal to urban audiences the appeal of the rural and the folk retain something of the antimodern character of earlier modernist writings themselves. This is where our perception of the varied standpoints of modernism has gone a bit awry, since, in addition to the formalist experiments of the high European modernists (with their generative disenchantment and often libertine sensibilities), there also looms the revolutionary modernism of the Soviets, which took its conceptual cues from endorsing rather than rejecting what the industrial age had to offer. Within the Soviet perspective modernism was the aesthetic counterpart to technological modernization, promising an opportunity to realize humanity's potential in the cultural sphere no less than in an industrial one. If the new socialist reality betokened a need for a radical rethinking of forms of signification, Ray's cinema also inherits this inflection to the modernist imperative, though it would be incorrect to propose that he was unambiguous about its destiny. Still, ambiguity or ambivalence is the mark of retrospection, and in taking up the Soviet project belatedly—and as a corrective to it—he signals both distance and fellowship.

Thus what becomes legible as merely an apolitical, even bourgeois, deployment of artistic innovation and investigation of technique is revived by Ray in an attempt to reawaken the political spirit of that which has been lost. Reversing the emphases in the Soviet experimental model, as well as its Western European equivalents, he leaves us with a self-dislocating encounter with modernism's dialectic. Consequently, his films are, in one way or another, experiments with forms of temporality and time-consciousness: from the use of the flashback as the central narrative device in a film like *Ghare Baire*, the return to the "primal" temporality of the village in *Pather Panchali* (Song of the Road, 1955), or the nonsynchronous coexistence of the rural and urban in *Agantuk* (The Stranger, 1991) to the dehiscent time of the goddess in *Devi* or the modern worker in *Mahanagar*. So I should say that I do not wish to claim a specifically late style for Ray, merely to thematize the stakes for reading his films on the terms of a concrete and materialistic sense of memory, time, and the possibility of the future, not merely the disappointments of the past. By inhabiting a critical negativity toward the predicament of Indian cinema and modernity that finds its way into an attenuated sense of form and often exaggeratedly discordant narratives, Ray gives us a new look at late style, though it is the newness of the anachronism that, despite its age, still intimates a futurity.

Much of what I have said is underwritten by a nonexceptionalist reading of historical emergence, even though the grounds for advancing my arguments are rooted in the specificities of Indian cinema and culture. By this light, to think seriously about postcoloniality is to think historically about the modern epoch as a whole, without prioritizing what came earlier as the defining criterion of value or, for that matter, celebrating belatedness as some sort of ontological proof of a resistant otherness. This in turn requires presupposing a temporal framework that twins the global emergence of formerly colonized societies and the world system of capitalism tethered to but by no means centered in the West. The way we *all*, as moderns, think about our place in history or, more precisely, the way we think about our place in time might thus represent an alternative rationale for my considerations here.

In the preceding chapters, as well as more proximately in this conclusion, my interest has been in speculating about what might come of recontextualizing the problem of lateness as a way to think about how aesthetic forms embed social content as well as a consciousness of their own historicity. This, after all, was Adorno's purpose in proposing the idea of late style. I would like to hope that such a recontextualization has something to contribute to a postcolonial conversation in going beyond the facile tarring of lateness with the brush of belatedness. For it can hardly be doubted that a certain common sense has prevailed in which to speak of being belated is necessarily to tarry with the ideological tendency of European thought to link the non-Western with the primitive or the backward. Against this the corrective has been to posit the "incommensurability" or "difference" of postcolonial alterity, the disjunctiveness of its temporality, and so on—conceits that fall apart no sooner than they are examined. The epistemological status of the primitive must surely be questioned. But this has happened all along, not just within postcolonial theory of the past two decades. As Robert Hullot-Kentor calls to our attention, the concept of the primitive in fact organizes the full array and force of Adorno's thinking about modernism. That is to say, the primitive articulates what was hitherto inconceivable within Western thought and generates a way to survive beyond parochialism rather than to reinforce it. Adorno's insight into the "primitive in us" is, in Hullot-Kentor's estimation, constellated at every turn in his conception of natural history, regression, the spell, the taboo, the ban, or magic. "Each [of these concepts] wants to reveal the

modern itself as the power of the primitive."[37] They are thus at the crux of
Adorno's recognition of modernism's leap forward into—rather than out
of—historicity. But the recursive dialecticism (not to mention difficulty) of
Adorno's thought has also intervened to prevent a true reckoning with it,
especially in critiques of modernism that see themselves thinking against
Eurocentrism. As a result, citations of Adorno now only travel as latter-
day *minima moralia* about the "culture industry," "dialectic of enlightenment," or "negative dialectic."

In the condensation of the primitive, the archaic, and the modern we
are given, however contrarily, the dialectical coordinates for a possible
revaluation of the category of lateness. Rather than designating the lack
of coevalness between West and non-West, it describes contingencies of
modern experience that Adorno, and somewhat differently, Said, regarded
as central to understanding our collective alienation in and through our
relationship to time.[38] Insofar as postcolonial thought evinces a thoroughgoing awareness of time-consciousness—above all the consciousness of
having come "after" and in the "post"—Ray's statements about cinema's
derangement of real time as reel time serve to highlight estrangements
constitutive of modern experience throughout what Giovanni Arrighi has
called "the long twentieth century."[39] If, to invoke another one of Said's
coinages, theories of modernism have emerged as an expression of "traveling theory," the routes of this travel have been charted via different means,
with a variety of terms used to account for its directions and tendencies.
So, from Houston Baker's effort to read the Harlem Renaissance by the
terms of a "liberating modernism," or Simon Gikandi's to articulate a
uniquely "Caribbean modernism" that reclaims "colonial modernism" for
itself, to Rey Chow's reading of the "translational" discourse of Chinese
cinema, and Charles W. Pollard's "new world modernisms" as a description
of Caribbean poetics, we get a wide range of possibilities.[40] There have also
been other ways to enter what would seem to be the infinitely capacious
echo-chamber of modernism—pluralized, hyphenated, modified, and
rectified. But through it all the determinate effects of European modernism on the dispositions of various nonmetropolitan cultural and literary
reengagements with it continue to be felt in ways that simply resist casting
the original aside.

Recalling Williams's critique (though he is seldom cited by the scholars just mentioned), modernism was the product of a "selective tradition," whose principles of inclusion and exclusion were invisible to itself
and whose aspiration to be construed as universal—as *the* literature of
modernity—was untrammeled. In the attempt to appropriate for itself the

energies and insights into the world-historical experience of modernity, what goes by the name of modernism demonstrates not that its terms are restricted to European or American authors and texts but only that the global flowering of a modernist sensibility and conceptual apparatus was displaced by policing the boundaries and referring to the experiments outside Europe or the United States as derivative or, at best, complementary. Thus, the retrospective lens one must, by definition, cast on modernism now needs to resituate what seems anachronistic or out of place as, in fact, illuminated by the same light and belonging in the same conversation that had hitherto reserved the pride of place in understanding modernity for itself. Hullot-Kentor has, I think, valuably derided "the gratuitous plural," and I, too, see no need to qualify Ray's cinema as one among a slew of "modernisms"—a pluralized, Indian, discrepant modernism, a variant of what James Clifford has called a "traveling culture."[41] For such a move banalizes what was most important about modernism as a claim on the modern—issued from different quarters and sometimes to oppositional ends. Ultimately, what remains most important in rethinking the concept of modernism is to insist on its explanatory force without relativizing it in the same move.

In one of many interviews in which he was asked to "define his relationship with the West," Ray responded by saying, "The more I pondered, the more I realised how hopeless it was. There was nothing to suggest that, outside the field of specialisation, the west took the slightest interest in India. The Taj Mahal drew the tourists, of course, as did the burning dead on the ghats at Benares. But there it ended. A vast sub-continent with one of the oldest and richest traditions of art, music, and literature, existed only to be ignored."[42] Some of this has changed in the past two decades, particularly with India's global emergence in the market no less than as the exemplum par excellence of curricular centrality for postcolonial initiatives in the academy. In either case, however, India's exemplarity is still only as good as the gold standard of market value. Seen from a muscular cosmopolitan perspective, things Indian are good these days: Ray as much as Gandhi (either the film or the man), chicken *tikka masala* as much as *bhangra* music. The primitive thus returns as the modern! But such entries into the global scene do not displace the value—always equal or higher—of their Western counterparts, and in the end such adjudications of civilizational accomplishment inevitably keep the value hierarchy intact.

On the face of it this point may seem to be only about the representation of otherness, but it pertains at a deeper level and almost as an epistemological tic to a framework of thought in which non-European cultures exist either to be ignored or to be traduced. "Under Western eyes" (the title of the interview from which I quote Ray here) Indian culture has always been rendered in the bifurcated terms of relativist recognition or absolutist difference. As Ray put it with biting irony, "For a land where cows are holy and God is a phallus, anything will pass for the truth."[43] I take Ray to be implying that only if we reckon with the historical and epistemological blind spots in our collective forms of thinking can a more appropriate understanding of our age emerge, one that is prepared to take on the apparent anachronisms of the "foreign" as a fundamental challenge to preconceptions about the world but also impelled by the need to re-cognize what can otherwise pass us by as anachronism or appropriation—in this case, of the many valences of the term *modernism*.

Anachronisms are, of course, often not what they seem, and the appar-ent untimeliness of ideas can also hide the lessons provided by the past and other places to the future, albeit these lessons are unlikely to be assimilated by good intentions or newer labels. Understanding in the present must also accompany its negative, its own admission at having ignored so much for so long. If, in Ray's account, this is an impetus for the West, in our own moment it also means that it may be time to stop casting about for newly consecrated ideals of "alternative modernities" to which multicultural forms of modernism can now be affixed. As Jürgen Habermas so aptly put it, modernity was always an "incomplete project," and its aesthetic corol-laries were everywhere equally incomplete.[44] Sometimes this incomple-tion took the form of a late encounter with specific experiential questions; at other times it may well have been a timely vision now rendered residual by the proliferation of interpretive vocabularies to talk about it.[45]

In the context of thinking about cinematic modernism we can certainly say that the lateness emblematized by Ray's films has less to do with India's belated experience of this technologically mediated form than with the post hoc ways in which that experience and its modes of narrativiza-tion have both undergone a secondary mediation on the terms introduced by the emergent interests of new comparatism, a new globality, or, for that matter, a new modernist analytic that looks to clarify what was previously misunderstood. Nonetheless, even such a corrective and remedial stand-point is enjoined to be mindful about a too-easy synthesis.

And, finally, it is important to note that Ray's apparent imperious-ness toward the West was by no means a one-way street. The challenge he posed to his Western critics and followers is one that he also issued to those at home, exhorting his Indian interlocutors to confront the actuality of European achievements rather than wallow in various forms of self-congratulatory marginality. Despite knowing that a Westernized education was relatively common among the middle-class Indians who were his primary audience, he recognized its insufficiencies as well, leading him to propose that a substantial appreciation of Indian culture itself requires a closer acquaintance with its European counterparts, particularly when it comes to cinema and its increasingly visible influence on modern Indian society. The underlying suggestion here is that only if we reckon with historical and epistemological impasses as a whole can a self-conscious cinema, as well as a better understanding, emerge.

At least part of the charge of such an understanding is to be borne by the ways that lateness and anachronism provide the challenge to begin learning anew the lessons of the past for the future. Instead of acceding to the demand for transparent knowledge, the burden of reflexive thinking must, to echo a phrase from Adorno again, account for the "recalcitrance of the object," which I adapt here to refer to the resistance that the past or the other puts up against being appropriated as objects of knowledge. Ray captures this obdurately historical intransigence in more demotic terms that are all the more effective for it: "It is more important for the west now to see our films than to understand them. In any case, true understanding will take time. Slighted for so long, India will not yield up her secrets to the west so easily, for cows are still holy here, and God is still a phallus."[46] The relevance of an avant-garde vision able to grasp this contradictory reality, both more palpable and more elusive than the sights and sounds of high art or mass culture, is the reason to return to its terms of engagement.

Notes

1. The place of cinema within the discourse of modernism has been productively explored in Charney and Schwartz, *Cinema and the Invention of Modern Life*.

2. There are of course other variants in the story of modernism, understood as "peripheral," "alternative," or "postcolonial" modernisms, but a survey of those is outside the scope of this discussion, not least because I think such subcategories relativize the issue.

3. Williams, "The Politics of the Avant-Garde," 59.

4. Malcolm, "Satyajit Ray," 109.

5. See Jameson, "Postmodernism, or the Cultural Logic of Late Capitalism."

6. Williams, "The Politics of the Avant-Garde," 62.

7. Ibid., 50–52.

8. Ray, "The Odds against Us," 58–59.

9. Robinson, *Satyajit Ray*, 327.

10. Descriptors such as *independent* or *art cinema* or *underground* cinema, used to label Ray's works, are incomplete to the extent that they do not reckon with the medium as a mode of the circulation of intelligibility in institutional settings rather than as discrete objects.

11. Kapur, *When Was Modernism*, 146.

12. *Sant Tukaram* (Saint Tukaram) was directed by Vishnu Govind Damle and Sheikh Fattelal. Kapur makes much of the film's affinity with magic, an idea that I pursue in my discussion of Ray's *Devi* (chapter 3) though with reference to Sergei Eisenstein.

13. Kapur, *When Was Modernism*, 202.

14. Kapur relies on Partha Chatterjee's "qualified use" of passive revolution (see Kapur, *When Was Modernism*, 228n5), itself a symptom of what Timothy Brennan has called the pro forma "narrative act of allegiance" one finds these days within postcolonial criticism, where, says Brennan, "Gramsci's own the-

ses, styles of thinking, or points of departure are in these circles still received second hand" (Brennan, "The Southern Intellectual," 234).

15. See Gramsci, *Selections from Cultural Writings*. For secondary criticism relating to Gramsci's interest in the avant-garde see San Juan Jr., "Antonio Gramsci on Surrealism and the Avantgarde."

16. Kapur, for example, celebrates the "irregular modernism" of Ravi Varma (*When Was Modernism*, 153). Those familiar with his floridly sexualized imagery and voyeuristic representations of nubile goddesses and women might find this an audacious and unpredictable assessment since, from a certain point of view, Varma's art seems exactly to reflect the European bourgeoisie's fetish of negligees, semitransparent lace coverings, and the faux naturalism of pinkened complexions (especially odd in the context of painting Indian subjects). Still, Kapur valorizes him for introducing "a manner of 'truth' through an objective demonstration of life's protocol." And he is seen to "simply circumvent the pitched logic of a realist encounter" (157), leading in turn to her argument that "Ravi Varma succeeds in obliterating the forms in which the past has come to us" (159). The language here is of the kind we are more accustomed to hear in reference to artists and artworks whose modernist critique is less ambivalent in an orientalist sense, and certainly less commercial. In this case, using the mass-cultural cachet of market-oriented art as the sign of authentic modernist transgression risks opening itself up to the charge of mere intellectual play.

17. Partha Mitter's books have effectively and comprehensively shed light on the problems of nationalism, modernism, and aesthetic discourse in India. See his *Art and Nationalism in Colonial India, 1850–1922;* and *The Triumph of Modernism*. The former provides an especially clear-eyed evaluation of Ravi Varma's paintings. Readers may also wish to look at Guha-Thakurta, *The Making of a New "Indian" Art* for a different approach that places Varma by the light of popular styles of image-making associated with Indian calendar art.

18. Kapur, *When Was Modernism*, 201, 224; subsequent citations of this source are referenced parenthetically in the text.

19. In contrast to Ray, Ghatak, says Kapur, "would pitch his expressional ambiguities beyond the westernizing/narodnik [populist] paradigm and give the interrogative mode its political edge in the contemporary" (Kapur, *When Was Modernism*, 204).

20. It is worth noting that Rajadhyaksha is the influential coeditor, with Paul Willemen, of one of the most important resources on Indian cinema to date: *Encyclopedia of Indian Cinema*.

21. Rajadhyaksha, "Beyond Orientalism," 34.

22. Rajadhyaksha, "Beyond Orientalism," 35.

23. Kapur, *When Was Modernism*, 260.

24. We may recall here Benjamin's important footnote in his essay "Eduard Fuchs, Collector and Historian": "It is well known that Marx never explained in any detail how the relationship between superstructure and infrastructure should be thought of in individual cases. All we can determine is that he envis-

aged a series of mediations—transmissions, one might say—which interpolate between the material relationships of production and the remoter domains of the superstructure, which includes art" (294n45).

25. See Adorno, *Negative Dialectics*, 3.

26. See, e.g., Rodowick, *The Virtual Life of Film*.

27. Rajadhyaksha, "Beyond Orientalism," 35.

28. Schwarz, "Misplaced Ideas," 25.

29. Fredric Jameson has offered a sharp critique of the tendency in postcolonial criticism to talk of "alternative modernities" in ways that thoroughly evacuate the term *modernity* of its conceptual force. In *A Singular Modernity* he rightly dismisses the voluntarism of the culturalist belief that "you can fashion your own modernity differently" (12) and reiterates the value of a structural understanding of modernity as the system of worldwide capitalism, which, at least in Marx's writings, was never about the normative status of Europe (or, more particularly, England) but about the contingently determined roads taken by capital under unique national circumstances.

30. Schwarz, "Misplaced Ideas," 29.

31. Briefly, and somewhat telegraphically, Hegel emphasizes the distinction (crucial for both historical and subjective development) between *Ansichseyn*, or any status quo whose positive content only promises other possibilities, and *Fürsichseyn*, which he proposes as the movement of an in-itself toward actualization; thus, an alienation from explicit content and an extension toward implicit and future potentialities. Howard P. Kainz explicates this and other Hegelian concepts in *Hegel's Phenomenology of Spirit*.

32. See, e.g., Chakrabarty, *Provincializing Europe*.

33. Pascale Casanova has referred to the cross-fertilization of global literary forms as constituting a "world republic of letters." See her book, *The World Republic of Letters*.

34. See Benjamin, "Surrealism," 181.

35. Aragon, *Paris Peasant*, 14.

36. See Kracauer, *Theory of Film*, xlix.

37. Ibid., xlvii; subsequent citations of this source are referenced parenthetically in the text.

38. See Polan, *The Political Language of Film and the Avant-Garde*, 1.

39. Miriam Hansen, introduction to Kracauer, *Theory of Film*, xl.

40. Kracauer, *Theory of Film*, l.

41. In her masterful commentary Hansen has proposed that cinema is emblematic of the modern to the extent that the specific historical cultures from which it emerged also underwrote specific forms of attention, distraction, and collectivization that have come to be associated with modernity at large (see Hansen, introduction, vii–xlv).

42. It should be noted that in Kracauer's conceptualization film bears no resemblance either to the existentialist faith in "things" in a state of innocence or, by contrast, to the "always already" deferrals of meaning we have come to expect from various modes of '68ist theory.

43. Two recent books that provide different but largely conventional text-in-context interpretations of Ray's representations of tradition and modernity are Darius Cooper, *The Cinema of Satyajit Ray;* and Suranjan Ganguly, *Satyajit Ray.*

44. The objection is that auteur approaches place an unjustifiably humanist faith in the person of the filmmaker, who, far from being the author of a text, is interchangeable with other agents of production and is merely the place, so to speak, of the "author-effect."

45. For an effective critique of the idea of the "West" as a geopolitically or theoretically viable category see Lazarus, *Nationalism and Cultural Practice in the Postcolonial World.*

46. Ray, "Little Man, Big Book," 178.

1. CATASTROPHE AND UTOPIA

1. Even though Freud would grant the mutual reinforcement of Eros and Thanatos, the problem of happiness remains for him mired in the irresolvable standoff between self and society (as opposed to being conceived as a socially devisable outcome for the future).

2. In 1977 Louis Marin brilliantly pursued the idea of a negative or "degenerate" utopia in "Disneyland: A Degenerate Utopia"; Jameson followed up in 1979 with his essay "Reification and Utopia in Mass Culture," reprinted in his *Signatures of the Visible* (9–34).

3. See, e.g., Schwarz, "Sexing the Pundits"; and Sprinker, "Homeboys."

4. I take the term *conjuncture (conjoncture)*—in the sense specified within *Annales* historiography—to refer to a way of organizing historical time and analysis into a period that spans anywhere from ten to fifty years (roughly); such a time frame is not "epochal" (which requires being analyzed as the *longue durée*). Such a historiographic understanding of the conjuncture is to be distinguished from the view proffered by Louis Althusser, for whom a conjuncture is more muddlingly, not to say idealistically, to be thought of as a *philosophical* rather than a historical concept emerging as an imperative of philosophy rather than history and indicating the materiality of philosophical practice in a given situation. For a fuller elaboration of what to my mind is the more compelling (and original) formulation see, for instance, Marc Bloch's classic statements in *The Historian's Craft.*

5. See Koselleck, *Futures Past.*

6. Dana Polan has proposed that our ideas of what constitutes radicalism in film must be revised from resting on formal strategies of subversion or cinematic reflexivity to a different way of conceptualizing the relationship of film to history; we need, that is, to move away from looking for the insertions of history into the text and move toward the historicizing gesture of (and this is the connection between his point and mine) inserting the text into history. See Polan, *The Political Language of Film and the Avant-Garde*, 30.

7. In referring to the prevalence of the issue of temporality in cinematic

history, I am referring not to mainstream or classical Hollywood (and related) traditions but to the corpus of avant-garde and independent films, many of which bear on the ways that time expresses different forms of consciousness and vice versa. Gilles Deleuze is today regarded in some quarters as having made time-consciousness a salient and even paradigmatic marker of the shift from prewar to postwar cinema (in his *Cinema 1* and *Cinema 2* books). Nevertheless, the history of the literature on film would amply attest to the sustained elaboration of temporal effects on the moving image in everyone from Sergei Eisenstein and Lev Kuleshov to, certainly, Walter Benjamin, Siegfried Kracauer, and Béla Balázs, and well before any purported transition from the "movement-image" to the "time-image."

8. See Jameson, *The Geopolitical Aesthetic.*

9. See, for instance, Sprinker, "Homeboys"; and, from a very different perspective, Sangeeta Ray, "Woman as Nation and a Nation of Women," in her *En-Gendering India* (90–125).

10. The distinction between a mode of signification that is ideological or "mythic" and one that is explanatory-critical was given to us, we may recall, by Roland Barthes in his paradigmatic essays in *Mythologies*, especially in the methodological essay at the end of the collection, "Myth Today" (109–59).

11. William Pietz's three essays on this subject remain the most authoritative. See Pietz, "The Problem of the Fetish: Part 1"; "The Problem of the Fetish: Part II"; and "The Problem of the Fetish: Part III."

12. See Astruc, "The Birth of a New Avant-Garde."

13. See Hansen, introduction to Kracauer, *Theory of Film*, xvii.

14. Rachel Moore has offered a similar argument: "The fetish physically holds relationships and history that cannot be recovered. This insight provides a way of understanding the brilliant objectness of things often found in films whose characters have a dulled or muted subjectivity" (Moore, *Savage Theory*, 82).

15. In a footnote to his discussion of the postwar "conspiracy" film Jameson says, "I take it that Proust's great theme is not memory but rather our incapacity to experience things 'for the first time'; the possibility of genuine experience *(Erfahrung)* only the second time round (by writing rather than memory)" (Jameson, *The Geopolitical Aesthetic*, 83n10).

16. Benjamin, "The Storyteller," 98.

17. Anderson's now-classic monograph *Imagined Communities* lays out some of the experiential effects of modern temporality in terms precisely drawn from Benjamin's insights into the "homogeneous, empty time" of the modern (see Anderson, *Imagined Communities*, passim).

18. The relevant examples here, aside from Proust's classic (cited above), are *Hard Times* (Dickens, 1854), *Un chien andalou* (Buñuel and Dali, 1929), and *Modern Times* (Chaplin, 1936).

19. Susan Buck-Morss provides a highly suggestive discussion of Benjamin's use of the figures of the *flaneur*, the sandwichman, and the whore as "prototypes" in the representation of modernity. Benjamin, she says, tended

to avoid "more obvious social types and went to the margins" for his commentary on the present because "historical figures whose existence was precarious economically in their own time" are best able to elucidate the dangers inherent in the predicament of modernity because they represent the disappearance of certain modes of existence (see Buck-Morss, "The Flaneur, the Sandwichman and the Whore," 101).

20. See Pensky, *Melancholy Dialectics*.

21. I have been influenced in thinking along these lines by Christine Buci-Glucksmann's *Baroque Reason*.

22. Tagore, *The Home and the World*, 22.

23. Ibid., 49.

24. Take, for instance, Rosalind Krauss's arguments in her influential book, *The Originality of the Avant-Garde and Other Modernist Myths*. Her rendition of avant-garde aesthetics is intended precisely to blunt the edge of some key avant-garde principles, particularly those informed by Marxist ideas about the demystification of consciousness (e.g., shock and chance). So it is that she can assert the following: "The aesthetic field, as it was structured by the thinking of the twenties and thirties, was the collective semantic marker not for Art but for Man. The field was both thoroughly humanized and psychologized; its obsessive subjects either biological or psychic creation" (126). Although such a description may well suffice as a partial explanation of the avant-garde's investments, it does not capture anything of the movement's more revolutionary impulses (as evident in the works of the Russian Futurists, for example, or German Expressionists like Kandinsky or Klée, or even the surrealist zeal of Louis Aragon)—for all of whom the term *Revolution* is much better inserted than "Man" in the dialectic of matter and spirit that Krauss sees as subtending the axis of mimetic/abstract art in the 1920s and 1930s. I would contend that if an overall descriptor is at all necessary, a more accurate way to describe the period might be to think of its project as a series of (failed) experiments in addressing what happens to human beings under certain conditions—that is, as interventions into a historico-philosophical field rather than as a humanistic or psychologistic enterprise.

25. Benjamin, "A Small History of Photography," 255.

26. Hansen, introduction to Kracauer, *Theory of Film*, xxvii.

27. Tagore, *The Home and the World*, 41.

28. Ibid., 64–65.

2. THE (UN)MOVING IMAGE

This chapter is a substantially revised version of the essay "Carnal Knowledge: Visuality and the Modern in *Charulata*," which appeared in *Camera Obscura* 37 (Jan. 1996): 157–86.

1. Kenneth Tynan, writing in the (London) *Observer*, is quoted in Robinson, *Satyajit Ray*, 157; Howard Thompson's review, "Ray's 'Charulata' Given: Simple Story Makes Exquisite Movie," appeared in the *New York Times*, Sep. 11, 1965.

2. Houston, "Ray's *Charulata*," 33.

3. See Calhoon, "Blind Gestures."

4. In a later scene we witness Amal and Charu's wordplay in which Ray works the letter *B* into the complex visual and aural motif about becoming, first displayed here. In the alliterative exchange that Amal and Charu undertake, each sentence they utter contains a significant word beginning with *B* either in Bengali or English. It is interesting that each of the words—*Bardhaman* (a town in Bengal), *biyé* (marriage), *Bilet* (Britain), *barrister, Bengal, Black Native, bap bap bolé* (requesting reprieve), *Bankim*—rehearses the familiar cycle of the Anglicized Indian's predicament: at one level it is a generatively hybridized collocation of Bengali and English language and culture—marked, allusively, by references to people and places. It also connotes recognition of the substantive inability of the Bengali to get to the journey's putative end (as in the genre of the self-authorizing "Grand Tour" undertaken by the sovereign subject of European history). On the contrary, the native returns "back to Bengal" and to "Bankim," who also wrote the influential nationalist novel *Anandamath*—to take his *proper* place in the world: at home. An instance of the afterlife of a historical problematic, the question of location (home vs. world) becomes even more vexed after decolonization, in the latter half of the twentieth century.

5. Suranjan Ganguly has pointed out that although Ray was often charged with being a bourgeois filmmaker who was unable to bring out the full realities of Indian existence (urban squalor, poverty, political violence, and so on), this ignores the shifts in his filmmaking career—particularly in his later films (such as *Pratidwandi* [The Adversary, 1970], *Ashani Sanket* [Distant Thunder, 1973], or *Jana Aranya* [The Middleman, 1975]). More important for the philosophical orientation of my analysis (in this chapter and in the rest of the book) is the argument that we must learn to resist the anxiety about what constitutes an *adequate* form of politicality, to the extent that this search for adequation voids any understanding of immanent critique. See Suranjan Ganguly, *Satyajit Ray*, esp. 141–49.

6. Robinson glosses the importance of musical motifs in his cinema, saying, in relation to *Charulata*, that "two of Tagore's songs provide a basis for much of the music in the film, either in their original form or in snatches and phrases embroidered by Ray. The first of them . . . is a very simple, catchy tune with a spring in it, used to teach young girls dance-steps and to train beginners in Tagore-singing" (Robinson, *Satyajit Ray*, 163).

7. Ray, "Under Western Eyes," 272–73.

8. This is a point of some contention, especially among Indian critics who have regarded Ray's occasional self-positioning as a Bengali director to be disingenuous at best, provincial at worst. Aside from the fact that Ray *was* a Bengali director, such identitarian objections are ultimately banal. A more interesting treatment of the problem of location in relation to the politics of secularism is offered by Shyam Benegal, another of India's important filmmakers (and something of a disciple of Ray). See his "Secularism and Popular Indian Cinema."

9. Rajadhyaksha, "Beyond Orientalism," 32.

10. Ibid.

11. Colin MacCabe, "Dead Mothers, Patrick McCabe, Neil Jordan, and Mother Ireland" (lecture, University of Minnesota, Twin Cities, Department of Cultural Studies and Comparative Literature, March 30, 2007).

12. As discussed in chapter 1, my understanding of the past-present relation in conjunctural terms is taken from the demarcation given to it by the *Annales* historians, seeing it as a perspective on the past from the present in a way that is neither "historicist" (as this term has been bandied about) or "epochal" but organized with respect to "medium-term" sociohistorical developments—e.g., post-Independence India or the French Revolution.

13. Benjamin, *The Origin of German Tragic Drama*, 175.

14. Ibid.

15. See Buck-Morss, "Aesthetics and Anaesthetics"; Hansen, "Benjamin and Cinema"; and Hansen, "Benjamin's Aura."

16. Some recent works of criticism have attempted to redress this imbalance. See, e.g., Prendergast, *Film Music: A Neglected Art;* Buhler, Flinn, and Neumeyer, *Music and Cinema;* and Wojcik, *Soundtrack Available.* The classic study of film sound remains Chion, *Audio-Vision;* see also Chion's most recent volume, *Film, a Sound Art.*

17. This information is given in Robinson, *Satyajit Ray,* 164. My point about the allegorical stitching together of spatially and temporally distant discourses is relevant here as well. For while the syncretism of expressing Bengali sentiments in a Scottish ballad is apparent, the less visible "archival" reference is to the dance drama *Kalmrigaya* (the genre being a baroque appropriation itself), in which Tagore first put the tune to use. In it the song is part of a portrayal of an episode from an even earlier cultural source, the *Ramayana.* What we have, then, is neither the continuity nor the disruption of tradition, but its dispersed construction in the service of modernity.

18. Moinak Biswas has suggestively and informatively written about the relationship of Bengali film and literature in the context of *Charulata.* I am largely in agreement with his position, though I would continue to insist that insofar as film is not literature, the act of writing, as it appears in the film, takes on an independent existence, an independence that cannot be understood without reference to the moving image (as in the etymology of "cinematograph" = "moving writing"). See Biswas, "Bengali Film Debates."

19. This is an obvious allusion to Johannes Fabian's important book, *Time and the Other.*

20. Chattopadhyay, "Pracheena o Nabeena"; see also Sangari and Vaid, *Recasting Women.*

21. See Benjamin, "Eduard Fuchs, Collector and Historian," 266. The scope of Benjamin's writings about cinema and temporality are fully explored by Hansen, who also cites his Fuchs essay in stating that for Benjamin, "film is the only medium that might yet counter the catastrophic effects of humanity's (already) miscarried *[verunglückte]* reception of technology" (Hansen, "Benjamin and Cinema," 312).

22. See, for instance, Ben Nyce's description of Ray's cinematographic preoccupations:

Charulata is the film which best illustrates Ray's careful scenic preparation before shooting and the superb coordination he obtained with his long-time art director, Bansi Chandragupta. In an interview with Montage, Chandragupta talks about the detailed drawings Ray gave him concerning the interior space of Charulata's house. The quadrangular courtyard is flanked by verandas which look into the bedrooms. However, only three verandas were constructed because— given the carefully plotted camera positions Ray knew he would shoot from—only three were necessary to suggest a quadrangular space. Charu's bedroom and its adjoining veranda were built on a six-foot high platform in life-size scale, while the two other verandas were deliberately built smaller to convey a sense of distance and perspective and to accommodate the small (80-x-40-foot) floor space available in the studio. The wallpaper and other Victorian interior furnishings were found by Ray and Chandragupta after scouring the bazaars in Calcutta. Thus in Charulata, as in all of Ray's films, limitations were turned to advantages by careful planning before shooting began. (Nyce, Satyajit Ray, 93–94)

23. Quoted in Robinson, Satyajit Ray, 164 (my emphasis).

24. This point may also be compared to Benjamin's specification of cinematic perception: "For the entire spectrum of optical, and now also acoustical, perception, the film has brought about a similar deepening of apperception" (Benjamin, "The Work of Art in the Age of Mechanical Reproduction," 235).

25. Depardieu is quoted by Andrew Robinson in the New York Times, April 2, 1995, in an article entitled, "Works of a Master Made Whole Again" (about the Merchant Ivory–sponsored restoration and international redistribution of some Ray films).

26. It may be of some interest that in Webster's English Dictionary, carnal is defined etymologically as bodily, corporeal (rather than sexual). This meaning is derived from the Latin, carnalis, carn, caro—meaning flesh, and is akin to the Greek, keirein—to cut. Actually, only at the level of connotation does the word mark its relationship to sexuality and sensual pleasures though it hardly needs underscoring that the connotative signification has greater resonance for contemporary readers. It is only over time that sedimented meanings of carnality have come to relate to fetishized understandings of the body, not coincidentally, the female body.

27. The term bhadralok literally translates as "respectable folk." Partha Chatterjee has offered an interpretation of this emergent middle class and its role in colonial and nationalist debates in Bengal, commenting on the label's polysemy: "The terms middle class, literati, and intelligentsia all have been used to describe it. Marxists have called it a petty bourgeoisie, the English rendering of petit marking its character with the unmistakable taint of historical insufficiency. A favorite target of the colonizer's ridicule, it was once famously

described as 'an oligarchy of caste tempered by matriculation'" (Chatterjee, *The Nation and Its Fragments*, 35).

28. The hyperprivileging of the visual leads to what Christian Metz called the "scopic regime" of the cinema (see Metz, *The Imaginary Signifier*, 61–63). Within a discursive frame that everywhere betokens the dominance of visuality, cinema is a special case wherein this ocularcentrism can be expressed, as well as negated. My argument has been that Ray's films perform the kind of reflexive work required in doubling back on the articulation of a dominant discursive regime and historical truths.

29. Martin Jay has explored the simultaneous hypertrophy and suspicion of vision within modern thought (see Jay, *Downcast Eyes*).

30. In 1992, in a ritual held once every ten years since 1952, the British Film Institute's influential organ *Sight and Sound* published its "top ten" poll of films and filmmakers (as selected by academics, critics, directors, and reviewers). Ray appeared for the first time as one of the critics' choices for top directors. In a self-questioning mode, the journal reflects on this first-time entry and ponders the fact that "there seems to be a *geography* as much as a *history* of cinema at work." The epistemological bases of evaluative criteria or the insistent impulse to list and measure rarely get interrogated, and a positivist categorical imperative tends to overwhelm film studies (as this list reveals). In this connection it is ironic to find the elision of the question of the translatability of value-codings within feminist film criticism as well. Despite, and more cynically perhaps, *because of* their insistence on the importance of "difference" (predictably understood in purely gendered terms), even apparently reflexive feminist critiques of cinema remain largely indifferent to problems of cultural incommensurability. As examples of this indifference, see, e.g., Penley, *Feminism and Film Theory;* and Silverman, *The Acoustic Mirror*.

31. In *Signatures of the Visible* Fredric Jameson, for example, locates Ray in the "moment of modernism," which is also the "moment of emergence of the great *auteurs:* Hitchcock, Bergman, Fellini, Kurosawa, Renoir, Welles, Wajda, Antonioni, Satyajit Ray, etc." (199). Jameson is to be commended for having taken global cinema seriously, but it seems odd that only Ray is listed by both names (as if he might be in danger of being confused with someone else) even though this would surely defeat Jameson's purpose of designating the "great *auteurs"*). Quite apart from this overcompensation by means of which any discussion of Ray's practice is elided, the texture of the historical-cum-aesthetic confrontation Jameson wishes to stage is also flattened out in the process.

32. Benjamin, "The Work of Art in the Age of Mechanical Reproduction," 236.

33. Benjamin makes the case that the "field of perception" has itself been transformed as a result of the optical and acoustical insights made possible by the technical operations of the cinematic apparatus (Benjamin, "The Work of Art in the Age of Mechanical Reproduction," 235). Jameson, in *The Geopolitical Aesthetic*, also draws on Benjamin's analogy between cinema and surgery in his analysis of films such as *Blow Out* and *All the President's Men* (see Jameson, *The Geopolitical Aesthetic*, 78).

34. It is relevant here to reconnect the discussion with my earlier gloss on allegory. Here let me note its stress on the artificial suturing of past and present. This argument is made by Susan Buck-Morss in her reconstruction of Benjamin's unfinished Arcades Project. She characterizes the relationship of the modern to modernism as a dialectical one—in which repetition (experience in modernity) and representation (coming-to-consciousness of myth) are the two poles of a process sometimes constellated in new forms and at others in archaic variations. Buck-Morss draws on the work of Peter Bürger, who, in his analysis of Benjamin's *Trauerspiel*, comments: "The allegorist pulls one element out of the totality of the life context, isolating it, depriving it of its function. Allegory is therefore essentially fragment. . . . The allegorist joins the isolated fragments of reality and thereby creates meaning. This is posited meaning; it does not derive from the original context of the fragments." See Buck-Morss, *The Dialectics of Seeing*, 225.

35. Spivak, "Can the Subaltern Speak?" 306.

36. Julian Roberts's biography of Benjamin includes a useful discussion of the philosophical precedents and conceptual reasons behind the privileging of dialectical images in Benjamin's work. Briefly, by virtue of its momentary "flash" the image or picture is closer to anamnesis or remembrance. Not only is this mode particularly appropriate to a consideration of history or the past, but Benjamin's opposition between "sayable things" and "unsayable pictures" acquires an extra resonance in the context of analyzing a *moving picture* (see Roberts, *Walter Benjamin*, esp. 211).

37. I would like to thank Dipesh Chakrabarty for reminding me that, in fact, Tagore's long and varied writing career reflects shifts in his representations of modernity (including in his short stories). So the proposition here should be read as confined to his vision in "Nastanirh."

38. It is well known that the montage sequence was inspired by François Truffaut's *Les quatre cents coups* (1959).

39. Robinson, "Works of a Master Made Whole Again."

3. *DEVI*

Epigraph 1. The classical Sanskrit chant to the goddess in her various incarnations: "Salutations to Devi who manifests herself among worldly creatures [as wisdom, sleep, hunger, shadow, shakti (strength, force), thirst, patience, modesty, peace, devotion, beauty, wealth, mindfulness, memory, kindness, satisfaction, and mother]." Hindus repeat the verse, interpolating the different manifestations of the goddess with every repetition of the initial salutation.

1. Davis, *Lives of Indian Images*, 5–6.

2. It should be noted that the objects Davis examines are of exclusively Hindu provenance since there is a proscription in Islamic thought against proliferating likenesses of the divine (although this would not, by itself, explain the absence of other artifacts among his choices).

3. My reference here is to an essay by Martin Heidegger, "The Age of the World-Picture," which has come to serve as something of an article of faith

within contemporary evaluations of the hypostasy of the spectral—ranging from propositions that stitch together the "end of history" and the "end of representation" with the disappearance of depth and the denial of difference in rendering the world as picture. Aside from being unimpressed by its hyperbolic claims, I believe the centrality attributed to Heidegger's thought requires some modulation, particularly if we consider that his arguments not only repeat what earlier thinkers from Schopenhauer and Simmel to Husserl and Bloch had already said. We should also recall that his ideas were thoroughly and far more critically appraised at a time when right-wing existentialism was in less favor. See, for example, Theodor Adorno's attack on Heideggerian totalizations in Adorno, "Parataxis." Heidegger's "The Age of the World-Picture" can be found in his *The Question Concerning Technology and Other Essays*, 3–35.

4. See Benjamin, "The Work of Art in the Age of Mechanical Reproduction," esp. 221–23, 229.

5. For a highly critical appraisal of Benjamin's "Work of Art" essay, unusual for its heterodox stance on the inconsistencies and dead ends of Benjamin's thinking, see Hullot-Kentor, "What Is Mechanical Reproduction?"

6. This phrase obviously paraphrases Theodor Adorno's and Max Horkheimer's *Dialectic of Enlightenment*. The inflection given to myth as the prehistory of modernity—which is less about the existence of the archaic in modern life than an unmasking of the modern per se—can be found in a range of Benjamin's writings. One place is in his essay "Surrealism." A later elaboration appears in the entry numbered "N [Re The Theory of Knowledge, Theory of Progress]" from the Arcades Project. I have explored some of the connections drawn in critical theory between commodity culture and mythic history in Ganguly, "Profane Illuminations and the Everyday." The classic study of Benjamin's investment in materialist history under the category of "natural history" remains Buck-Morss, *The Dialectics of Seeing*.

7. Barthes, "The Third Meaning," 58.

8. Norman Holland reveals his complete lack of familiarity with Hindu iconography (though that does not prevent his inclusion in an anthology on Indian aesthetics and culture) when he remarks that the mask of Devi could be a Greek, Southeast Asian, or even Central American image! See Holland, "Ray's *Devi*," 139, for the relevant passage.

9. It should be said that even non-Hindus or nonobservant Hindus would be familiar with this ritual of goddess worship simply because it involves three consecutive official holidays, traffic jams, and merrymaking throughout Bengal (as well as other parts of India).

10. In a critical monograph that stands up to scrutiny almost thirty years after its original publication, Dana Polan enlarges on Eisenstein's investment in cinema as conceptual thinking—an "ideational" cinema that Eisenstein himself approximated to the German word *Begriff* (concept, idea). See Polan, *The Political Language of Film and the Avant-Garde*, 1, 33–52. Useful extracts of Eisenstein's arguments can be found in Braudy and Cohen, *Film Theory and Criticism*, 13–40.

11. Eisenstein, "Beyond the Shot," 13.

12. These ideas are explored in Eisenstein, *Film Sense,* 17.

13. Eisenstein, "Beyond the Shot," 14.

14. For instance, Rachel Moore takes the position that Eisenstein's directorial and theoretical impulses lay in the direction of "sensual thinking" (sparked, in part, by his encounter with Mexican society). She notes that his emphasis on the sensuous "became one side of an abiding tension," although she is less explicit on what might constitute its other side. My emphasis here—and elsewhere—is to mark the dialectical, *revolutionary* character of the tension. That is to say, the balance Eisenstein sought to achieve was through dialectics, a philosophical and political project that proceeds less by counterposing elements such as sensuousness and thought than, constitutively (since Hegel), through an elaboration of the sensuousness *of* thought. Eisenstein sought to express his dialectical intentions in his films and writings, though the point is less to adjudicate whether they were realized (clearly they were not, after the interlude of Proletkult) than to evaluate the ways that dialectical thinking not only presupposes the sensuous and the existent as constitutive of intellectual effort but also lives on in subsequent cinematic practices, such as Ray's. See Moore, *Savage Theory,* esp. 19.

15. See Eisenstein, "Beyond the Shot," 15.

16. Ibid., 14, 28.

17. Eisenstein had intensively studied Renaissance art and was thus well acquainted with the tradition of European "high art." Vjačeslav Vsevolodovič Ivanov tells us that Eisenstein had also studied Oriental languages. See Ivanov, in *On Signs,* ed. Blonsky, 221–35.

18. Eisenstein, "Beyond the Shot," 18. It is of passing interest perhaps that Eisenstein's predilection was toward constructivism, a modality of thinking about aesthetics and politics that not only took its inspiration from the movement (roughly extending from the Russian Revolution to the 1940s) but also from his training as a civil engineer and his study of Oriental languages.

19. Barthes, "The Third Meaning," 52.

20. Ibid.

21. Eisenstein, "The Dramaturgy of Film Form," 24–26 (my emphasis).

22. Barthes, "The Third Meaning," 60; subsequent citations of this source are referenced parenthetically in the text.

23. See figures XVII and XVI, respectively, in the gallery following page 52 of "The Third Meaning."

24. Barthes, "The Third Meaning," 54.

25. This view of the workings of language depends on a linguistic theory that has these days fallen out of favor. Nonetheless, it charts a course of possibilities that, to my way of thinking, not only corrects the excesses of post-Saussurean approaches to language but also is perhaps more specifically appropriate for understanding a cinematic repertoire that remains resolutely outside the parameters of semiotics. For an incisive critique of the mode of thinking ushered in by Saussure see Williams, "Problems of Materialism."

26. Hansen, introduction to Kracauer, *Theory of Film,* xxvii.

27. I am referring to the *Devī-māhātmya* (Specific Greatness [or Virtue] of the Goddess), an ancient, extant text illustrating the words, images, and

concepts associated with the demotic practices of goddess worship in India. For an erudite account of this text and its own afterlife see Coburn, *Encountering the Goddess*.

28. The annual festival of the goddess, in her incarnation as Durga, is the most important religious festival in Bengal, although it signifies less as ascetic practice than as the carnivalesque. Durga Puja commences with the now-historical broadcast of *Mahalaya* (the recitation of verses to the goddess heralding her appearance) on All India Radio. My point in alluding to it here is to mark its extratextual presence in signifying the intelligibility of Ray's use of the Devi image.

29. See Horkheimer and Adorno, *Dialectic of Enlightenment*, esp. 1–34.

30. Viewers familiar with *ragas* in Hindustani classical music would also associate the nondiegetic detail of the *sarod* playing the *ragini* (feminine mood) named Durga during the credit sequence with the image of the goddess it evokes.

31. See Marcuse, "The Affirmative Character of Culture," 102.

32. Ibid., 132.

33. Robinson, *Satyajit Ray*, 126.

34. See www.filmref.com/directors/dirpages/ray.html (maintained by Acquarello and accessed on Aug. 5, 2009).

35. Nyce, *Satyajit Ray*, 52.

36. Ray, "Calm Without, Fire Within," 160.

37. Barthes, "The Third Meaning," 54.

38. Ray, "What Is Wrong with Indian Films?" 19.

39. Ghosh, "Satyajit Ray's *Devi*," 166; subsequent citations of this source are referenced parenthetically in the text.

40. Continuing in this vein, she says: "Thus, when I speak of ideology in *Devi*, I am speaking primarily of the ideology of sexual difference and not the overt confrontation between rationalism and religious orthodoxy" (ibid., 168).

41. The reference is to Pam Cook's and Claire Johnston's take on Julia Kristeva's attempt to revise Freudian psychoanalysis by means of the notion of a semiotic "chora" that both precedes and explodes the Oedipal order. See Cook and Johnston, "The Place of Women in the Films of Raoul Walsh."

42. Pertinent here is Gayatri Chakravorty Spivak's essay "Moving Devi." Spivak draws attention to the epistemic violence involved in reading female sexuality exclusively through the "optic" of psychoanalytic criticism—detailing in the process a reading of Devi worship outside the parameters of Freud's failure to de-essentialize the feminine.

43. Quoted in Robinson, *Satyajit Ray*, 123.

44. Kael, *I Lost It at the Movies*, 253.

45. Gilliatt, "A Genius and Something Less at Large on the Subcontinent," 56.

46. See Freud, "The Uncanny." In Freud's essay (written in 1919) the phenomenon of the uncanny *(das Unheimliche)* is said to subsume the territory of dream imagery, as well as the topoi of consciousness—as in the experience of a train journey, losing oneself in a strange city, a certain sight of twins and other freakish forms of doubleness, and so on.

47. Abbas, "On Fascination," 47.
48. Ibid., 50.
49. Ghosh, "Satyajit Ray's *Devi*," 165.
50. Those familiar with mainstream Hindi cinema will recognize the young Sharmila Tagore as Doya (Tagore went on to star in scores of Bollywood extravaganzas and to marry the captain of the Indian national cricket team). Her "star image" was, however, only established later, and Ray was the one who initially "discovered" her, casting her as Apu's wife in *Apur Sansar* (The World of Apu, 1959), released the year before *Devi*.
51. It is important to recognize that the song, written by the eighteenth-century poet-saint Ramprasad Sen, belongs in the devotional music tradition in Bengal that dates back to various *bhakti* and *tantric* movements and continues uninterrupted into the present. Ramprasad was particularly influential in the formulation of a critique of high Hinduism with its caste prejudices. Of particular interest here is that this musical tradition is largely centered on a popular discourse based on the indigenous form of Kali worship and offers a resistance against the imperatives of a canonical and patriarchal Hinduism through its emphasis on everyday practices regarding the protection of nature, the celebration of femininity, and the ecstasy of love, both carnal and spiritual. I will pick up on the suggestiveness of music in general in my discussion of *Jalsaghar* (chapter 4).
52. Some implications of Kracauer's use of "redemption" as a nonmetaphysical modality of the cinema are discussed in my introduction. To consult the original, readers are directed to Kracauer, *Theory of Film*, especially to the introduction by Hansen (vii–xlv).
53. This is Darius Cooper's perspective in *The Cinema of Satyajit Ray*. Readers may also wish to consult my review of Cooper's book (see Ganguly, "Satyajit Ray and Indian Modernity").
54. Ray, "What Is Wrong with Indian Films?" 21.
55. Ibid.
56. See Naficy, *An Accented Cinema*.

4. THE MUSIC ROOM REVISITED

1. See Eisenstein, "The Montage of Attractions."
2. See Gunning, "The Cinema of Attractions."
3. Quoted in Fore, "Soviet Factography," 19.
4. Tret'iakov, "The Theater of Attractions," 20, 23 (Tret'iakov's emphasis).
5. Ibid., 23–24 (Tret'iakov's emphasis).
6. Ibid., 24.
7. In "Winding Road to a Music Room" Ray comments wryly on the opportunity to insert singing and dancing into his films—albeit with a difference. As he puts it, "Here was a dramatic story which could be laced legitimately with music and dancing, and distributors loved music and dancing" (45).
8. In a collection of his essays in Bengali entitled *Bishoy Chalachitra* Ray enlarges on the influence of Soviet cinema on his thinking and filmmaking.

Gopa Majumdar has translated this collection into English as *Speaking of Film*.

9. Ray, "Satyajit Ray: In Retrospect," 385.

10. Georges Méliès, *Le voyage dans la lune* (1902) and *Le cake-walk infernal* (1903).

11. The difficulties of this work include its authorship (it was first published only under Eisler's name in 1947 because Adorno wanted to avoid being implicated in the House Un-American Activities Committee's investigations of Eisler's "communist sympathies"). Other problems have to do with the distinctive and disjunctive writing styles.

12. Adorno and Eisler, *Composing for the Films*, 76; subsequent citations of this source are referenced parenthetically in the text.

13. Adorno and Eisler argue that speech in motion pictures is actually the heir to the caption, its artificiality as marked: "it is a roll *[sic]* retranslated into acoustics, and that is what it sounds like even if the formulation of the words is not bookish but rather feigns the 'natural'" (77).

14. Ray, "Those Songs," 72.

15. Ibid., 73.

16. Ibid., 74.

17. Adorno and Eisler, *Composing for the Films*, 23.

18. Ray, "Those Songs," 75.

19. In an essay originally written in 1966 (reprinted in *Our Films, Their Films*) Ray notes that since *Teen Kanya* (Three Daughters, 1961) he composed his own music, noting that "the reason I do not work with professional composers any more is that I get too many musical ideas of my own, and composers, understandably enough, resent being guided too much" (Ray, "Some Aspects of My Craft," 71).

20. Ray, "Those Songs," 71; Adorno and Eisler, *Composing for the Films*, 71.

21. The *tappa* is an expansive form whose content ranges from raunchy love songs to *bhakti* (devotional) music), including *kirtans*. The *tappa* heard in this scene is a *kirtan* advocating a renunciatory mode of life. In its syncretism the song expresses one of the characteristics of Nidhu Babu's *tappas*, the hallmark of Bangla tappas (deriving from Punjabi antecedents), taking its leads in terms of lyrical content from the *bhakti sangeet* brought into vogue by the Naba Vidhan Brahmo Samaj directed by Keshab Chandra Sen (1838–84). In a minor though consistent way this song also attests to Ray's penchant for yoking together the old and the new. And its placement within the narrative is in keeping with his general disposition—which sought to invoke the bygone imperatives of the Brahmo Samaj and its program of general social inculcation with his avant-garde desire to take a new look at the old in order to provoke a different horizon of meanings. My thanks to Bhaskar Sarkar for prompting me to think more carefully about the relationship between *tappa* and *kirtan*.

22. This is a predicament Ray also captures in *Shatranj Ke Khilari* (The Chess Players, 1977), a story by Premchand, set in 1856, where the *nawabs* are shown playing chess while the British forces of General Outram institute a takeover of Avadh.

23. Barthes speaks of Garbo as "a sort of Platonic idea of the human creature" and as "an Idea," taken from a "fragile moment when the cinema is about to draw an existential from an essential beauty." I might add that in emblematizing this essential appeal, Garbo—whose makeup "has the snowy thickness of a mask: it is not a painted face but one set in plaster"—conjures up an attraction (in the specifically cinematic sense) of a tactile, plastic sort. See Barthes, "The Face of Garbo." Ray himself commented that after Biswas's death there were no other actors who could convey the "monumental" aspects of existence—by which I take him to suggest a distinction, similar to Barthes' description of Garbo, between personality and person. See Ray, "Duti Samasya" (Two Problems), in *Bishoy Chalachitra*, 69.

24. Gillian Rose reminds us that the "phantasmagoric" in Marx alludes to "the personifications as well as strangeness of the form in which relations between men appear [under capitalism]." See Rose, *The Melancholy Science*, 31.

25. Quoted in Robinson, *Satyajit Ray*, 113.

26. McCann, "New Introduction," xxxv.

27. In drawing the distinction between the filmic and nonfilmic, I am again referring to its use by Christian Metz, who identified "the 'profilmic' spectacle" as everything that can be put in front of the camera in order, specifically, to shoot it (Metz, *Film Language*, 100n).

28. Ray writes suggestively about problems of music and sound in "Abohosangeet Prasangey" (About Background Music). See Ray, *Bishoy Chalachitra*, 62–67.

29. This is a rough paraphrase of Ray's opinions on the use of classical *ragas* as background music. See Ray, *Bishoy Chalachitra*, 65.

30. Ibid., 66 (my translation).

31. Rajadhyaksha, "Beyond Orientalism," 35.

32. Rajadhyaksha ends his retrospection on Ray by quoting another critic who regarded the last films, apparently "sympathetically," as the product of "an armchair liberal functioning as a simple humanist who now viewed society in terms of a naïve individual-versus-society conflict and placed his hopes and disillusionment either in some grassroots cultural activity or the travails of innocent children, sensitive but mentally retarded figures and maverick outsiders" (Rajadhyaksha, "Beyond Orientalism," 35).

33. Ibid.

34. Adorno and Eisler, *Composing for the Films*, 66.

5. TAKE TWO

1. In his review of the film in the *New York Times*, Bosley Crowther was apparently unable to distinguish between Indian cities and refers to the "big city" in question as "evidently New Delhi." The point, of course, is not that the location is fixed for the film to acquire its meaning but that such carelessness has been the mark of the West's reception of the Indian locales and other details in Ray's films. See Crowther, " 'Mahanagar' Relates Story of a Family."

2. My thanks to Dilip Basu for pointing me to the necessity of indicating the denotative meaning of the title.

3. This, of course, represents the grounds on which socialist feminism has distinguished itself from other feminist discourses, though the position has lost some of its force with the rise in recent years of "body talk" within various postmodern theories of sexual difference.

4. Colin MacCabe has defined *metalanguage* as "the knowledge which the film provides of how things really are"—that is to say, the film's own ideological perspective (see MacCabe, *Tracking the Signifier*, 38).

5. Interestingly, Ray had originally proposed the title of *A Woman's Place* (instead of *The Big City*) for the subtitled English version of the film.

6. Ray's investment in arranging his characters and props down to the last detail is well known. Here we may note the kinship between his ideas about the autonomy of the "three-legged instrument" and Kracauer's argument that characters in films take on the aspect of objects (rather than fully fleshed out personalities) since cinema is the modern form that best encapsulates the reification of all forms, including humans. For an enlargement see Kracauer, *Theory of Film*, esp. 45–46, 97.

7. Along these lines, some of Ray's other films also take heterodox (though emphatically not "reformist") positions on modern pieties that have come to be taken for granted; for instance, he does not present the traditional bourgeoisie as purely retrograde, the precolonial past as an unblemished pastoral, or the postcolonial present as a triumph of the new nation.

8. Adorno, "Situation," 31.

9. Following is a summary of Fritz Lang's *Metropolis:*

Around the year 2027 the ruling class lives in towering luxury skyscrapers while slave laborers toil underground. The hero, Freder, is the pampered son of Fredersen, one of the most egregious of the oppressive rulers. Freder is reformed when he meets Maria, the loveliest of the subterranean dwellers, and falls in love with her. Traveling incognito below ground, Freder, appalled by the laborers' squalid living conditions, immediately begins campaigning for humanitarian reforms. Evil industrialist Rotwang cannot let this happen, so he plots to turn the slaves against the reformers. In his neon-dominated laboratory Rotwang creates a robot in the image of Maria, designed as a false prophet to lead the rabble astray. After a destructive uprising and an underground flood of biblical proportions, the despotic Fredersen sees the light, and agrees in the future to treat the working class with equanimity and compassion. (www.starpulse.com/Movies/Metropolis/Summary/; description slightly modified)

10. The allusion is to Adorno's *Minima Moralia.*

11. Quoted at SatyajitRay.org (www.satyajitray.org/films/mahanag.htm).

12. See Barthes, *Writing Degree Zero.*

13. Ray, "The Odds against Us," 57.

14. Barthes himself, high European theorist that he was, came to propose that the language and aesthetics of European culture had exhausted themselves; that, in fact, what was needed for properly comprehending the collective experience of capitalist modernity was an "other" mode of expression and habitation approximated only by non-Western, particularly Eastern, aesthetic forms. See, for instance, the article he published in 1974 after a visit to China entitled "Alors, la Chine?" ("Well Then, China?") in the French daily newspaper, Le monde, May 27; or his collection of essays Empire of Signs.

15. Ray, "The Odds against Us," 61–62.

16. Thanks to Leo Chen for clarifying the mechanics of Ray's use of a camera with an Arriflex lens mounted on top of the cable car.

17. Alfred Hitchcock famously distinguished between "suspense" and "surprise" and the different effects particular to each. Here, the fact that Hitchcock's early training was at the Babelsberg Studios in Berlin (and under F. W. Murnau) may be relevant in considering the influence of German Expressionism on his preference for surprise—given that it must, like other deductive principles, be built up. Formed under its influence, Hitchcock (like Ray) looked for visual strategies to depict inner, expressive truths, an orientation he later domesticated into the production of textual anxiety that is of course more superficial than Ray's interest in immanent truths.

18. Wagner's concept of the Gesamtkunstwerk ("total work of art") rests on the principle of the unity of the arts. In his compositions this unity is deployed in the service of an enclosed form of experience, one that permits withdrawing from the social world and into the sublime experience of an aesthetic emotionality. The point of my connection, however, is to call attention to Ray's extreme deftness in unifying the conditions of both production and reception—thus giving new meaning to the totality of cinematic expression.

19. See Pines and Willemen, Questions of Third Cinema.

20. Originally published in Cine Cubano 66/67 (1969), García Espinosa's essay has been reprinted in Stam and Miller, Film and Theory.

21. Stam and Miller, Film and Theory, 295.

22. Eagleton establishes in undeniable ways (perhaps the reason why his work is so rarely found in aesthetics curricula these days) that, in fostering a connection between aesthetics and subjective being, the work of art comes to be seen as a "kind of subject" paralleling the self-referentiality and self-determination of the author. In this way the realm of the aesthetic has become, since the eighteenth century, more subject to (pun intended) social control than to its overthrow. See Eagleton, The Ideology of the Aesthetic, 9.

23. The list of works inspired by the turn to postmodern theorizations of global flows, transnational border-crossings, postnational hybridity, nomadic subjectivity and opposition to capitalism, and other related ideas is too numerous (and interchangeable) to be cited here. For some early avatars readers may wish to look at Deleuze and Guattari, A Thousand Plateaus; any recent issue of the journal boundary 2; or the debates in cultural studies about "new times."

24. See Marx, "Theses on Feuerbach."

6. CINEMA AND UNIVERSALITY

This chapter is a revised version of my essay "Cinema and Universality."
1. Bazin, "De Sica," 180.
2. Ibid., 181.
3. Kracauer, *Theory of Film*, 310–11.
4. Ibid., 311.
5. Hansen, introduction to Kracauer, *Theory of Film*, xxxi.
6. Kracauer, *Theory of Film*, l.
7. Ibid.
8. Ibid.
9. Robinson, *Satyajit Ray*, 99.
10. Ray, quoted in Basu, "Mastering the Language of Cinema."
11. Ray, "A Long Time on the Little Road," 33–34.
12. Kracauer, *Theory of Film*, 71.
13. Ibid., 31.
14. Ibid., 304.
15. Macdonald, "Short Takes."
16. Amis, "Several Splendid Evenings," 43.
17. I am grateful to Timothy Brennan for his insightful critique of the aesthetics of complexity in "Cosmopolitanism and Method" (see Brennan, *At Home in the World*, 66–81).
18. In one of his rare retorts to critics Ray takes to task the columnist of a popular Bengali magazine, *Desh* (Nation) for misunderstanding the fundamental difference between a good film that "adapts" a novel—redeeming, as it were, its hidden dimensions—and a bad or indifferent adaptation that merely mimics the novel's representation of characters, places, and events. See *"Apur Sansar* Prasangey" (About *The World of Apu*), in *Bishoy Chalachitra*, 75–78 ("On *Apur Sansar*," in *Speaking of Films*, 136–41).
19. Hood, *The Essential Mystery*, 60–61.
20. See Kapur, *When Was Modernism*.
21. See Mitter, *The Triumph of Modernism*.
22. See Kracauer's study for his comment at the end: "Béla Balázs's thesis that the cinema comes into its own only if it serves revolutionary ends is as untenable as are the kindred views of those schools of thought, neorealistic and otherwise, which postulate an intimate relationship between the medium and socialism or collectivism" (Kracauer, *Theory of Film*, 309).
23. See Bürger, *Theory of the Avant-Garde*.
24. I am referring to such films as Ashutosh Gowariker's *Lagaan* (2001), a sentimental allegory of anticolonial resistance set in British India and depicted via a cricket match between a motley crew of Indian villagers and an English team of colonial officers from the local British cantonment. The Indian team wins, improbably if heroically (though only with help from a fair-minded Englishwoman), giving viewers equal parts populism, visual cliché, and song-and-dance routines.
25. Ray, "Under Western Eyes," 273.

CONCLUSION

1. Ray, *The Cineaste Interviews*, 382; the interview is also available online at www.satyajitray.org/about_ray/ray_on_ray.htm (accessed March 12, 2008).

2. In the early 1950s Ray had intended *Ghare Baire* to be his debut film but could not make progress on it because of lack of financial backing. It was not made until the National Film Development Corporation (a government-funded, public sector entity) finally helped to produce it, though only decades later, after Ray's reputation had been fully established abroad with his early films. See Rajadhyaksha and Willemen, *Encyclopedia of Indian Cinema*, 465.

3. See Robinson, *Satyajit Ray*, 270–71.

4. Quoted in Robinson, *Satyajit Ray*, 272. The fact that Ray had tried much earlier to produce an adaptation of *Ghare Baire* for the screen does not negate the specific point about the form that its eventual appearance takes or the implications for an understanding of his late style.

5. I would like to thank Patrick Flanagan for bringing this idea to my attention.

6. Robinson has this to say about *Ghare Baire:* "The real awkwardness of the film lies . . . in Ray's (and Tagore's) conception of the characters, which the performances cannot quite overcome, and which is responsible for the common criticism that the film is too 'talkative.' It is as if 'intuition,' a modern English word for a very old sensation, to which Sandip, Nikhil and Bimala all pay tribute and which none of them truly possesses, has also, for once, eluded Ray too. They none of them seem to come alive quite in the way that Amal, Bhupati and Charu do in the earlier film" (Robinson, *Satyajit Ray*, 271).

7. I am mindful of the biographical fact that Ray was in poor health by the time of the making of *Ghare Baire*, but this fact only reinforces the point I subsequently make about lateness and decline.

8. Ray, *The Cineaste Interviews*, 389.

9. Adorno, *Beethoven*, 14, viii. Adorno's estimation was that Beethoven should be seen as a musical correlate to Hegel in the ways that his works defied a sense of progression and exemplified, rather, the *discontinuities* of experience under capitalism (particularly the later works). Offering his own Hegelian perspective on the nature of aesthetic experience as an aspect of the disjunction of subject and object, Adorno considered that Hegel's most important lesson was far from developmentalist or teleological. I should add that this is far from the formulaic, if mistaken, view of Hegel. Thus, if Hegel proposed that history's owl flies at dusk, this meant only that historical insight is produced belatedly.

10. Ibid., 9.

11. Ibid. (Adorno's emphasis). This proposition echoes others in Adorno such as the "whole is the untrue." For a clear exposition of his dialectical method see Rose, *The Melancholy Science*.

12. Jameson, *Late Marxism*, 11.

13. Aside from his highly critical assessments of film in *Minima Moralia* or *Dialectic of Enlightenment*, there are a few occasions on which Adorno

speaks of the utopian dimensions of cinema along lines that resemble what he had to say at far greater length about music (and which would accommodate my readings of Ray). See, e.g., Adorno, "Chaplin Times Two"; and Adorno, "Transparencies on Film."

14. This historical resonance is, I might add, much stronger than is customarily available in reading, say, subaltern consciousness via Jacques Derrida's ideas or diasporic culture from Michel Foucault's or Jacques Lacan's perspective (such readings are quite common in film or postcolonial studies, whereas turning to Adorno is much more likely to raise eyebrows on the grounds of an alleged lack of theoretical fit).

15. Adorno, *Beethoven*, 126.

16. Rose, *The Melancholy Science*, 2.

17. Speaking of Ray's film *Seemabaddha* (Company Limited, 1970) and others made in the same decade, Rajadhyaksha observes: "Sequences like these [disjunctive insertions that interrupt the 'comfortably naturalist' vision of the later films] reveal Ray's increasing mistrust, into and through the 70s, of his cinematic apparatus. By a logic startlingly clear in retrospect, it appears that the sense of control he invested in that apparatus in the idealism of the 50s had given way to ideological associations that, as he said, 'keep changing all the time.' He was still in the middle of his Calcutta films . . . and was signaling with growing frustration a reality that appeared too complicated to handle. This well-documented crisis has now become part of Ray lore" (Rajadhyaksha, "Beyond Orientalism," 35).

18. Ray made twenty-eight feature films in his career, of which four are in the genre of fantasy or adventure (*Goopy Gyne Bagha Byne* [The Adventures of Goopy and Bagha, 1968], *Sonar Kella* [The Golden Fortress, 1974], *Joy Baba Felunath* [The Elephant God, 1978], and *Hirak Rajar Deshe* [The Kingdom of Diamonds, 1980]).

19. Adorno, *Beethoven*, 157.

20. MacCabe, preface to Jameson, *The Geopolitical Aesthetic*, xiii.

21. Said, "A Note on Modernism," 188.

22. Ibid. What ought to interest us (although it is by no means surprising given Said's acknowledged debts to Williams) is that he, too, locates the future of criticism on the reach of modernism into the present, though different agents, politics, and traditions have now to be counted as its principal entailments. On this point see Lecia Rosenthal, "Between Humanism and Late Style."

23. Part of the problem with Jameson's discussion of national allegory is that he does not thematize its dependence on Benjamin's idea that modern time is marked by calendrical homogeneity or that it represents what he calls "homogeneous empty time." Against this emptiness Jameson poses a different or heterogeneous temporality in the Third World that corresponds to a collective and allegorical imperative rather than an individualistic or libidinal one. Benjamin was, in turn, relying on Bloch's formulation of "nonsynchronousness" *(Ungleichzeitigkeit)* to differentiate between modes of subjective exis-

tence, saying, "not all people exist in the same Now." Unfortunately, Benjamin and Bloch's multilayered propositions are dimmed from view here—seeming to appear in Jameson's contentions as a theory of Third World backwardness. See Benjamin, "On the Concept of History"; and Bloch, "Nonsynchronism and the Obligation to Its Dialectics." Jameson's essay, which attracted controversy on its appearance because many critics misunderstood the conceptual underpinnings of his argument, is entitled "Third-World Literature in the Era of Multinational Capitalism."

24. See Jameson, *The Geopolitical Aesthetic*, 186–213.

25. Timothy Brennan reminds me that with the exception of a few insertions about C. L. R. James, Tayib Salih, and the like, in the relatively late work *Culture and Imperialism*, Said did not have much to say in the way of promoting postcolonial writing. See Said, *Culture and Imperialism*.

26. See Said, "Adorno as Lateness Itself."

27. Recent work on Said's legacy and his specific contributions to a humanist mode of scholarship that pays attention to questions of exploitation, exile, and emancipation without semanticizing them has taken up his development of the idea of lateness and related it to future directions in postcolonial criticism. See, e.g., Hussein, *Edward Said;* Rubin, "Techniques of Trouble"; and Rosenthal, "Between Humanism and Late Style." Most of this work, by younger or later scholars, is promising and energetic in its efforts to solidify the future of Saidian scholarship, though, by the same token, its engagement with Adorno (or critical theory) is somewhat mediated.

28. Said, *On Late Style*, 7.

29. Ibid.

30. The reference here is to Said, *The World, the Text, and the Critic*.

31. Nicholsen, *Exact Imagination, Late Work*, 32.

32. Ibid., 7.

33. Ibid.

34. Ibid., 41 (my emphasis). Nicholsen is circumspect about the authors of the "popular" view, marking her difference from them by underscoring the importance of formal elements of composition rather than authorial subjectivity in Adorno's thinking.

35. Adorno, *Beethoven*, 123. Here Adorno does not explicitly link Marx's conception of alienation as the dyad of dead labor/deadened consciousness with his own image of the petrified subjectivity of late work—showing "more traces of history than of growth." Nonetheless, the force of his rendering of late work as overripe but unsweet fruit depends on Marx's understanding of the twinning of subjective or spiritual alienation *(Entäusserung)* and objective or historical alienation *(Entfremdung)* in the experience of late capitalism.

36. Ibid., 8.

37. Hullot-Kentor, "The Exact Sense in Which the Culture Industry No Longer Exists," 146.

38. Johannes Fabian has proposed the idea of "allochronism" to describe the denial of coevalness. See his *Time and the Other*.

39. Arrighi, *The Long Twentieth Century.*

40. See Baker, *Modernism and the Harlem Renaissance;* Gikandi, *Writing in Limbo;* Chow, *Primitive Passions;* and Pollard, *New World Modernisms.*

41. See Clifford, *Routes,* esp. 17–46.

42. Ray, "Under Western Eyes," 270.

43. Ibid., 271.

44. See Habermas, "Modernity—An Incomplete Project."

45. See, e.g., Neil Lazarus's "The Politics of Postcolonial Modernism." Lazarus offers a trenchant analysis of the restricted terms of analysis within postcolonial criticism that seek to maximize the cachet of the field itself while minimizing the actual ambitions of a wide variety of writers and texts that do not see themselves in its orbit.

46. Ray, "Under Western Eyes," 274.

Select Bibliography

PRIMARY ARTICLES AND BOOKS ON AND BY RAY

Amis, Kingsley. "Several Splendid Evenings: The Reality Is There, but Not the Stimulation." *Esquire*, May 1959, 43–44.

Banerjee, Surabhi. *Satyajit Ray: Beyond the Frame*. New Delhi: Allied Publishers, 1996.

Basu, Dilip K. "Mastering the Language of Cinema." http://satyajitray.ucsc.edu/articles/language.html.

Biswas, Moinak. "Bengali Film Debates: The Literary Liaison Revisited." *Journal of the Moving Image*, no. 1 (autumn 1999): 1–13.

Cooper, Darius. *The Cinema of Satyajit Ray: Between Tradition and Modernity*. Cambridge, UK: Cambridge University Press, 2000.

Crowther, Bosley. " 'Mahanagar' Relates Story of a Family." *New York Times*, Sep. 28, 1964.

Das, Santi, ed. *Satyajit Ray: An Intimate Master*. New Delhi: Allied Publishers, 1998.

Das Gupta, Chidananda. *The Cinema of Satyajit Ray*. New Delhi: Vikas, 1980.

Dasgupta, Kurchi, ed. *Satyajit Ray: A Glimpse*. Kolkata: Lotus Print, 2001.

Dirks, Nicholas B. "The Sovereignty of History: Culture and Modernity in the Cinema of Satyajit Ray." In *Questions of Modernity*, ed. Timothy Mitchell, 148–65. Minneapolis: University of Minnesota Press, 2000.

Dube, Reena. *Satyajit Ray's "The Chess Players" and Postcolonial Theory: Culture, Labour, and the Value of Alterity*. London: Palgrave MacMillan, 2005.

Ganguly, Keya. "Carnal Knowledge: Visuality and the Modern in *Charulata*." *Camera Obscura* 37 (Jan. 1996): 157–86.

———. "Cinema and Universality: On Satyajit Ray's *Apur Sansar*." *Race and Class* 44, no. 2 (2002): 57–70.

———. "Satyajit Ray and Indian Modernity." Review of *The Cinema of Satyajit Ray: Tradition and Modernity*, by Darius Cooper. *Journal of Commonwealth and Postcolonial Studies* 8, nos. 1 and 2 (2001): 223–29.

Ganguly, Suranjan. *Satyajit Ray: In Search of the Modern.* Lanham, MD: Scarecrow Press, 2000.

Ghosh, Bishnupriya. "Satyajit Ray's *Devi*: Constructing a Third-World Feminist 'Critique.'" *Screen* 33, no. 2 (summer 1992): 165–73.

Ghosh, Nemai. *Manikda.* Calcutta: Bingsha Shatabdi, 2000.

Gilliatt, Penelope. "A Genius and Something Less at Large on the Subcontinent." *New Yorker,* July 23, 1973, 56–58.

Holland, Norman. "Ray's *Devi*." In *Literary India: Comparative Studies in Aesthetics, Colonialism, and Culture,* ed. Patrick Colm Hogan and Lalita Pandit, 135–40. Albany: SUNY Press, 1995.

Houston, Penelope. "Ray's *Charulata*." *Sight and Sound* 35, no. 1 (winter 1965/66): 31–33.

Malcolm, Derek. "Satyajit Ray." *Sight and Sound* 51, no. 2 (spring 1982): 106–9.

Nandy, Ashis. "Satyajit Ray's Secret Guide to Exquisite Murders: Creativity, Social Criticism, and the Partitioning of the Self." In *The Savage Freud and Other Essays on Possible and Retrievable Selves,* 237–66. New Delhi: Oxford University Press, 1995.

Nyce, Ben. *Satyajit Ray: A Study of His Films.* New York: Praeger, 1988.

Ray, Satyajit. *Bishoy Chalachitra.* Calcutta: Ananda Publishers, 1982.

———. "Calm Without, Fire Within." 1963. In *Our Films, Their Films,* 152–61.

———. "Film Making." 1965. In *Our Films, Their Films,* 48–56.

———. "Little Man, Big Book." 1964. In *Our Films, Their Films,* 172–79.

———. "A Long Time on the Little Road." 1957. In *Our Films, Their Films,* 30–37.

———. "The Odds against Us." 1966. In *Our Films, Their Films,* 57–62.

———. *Our Films, Their Films.* New York: Hyperion, 1994.

———. "Satyajit Ray: In Retrospect." Interview by Udayan Gupta. In Georgakas and Rubenstein, *The Cineaste Interviews,* 381–89.

———. "Some Aspects of My Craft." 1966. In *Our Films, Their Films,* 63–71.

———. "Some Italian Films I Have Seen." 1951. In *Our Films, Their Films,* 120–27.

———. *Speaking of Films.* Trans. Gopa Majumdar. New Delhi: Penguin India, 2005.

———. "Those Songs." 1967. In *Our Films, Their Films,* 72–75.

———. "Under Western Eyes." *Sight and Sound* 51, no. 4 (fall 1982): 268–74.

———. "What Is Wrong with Indian Films?" 1948. In *Our Films, Their Films,* 19–24.

———. "Winding Road to a Music Room." 1963. In *Our Films, Their Films,* 44–47.

Robinson, Andrew. *Satyajit Ray: The Inner Eye.* Berkeley: University of California Press, 1989.

———. "Works of a Master Made Whole Again." *New York Times,* April 2, 1995.

Sarkar, Bidyut. *The World of Satyajit Ray.* New Delhi: UBS Publishers, 1992.

Sen, Amartya. "Satyajit Ray and the Art of Universalism: Our Culture, Their Culture." *New Republic*, April 27, 1996, 27–34.

Seton, Marie. *Portrait of a Director: Satyajit Ray.* Bloomington: Indiana University Press, 1971.

Sil, Narasingha P. "Tagore's *Broken Nest* vs. Ray's *Charulata*: A Critique." *Asian Cinema* 10, no. 2 (spring/summer 1999): 130–44.

Thompson, Howard. "Ray's 'Charulata' Given: Simple Story Makes Exquisite Movie." *New York Times*, Sep. 11, 1965.

Wood, Robin. *The Apu Trilogy.* New York: Praeger, 1971.

SECONDARY WORKS

Abbas, Ackbar. "On Fascination: Walter Benjamin's Images." *New German Critique*, no. 48 (autumn 1989): 43–62.

Adorno, Theodor. *Beethoven: The Philosophy of Music.* Ed. Rolf Tiedemann. Trans. Edmund Jephcott. Stanford, CA: Stanford University Press, 1998.

———. "Chaplin Times Two." Trans. John McKay. *Yale Journal of Criticism* 9, no. 1 (1996): 57–61.

———. *Minima Moralia: Reflections from Damaged Life.* Trans. E. F. N. Jephcott. London: Verso, 1974.

———. *Negative Dialectics.* Trans. E. B. Ashton. New York: Continuum, 1990.

———. *Notes to Literature.* Vol. 2. Trans. Shierry Weber Nicholsen. New York: Columbia University Press, 1992.

———. "Parataxis: On Hölderlin's Late Poetry." In *Notes to Literature*, 2:109–49.

———. "Resignation." In *Critical Models: Interventions and Catchwords.* Trans. Henry W. Pickford, 289–93. New York: Columbia University Press, 1998.

———. "Situation." In *Aesthetic Theory.* Ed. Gretel Adorno and Rolf Tiedemann. Trans. C. Lenhardt, 23–67. London: Routledge and Kegan Paul, 1984.

———. "Transparencies on Film." Trans. Thomas Levin. *New German Critique*, no. 24/25 (autumn 1981-winter 1982): 199–205.

Adorno, Theodor W., and Hanns Eisler, *Composing for the Films.* Trans. George MacManus and Norbert Guterman. London: Athlone, 1994.

Althusser, Louis. *For Marx.* Trans. Ben Brewster. London: Verso, 1990.

———. *The Spectre of Hegel: Early Writings.* Trans. G. M. Goshgarian. London: Verso, 1997.

Anderson, Benedict. *Imagined Communities: Reflections on the Origins and Spread of Nationalism.* London: Verso, 1991.

Anderson, Perry. *Considerations on Western Marxism.* London: Verso, 1976.

———. *A Zone of Engagement.* London: Verso, 1992.

Aragon, Louis. *Paris Peasant.* Trans. Simon Watson Taylor. London: Exact Change, 2004.

Arrighi, Giovanni. *The Long Twentieth Century: Money, Power, and the Origins of Our Times.* London: Verso, 1994.

Astruc, Alexandre. "The Birth of a New Avant-Garde: *Le caméra-stylo.*" 1948. In *The New Wave: Critical Landmarks*, ed. Peter Graham, 17–23. Garden City, NY: Doubleday, 1968.

Baker, Houston. *Modernism and the Harlem Renaissance.* Chicago: University of Chicago Press, 1987.

Barnouw, Dagmar. *Critical Realism: History, Photography, and the Work of Siegfried Kracauer.* Baltimore: Johns Hopkins University Press, 1994.

Barnouw, Erik, and S. Krishnaswamy. *Indian Film.* 2nd ed. New York: Oxford University Press, 1980.

Barthes, Roland. *Empire of Signs.* Trans. Richard Howard. New York: Hill and Wang, 1983.

———. "The Face of Garbo." 1957. In *Mythologies*, 56–57.

———. *Image-Music-Text.* Trans. Stephen Heath. New York: Hill and Wang, 1977.

———. *Mythologies.* Trans. Annette Lavers. New York: Hill and Wang, 1972.

———. "The Third Meaning: Research Notes on Some Eisenstein Stills." In *Image-Music-Text*, 52–68.

———. *Writing Degree Zero.* Trans. Annette Lavers and Colin Smith. New York: Hill and Wang, 1968.

Bazin, André. "De Sica: Metteur-en-scène." In Braudy and Cohen, *Film Theory and Criticism*, 174–82.

Benegal, Shyam. "Secularism and Popular Indian Cinema." In *The Crisis of Secularism in India*, ed. Anuradha Dingwaney Needham and Rajeswari Sunder Rajan, 225–38. Durham, NC: Duke University Press, 2007.

Benjamin, Walter. "Eduard Fuchs, Collector and Historian." In *Walter Benjamin: Selected Writings.* Vol. 3. Trans. Edmund Jephcott, Howard Eiland, and others, 260–302. Cambridge, MA: Harvard University Press, 2003.

———. *Illuminations.* Trans. Harry Zohn. New York: Schocken, 1968.

———. "N [Re The Theory of Knowledge, Theory of Progress]." In *Benjamin: Philosophy, Aesthetics, History*, ed. Gary Smith, 43–83. Chicago: University of Chicago Press, 1983.

———. *One-Way Street and Other Writings.* Trans. Edmund Jephcott and Kingsley Shorter. London: Verso, 1979.

———. "On the Concept of History." 1940. In *Walter Benjamin: Selected Writings.* Vol. 4, 389–400. Trans. Edmund Jephcott and others. Cambridge, MA: Harvard University Press, 2003.

———. *The Origin of German Tragic Drama.* Trans. John Osborne. London: Verso, 1977.

———. *Reflections.* Trans. Edmund Jephcott. New York: Schocken, 1978.

———. "A Small History of Photography." 1931. In *One-Way Street and Other Writings*, 240–57.

———. "The Storyteller: Reflections on the Works of Nikolai Leskov." 1936. In *Illuminations*, 83–109.

———. "Surrealism." In *Reflections*, 177–92.

———. "The Work of Art in the Age of Mechanical Reproduction." 1936. In *Illuminations*, 217–51.

Bloch, Ernst. *Heritage of Our Times*. Trans. Neville and Stephen Plaice. Berkeley: University of California Press, 1990.

———. "Nonsynchronism and the Obligation to Its Dialectics." 1932. Trans. Mark Ritter. *New German Critique*, no. 11 (spring 1977): 22–38.

———. *The Spirit of Utopia*. Trans. Anthony Nassar. Stanford, CA: Stanford University Press, 2000.

Bloch, Marc. *The Historian's Craft*. Trans. J. E. Anderson. Cambridge, UK: Cambridge University Press, 1964.

Blonsky, Marshall, ed. *On Signs*. Baltimore: Johns Hopkins University Press, 1985.

Braudy, Leo, and Marshall Cohen, eds. *Film Theory and Criticism*. 6th ed. New York: Oxford University Press, 2004.

Brecht, Bertolt. *Die Neuen Zeitalter* (New Ages). In *Poems: 1913–1956*. New York: Methuen, 1976.

Brennan, Timothy. *At Home in the World: Cosmopolitanism Now*. Cambridge, MA: Harvard University Press, 1997.

———. "The Southern Intellectual." In *Wars of Position: The Cultural Politics of Left and Right*, 233–71. New York: Columbia University Press, 2006.

Buchloh, Benjamin H. D. *Neo-Avantgarde and Culture Industry: Essays on European and American Art from 1955–1975*. Cambridge, MA: MIT Press, 2003.

Buci-Glucksmann, Christine. *Baroque Reason: The Aesthetics of Modernity*. Trans. Patrick Camiller. London: Sage, 1994.

Buck-Morss, Susan. "Aesthetics and Anaesthetics: Walter Benjamin's Artwork Essay Reconsidered." *New Formations*, no. 20 (summer 1993): 123–43.

———. *The Dialectics of Seeing: Walter Benjamin and the Arcades Project*. Cambridge, MA: MIT Press, 1991.

———. "The Flaneur, the Sandwichman and the Whore: The Politics of Loitering." *New German Critique*, no. 39 (fall 1986): 99–140.

Buhler, James, Caryl Flinn, and James Neumeyer, eds. *Music and Cinema*. Hanover, NH: Wesleyan University Press, 2000.

Bürger, Peter. *Theory of the Avant-Garde*. Trans. Michael Shaw. Minneapolis: University of Minnesota Press, 1984.

Calhoon, Kenneth. "Blind Gestures: Chaplin, Diderot, Lessing." *MLN* 115, no. 3 (April 2000): 381–402.

———, ed. *Peripheral Visions: The Hidden Stages of Weimar Cinema*. Detroit: Wayne State University Press, 2001.

Calinescu, Matei. *Five Faces of Modernity: Modernism, Avant-garde, Decadence, Kitsch, Postmodernism*. Durham: Duke University Press, 1987.

Casanova, Pascale. *The World Republic of Letters*. Cambridge, MA: Harvard University Press, 2007.

Chakrabarty, Dipesh. *Provincializing Europe: Postcolonial Thought and Historical Difference*. Princeton, NJ: Princeton University Press, 2000.

Charney, Leo, and Vanessa R. Schwartz, eds. *Cinema and the Invention of Modern Life*. Berkeley: University of California Press, 1995.

Chatterjee, Partha. *The Nation and Its Fragments: Colonial and Postcolonial Histories*. Princeton, NJ: Princeton University Press, 1993.

Chattopadhyay, Bankim Chandra. "Pracheena o Nabeena." 1879. In *Bibidha Prabandha* [Selected Essays]. Calcutta: Basumati Sahitya Mandir, 1930.

Chion, Michel. *Audio-Vision: Sound on Screen*. Trans. Claudia Gorbman. New York: Columbia University Press, 1994.

———. *Film, a Sound Art*. Trans. Claudia Gorbman. New York: Columbia University Press, 2009.

Chow, Rey. *Primitive Passions: Visuality, Sexuality, Ethnography, and Contemporary Chinese Cinema*. New York: Columbia University Press, 1995.

Clark, T. J. *Farewell to an Idea: Episodes from a History of Modernism*. New Haven, CT: Yale University Press, 1999.

Clifford, James. *Routes: Travel and Translation in the Late Twentieth Century*. Cambridge, MA: Harvard University Press, 1997.

Coburn, Thomas B. *Encountering the Goddess: A Translation of the Devī-māhātmya and a Study of Its Interpretation*. Albany: SUNY Press, 1991.

Cook, Pam, and Claire Johnston. "The Place of Women in the Films of Raoul Walsh." In *Feminism and Film Theory*, ed. Constance Penley, 25–35. New York: Routledge, 1998.

Davis, Richard H. *Lives of Indian Images*. Princeton, NJ: Princeton University Press, 1999.

Dehejia, Vidya, ed. *Devi, the Great Goddess: Female Divinity in South Asia*. Washington, DC: Arthur M. Sackler Gallery, Smithsonian Institution, in association with Mapin Publishing (Ahmedabad) and Prestel Verlag (Munich), 1999.

Deleuze, Gilles. *Cinema 1: The Movement-Image*. Minneapolis: University of Minnesota Press, 1986.

———. *Cinema 2: The Time-Image*. Minneapolis: University of Minnesota Press, 1989.

Deleuze, Gilles, and Felix Guattari. *A Thousand Plateaus: Capitalism and Schizophrenia*. Trans. Brian Massumi. Minneapolis: University of Minnesota Press, 1987.

Doane, Mary Anne. *The Emergence of Cinematic Time: Modernity, Contingency, the Archive*. Cambridge, MA: Harvard University Press, 2002.

Dunne, Jean-Antoine, and Paula Quigley, eds. *The Montage Principle: Eisenstein in New Cultural and Critical Contexts*. Amsterdam: Rodopi, 2003.

Eagleton, Terry. *The Ideology of the Aesthetic*. Oxford: Blackwell, 1990.

Eisenstein, Sergei M. "Beyond the Shot [The Cinematic Principle and the Ideogram]." 1929. In Braudy and Cohen, *Film Theory and Criticism*, 13–23.

———. "The Dramaturgy of Film Form [A Dialectic Approach to Film Form]." 1929. In Braudy and Cohen, *Film Theory and Criticism*, 23–40.

———. *Film Sense*. 1943. Trans. Jay Leyda. London: Faber and Faber, 1986.

————. "The Montage of Attractions." 1923. In *Selected Works*. Ed. and trans. Richard Taylor, 33–38. London: BFI, 1988.

Fabian, Johannes. *Time and the Other: How Anthropology Makes Its Object*. New York: Columbia University Press, 1983.

Fanon, Frantz. *Black Skin, White Masks*. Trans. Charles Lam Markmann. New York: Grove, 1982.

Fore, Devin, ed. "Soviet Factography." Special issue, *October* 118 (fall 2006).

Freud, Sigmund. "The Uncanny." In *The Standard Edition of the Complete Psychological Works of Sigmund Freud*. Trans. James Strachey. Vol. 27, 217–56. London: Hogarth, 1955.

Ganguly, Keya. "Profane Illuminations and the Everyday." *Cultural Studies* 18, no. 2/3 (March–May 2004): 255–70.

García Espinosa, Julio. "For an Imperfect Cinema." In Stam and Miller, *Film and Theory*, 287–97.

Georgakas, Dan, and Lenny Rubenstein, eds. *The Cineaste Interviews: On the Art and Politics of the Cinema*. Chicago: Lake View Press, 1983.

Gikandi, Simon. *Writing in Limbo: Modernism and Caribbean Literature*. Ithaca, NY: Cornell University Press, 1983.

Gramsci, Antonio. *Selections from Cultural Writings*. Trans. William Boelhower. Cambridge, MA: Harvard University Press, 1985.

Greenberg, Clement. *Late Writings*. Ed. Robert C. Morgan. Minneapolis: University of Minnesota Press, 2003.

Guha-Thakurta, Tapati. *The Making of a New "Indian" Art*. Cambridge, UK: Cambridge University Press, 1992.

Gunning, Tom. "The Cinema of Attractions: Early Cinema, Its Spectator, and the Avant-Garde." *Wide Angle* 8, no. 3/4 (1986): 63–70.

Habermas, Jürgen. "Modernity—An Incomplete Project." Trans. Seyla BenHabib. In *The Anti-Aesthetic: Essays on Postmodern Culture*, ed. Hal Foster, 3–15. Port Townsend, WA: Bay Press, 1983.

Hansen, Miriam. "Benjamin and Cinema: Not a One-Way Street." *Critical Inquiry* 25, no. 2 (winter 1999): 306–43.

————. "Benjamin's Aura." *Critical Inquiry* 34, no. 2 (winter 2008): 336–75.

————. Introduction to Kracauer, *Theory of Film*, vii–xlv.

Hegel, Georg Wilhelm. *Science of Logic*. 1812. Trans. A. V. Miller. New York: Prometheus, 1998.

Heidegger, Martin. *The Question Concerning Technology, and Other Essays*. Trans. William Lovitt. New York: Harper Torchbooks, 1977.

Hewitt, Andrew. *Fascist Modernism: Aesthetics, Politics, and the Avant-Garde*. Stanford: Stanford University Press, 1993.

Hood, John W. *The Essential Mystery: The Major Filmmakers of Indian Art Cinema*. New Delhi: Orient Longman, 2000.

Hohendahl, Peter Uwe. *Reappraisals: Shifting Alignments in Postwar Critical Theory*. Ithaca, NY: Cornell University Press, 1991.

Horkheimer, Max, and Theodor Adorno. *Dialectic of Enlightenment: Philosophical Fragments. 1944. Trans. Edmund Jephcott. Stanford, CA: Stanford University Press, 2002.

Hullot-Kentor, Robert. "The Exact Sense in Which the Culture Industry No Longer Exists." Cultural Critique 70 (fall 2008): 137–57.

———. Things beyond Resemblance: Collected Essays on Theodor W. Adorno. New York: Columbia University Press, 2006.

———. "What Is Mechanical Reproduction?" In Hullot-Kentor, Things beyond Resemblance, 136–53.

Hussein, Abdirahman A. Edward Said: Criticism and Society. London: Verso, 2002.

Huyssen, Andreas. "Adorno in Reverse: From Hollywood to Richard Wagner." In Adorno: A Critical Reader, ed. Nigel C. Gibson and Andrew Rubin, 29–56. Malden, MA: Blackwell, 2002.

Ivanov, Vjačeslav Vsevolodovič. "Eisenstein's Montage of Hieroglyphic Signs." In On Signs, ed. Marshall Blonsky, 221–35.

James, C. L. R. Notes on Dialectics. New York: Lawrence Hill, 1981.

Jameson, Fredric. Cinema and the Invention of Modern Life. Ed. Leo Charney and Vanessa R. Schwartz. Berkeley: University of California Press, 1995.

———. The Geopolitical Aesthetic: Cinema and Space in the World System. London: BFI, 1992.

———. Late Marxism: Adorno, or, the Persistence of the Dialectic. London: Verso, 1990.

———. "Postmodernism, or the Cultural Logic of Late Capitalism." New Left Review I/146 (July-August 1984): 59–92.

———. Signatures of the Visible. New York: Routledge, 1990.

———. A Singular Modernity. London: Verso, 2002.

———. "Third-World Literature in the Era of Multinational Capitalism." Social Text 15 (1986): 65–88.

Jay, Martin. Downcast Eyes: The Denigration of Vision in Twentieth-Century French Thought. Berkeley: University of California Press, 1993.

Kael, Pauline. I Lost It at the Movies. Boston: Little, Brown, 1965.

Kainz, Howard P. Hegel's Phenomenology of Spirit: Selections. University Park: Pennsylvania State University Press, 1994.

Kapur, Geeta. When Was Modernism: Essays on Contemporary Cultural Practice in India. New Delhi: Tulika, 2000.

Koselleck, Reinhart. Futures Past: The Semantics of Historical Time. Trans. Keith Tribe. New York: Columbia University Press, 2004.

Kracauer, Siegfried. From Caligari to Hitler: A Psychological History of the German Film. Princeton, NJ: Princeton University Press, 2004.

———. Theory of Film: The Redemption of Physical Reality. 1960. Princeton, NJ: Princeton University Press, 1997.

Krauss, Rosalind. The Originality of the Avant-Garde and Other Modernist Myths. Cambridge, MA: MIT Press, 1994.

Larsen, Neil. Modernism and Hegemony: A Materialist Critique of Aesthetic Agencies. Minneapolis: University of Minnesota Press, 1990.

Lazarus, Neil. *Nationalism and Cultural Practice in the Postcolonial World.* Cambridge, UK: Cambridge University Press, 1999.

———. "The Politics of Postcolonial Modernism." *European Legacy* 7, no. 6 (2002): 771–82.

Leslie, Esther. *Hollywood Flatlands: Animation, Critical Theory and the Avant-Garde.* London: Verso, 2002.

Lukács, Georg. *A Defence of History and Class Consciousness: Tailism and the Dialectic.* 1925–26. Trans. Esther Leslie. London: Verso, 2000.

MacCabe, Colin. Preface to Jameson, *The Geopolitical Aesthetic,* ix–xvi.

———. *Tracking the Signifier: Theoretical Essays: Film, Linguistics, Literature.* Minneapolis: University of Minnesota Press, 1985.

Macdonald, Dwight. "Short Takes." *Esquire,* May 1960, 42.

Marcuse, Herbert. "The Affirmative Character of Culture." 1936. In *Negations: Essays in Critical Theory.* Trans. Jeremy J. Shapiro, 88–133. London: Allen Lane, 1968.

Marin, Louis. "Disneyland: A Degenerate Utopia." *Glyph* 1 (1977): 50–66.

Marx, Karl. *Capital: Volume One: A Critique of Political Economy.* 1867. Trans. Ben Fowkes. London: Penguin Classics, 1990.

———. "Theses on Feuerbach." 1845. *Marx/Engels: Selected Works.* Vol. 1, 13–15. Trans. W. Lough. Moscow: Progress Publishers, 1969.

McCann, Graham. "New Introduction." In Adorno and Eisler, *Composing for the Films,* vii–xlvii.

Mellencamp, Patricia, and Philip Rosen. *Cinema Histories, Cinema Practices.* Frederick, MD: University Publications of America, 1984.

Metz, Christian. *Film Language: A Semiotics of the Cinema.* Trans. Michael Taylor. Chicago: University of Chicago Press, 1974.

———. *The Imaginary Signifier: Psychoanalysis and the Cinema.* Trans. Celia Britton, Annwyl Williams, Ben Brewster, and Alfred Guzzetti. Bloomington: Indiana University Press, 1977.

———. "Photography and Fetish." *October* 34 (fall 1985): 81–90.

Michelson, Annette. "Bodies in Space: Film as Carnal Knowledge." *Artforum,* Feb. 1969, 54–63.

Mitchell, W. J. T. *Iconology: Image, Text, Ideology.* Chicago: University of Chicago Press, 1986.

Mitter, Partha. *Art and Nationalism in Colonial India, 1850–1922: Occidental Orientations.* Cambridge, UK: Cambridge University Press, 1995.

———. *The Triumph of Modernism: India's Artists and the Avant-Garde, 1922–1947.* London: Reaktion, 2007.

Moore, Rachel O. *Savage Theory: Cinema as Modern Magic.* Durham, NC: Duke University Press, 2000.

Naficy, Hamid. *An Accented Cinema: Exilic and Diasporic Filmmaking.* Princeton, NJ: Princeton University Press, 2001.

Nicholsen, Shierry Weber. *Exact Imagination, Late Work: On Adorno's Aesthetics.* Cambridge, MA: MIT Press, 1997.

Osborne, Peter. *The Politics of Time: Modernity and Avant-Garde*. London: Verso, 1996.

Penley, Constance, ed. *Feminism and Film Theory*. London: Routledge, 1988.

Pensky, Max, ed. *Globalizing Critical Theory*. Lanham, MD: Rowman and Littlefield, 2005.

———. *Melancholy Dialectics: Walter Benjamin and the Play of Mourning*. Amherst: University of Massachusetts Press, 2001.

Pietz, William. "The Problem of the Fetish: Part I." *Res* 9 (1985): 5–17.

———. "The Problem of the Fetish: Part II." *Res* 13 (1987): 23–45.

———. "The Problem of the Fetish: Part III." *Res* 16 (1988): 105–23.

Pines, Jim, and Paul Willemen, eds. *Questions of Third Cinema*. London: BFI, 1989.

Poggioli, Renato. *The Theory of the Avant-Garde*. Trans. Gerald Fitzgerald. Cambridge, MA: Harvard University Press, 1981.

Polan, Dana. *The Political Language of Film and the Avant-Garde*. Ann Arbor, MI: UMI Research Press, 1985.

Pollard, Charles W. *New World Modernisms: T. S. Eliot, Derek Walcott, and Kamau Brathwaite*. Charlottesville: University of Virginia Press, 2004.

Prendergast, Roy M. *Film Music: A Neglected Art: A Critical Study of Music in Films*. New York: Norton, 1992.

Rajadhyaksha, Ashish. "Beyond Orientalism." *Sight and Sound* 2, no. 4 (Aug. 1992): 32–35.

Rajadhyaksha, Ashish, and Paul Willemen, eds. *Encyclopedia of Indian Cinema*. New rev. ed. London: BFI, 1999.

Ray, Sangeeta. *En-Gendering India: Women and Nation in Colonial and Postcolonial Narratives*. Durham, NC: Duke University Press, 2000.

Roberts, Julian. *Walter Benjamin*. London: Macmillan, 1982.

Rodowick, D. N. *The Virtual Life of Film*. Cambridge, MA: Harvard University Press, 2007.

Rose, Gillian. *The Melancholy Science: An Introduction to the Thought of Theodor W. Adorno*. New York: Columbia University Press, 1978.

Rosen, Philip. *Change Mummified: Cinema, Historicity, Theory*. Minneapolis: University of Minnesota Press, 2001.

Rosenthal, Lecia. "Between Humanism and Late Style." *Cultural Critique* 67 (fall 2007): 107–40.

Rubin, Andrew. "Techniques of Trouble: Edward Said and the Dialectics of Cultural Philology." *South Atlantic Quarterly* 102 (2003): 861–76.

Rush, Fred Leland, ed. *The Cambridge Companion to Critical Theory*. Cambridge, UK: Cambridge University Press, 2008.

Said, Edward W. "Adorno as Lateness Itself." In *Apocalypse Theory and the Ends of the World*, ed. Malcolm Bull, 264–81. Oxford: Blackwell, 1995.

———. "A Note on Modernism." In *Culture and Imperialism*, 186–90. New York: Alfred A. Knopf, 1993.

———. *On Late Style: Music and Literature against the Grain*. New York: Pantheon, 2006.

———. *The World, the Text, and the Critic.* Cambridge, MA: Harvard University Press, 1983.

Sangari, Kumkum, and Sudesh Vaid, eds. *Recasting Women: Essays in Colonial History.* New Delhi: Kali for Women, 1989.

San Juan Jr., E. "Antonio Gramsci on Surrealism and the Avantgarde." *Journal of Aesthetic Education* 32, no. 2 (summer 2003): 31–45.

Schwarz, Henry. "Sexing the Pundits: Gender, Romance, and Realism in the Cultural Politics of Colonial Bengal." In Schwarz and Dienst, *Reading the Shape of the World,* 224–58.

Schwarz, Henry, and Richard Dienst, eds. *Reading the Shape of the World: Toward an International Cultural Studies.* Boulder: Westview Press, 1996.

Schwarz, Roberto. "Misplaced Ideas: Literature and Society in Late-Nineteenth-Century Brazil." In *Misplaced Ideas: Essays on Brazilian Culture,* ed. John Gledson, 19–32. London: Verso, 1992.

Shohat, Ella, and Robert Stam. *Unthinking Eurocentrism: Multiculturalism and the Media.* London: Routledge, 1994.

Silverman, Kaja. *The Acoustic Mirror: The Female Voice in Psychoanalysis and Cinema.* Bloomington: Indiana University Press, 1988.

Spivak, Gayatri Chakravorty. "Can the Subaltern Speak?" In *Marxism and the Interpretation of Culture,* ed. Cary Nelson and Lawrence Grossberg, 271–313. Urbana: University of Illinois Press, 1988.

———. "Moving Devi." *Cultural Critique* 47 (winter 2001): 120–163.

Sprinker, Michael. "Homeboys: Nationalism, Colonialism, and Gender in Rabindranath Tagore's *The Home and the World.*" In Schwarz and Dienst, *Reading the Shape of the World,* 202–23.

Stam, Robert, and Toby Miller, eds. *Film and Theory: An Anthology.* London: Blackwell, 2004.

Tagore, Rabindranath. *The Home and the World.* Trans. Surendranath Tagore. 1915. Introduction by Anita Desai. New York: Penguin, 1996.

Tret'iakov, Sergei. "The Theater of Attractions." 1923. Trans. Kristin Romberg. *October* 118 (fall 2006): 19–26.

Williams, Raymond. "The Politics of the Avant-Garde." In *The Politics of Modernism,* 49–80.

———. *The Politics of Modernism: Against the New Conformists.* London: Verso, 1989.

———. *Problems in Materialism and Culture.* London: Verso, 1980.

———. "Problems of Materialism." In *Problems in Materialism and Culture,* 103–22.

Wojcik, Pamela Robertson, ed. *Soundtrack Available: Essays on Film and Popular Music.* Durham, NC: Duke University Press, 2001.

Zipes, Jack. *Happily Ever After: Fairy Tales, Children, and the Culture Industry.* New York: Routledge, 1998.

Žižek, Slavoj. *The Parallax View.* Cambridge, MA: MIT Press, 2006.

Index

Text: 10/13 Aldus
Display: Aldus
Compositor: BookMatters, Berkeley
Printer and binder: Transcontinental Printing